TRANSFORMING CORPORATIONS

take action now!

Transforming Corporations

take action now!

DAN BALAN

A FOUR DIAMOND Publication
Chicago

© 2002 by Dan Balan
All Rights reserved. No part of this book may be reproduced or transmitted on any form or by any means, electronic or mechanical, including photocopying, recording, or by any information storage and retrieval system, without written permission from the author, except for the inclusion of brief quotations in review.
11 10 09 08 07 06 05 04 03 02   1 2 3 4 5

FOUR DIAMOND Publication
Chicago IL 60661

Library of Congress Cataloging in–Publication Data – Pending
ISBN 0-615-12031-8
Business Non-Fiction
First publication 2002

TRANSFORMING CORPORATIONS
take action now !

© Dan (Dorairaj) Balan

FOUR DIAMOND books are available at special discounts for bulk purchases for sales promotions, corporations, premiums, fund-raising, or educational use.

For more information, contact

TRANSFORMING CORPORATIONS
A FOUR DIAMOND Publication
Toll Free : 1-877-762-8669
Tel : (312) 775-7777

Printed in the United States of America

Contents

I dedicate *Transforming Corporations* to

G.
Thank you for giving me the gift of analysis, speech, writing...
and giving me the mad passion to change whatever I can for the
better.

My mother, Sita Devi, and
my father, Valady Krishnaswami Dorairaj

My Grandparents

My Godchildren

My sisters and their husbands

My dear departed uncle, Sivaskandan

I attribute my own journey to the inspiration and illumination I derived from the contributions of the following – some living, some dead. They are

Rahul Dev Burman, Kishore Kumar, Lata Mangeshkar, Asha Bhonsle, P. Sushila, T. M. Soundarajan, K.J. Yesudas, Kannadasan, Jalal Rumi, Pablo Neruda, Shakespeare, Og Mandino, Richard Bandler, Miles Davis, Muddy Mississippi Waters, M.C. Escher, Claude Monet, Beethoven, Mozart, Albert Einstein, Napoleon Hill, Paul Simon, Big Band Players, The Beatles, Jimmy Connors, Michael Jordan, Rosa Parks, Tony Robbins, Mark Victor Hansen, John F. Kennedy, The Life Training Foundation.

Acknowledgements

After years of agonizing over the gaping and growing disconnect between industry, academia, technology, and actual life, I decided to write a straightforward book that would be powerful, easy to understand, exciting to apply, and effective in producing dramatic results that would help anyone in any company in any industry in any country.

Well, it is one thing to aspire to solve world hunger but quite another to find the skillets, the stoves, the recipes, and the polyethylene bags to pack the food.

Writing is like weight lifting. You lift, then rest, lift again, rest, then lift again and rest, so you can lift again.

No man ever arrives at his station without the help of friends and good people. I wish to thank the following people who have helped me over the years with their friendship, guidance, knowledge, and inspiration: John Cannington, Steve Koporec, Jim Keller, John Boatman, Larry Beamer, Sanford Markin, Gregg Mckee, Andy Zoldan, Mayur Shah, John Kohlmeyer, Keith Peterson, Kimberly Horstmann, Glenn Habib, Sanjiv Sidhu, Steve Cole, Hiten Varia, Ken Kline, Christopher Russell, Mac McDougall, Mike Wilson, Terry Murphy, Mark Power, Manny Singh, David Caruso, David Waller, and Scott Brown.

Creation of a book is truly a very twisted supply chain. In writing *Transforming Corporations*, I wish to thank the following individuals for their contribution:

> Jennifer Siner – for her everready enthusiasm and her extraordinary graphics and layout.

> Dana and Andrea Meyer – for working with me on the initial aspects of the book.

> Peter Balbus – for acting as a sounding board on myriad issues.

> Andrew Grossman – for taking my zany mental excesses and turning them into fabulous cartoons.

> Nikhil Jhaveri – for his unflinching loyalty, his understanding of business issues, and his kind gesture to feed me countless times with the delicious Indian dish *Dal palak*, cooked by his lovely wife, Dr. Asavari.

Juanita Raman – for editing two chapters of the book at the beginning of the project.

Sheldon Liebman – one Chicago Bull of an editor, your editorial skills are matchless. You are the best.

Sylvia Hecimovich – for being ever so gracious and guiding me through the mine-filled publishing industry.

Deborah Hawkins – for helping me burnish some aspects of the book and also for your incisive insight.

My students from several companies – for absorbing, appreciating, and avowing to apply what I have set forth in the book.

Vishal Badani and Murtaza Poonawala – for being my eyes and ears and supporting me on innumerable matters including brain storming and proofreading, and passionately managing every aspect of this project. These two young men are rising stars.

Far too numerous to mention here, I wish to thank all my former colleagues from SAP and i2 Technologies.

I also wish to thank Dr. Myrna Hammermann, my dear friend, to whom I first disclosed that I wanted to write a book. Her support and loving counsel, especially during the tumultuous years of my life are unforgettable.

Lastly, I wish to thank Barbara Stepp for helping me rebuild my health with hypnosis. The Indian chief is cooking on all eight cylinders.... He will have it no other way.

"Make things simple, not simpler"

- *Albert Einstein*

Introduction

The American Corporate Rock goes thus:

Sliding revenues	....lay people off
Reduced profits	....lay people off
Increasing costs	....lay people off
Legal problems	....lay people off
Ill-advised mergers	....lay people off
Bad investments	....lay people off
Falling stock prices	....lay people off
Leadership vacuum	....lay people off
Lack of innovation	....lay people off
Falling morale	....lay the whiners off

This familiar jazz has rocked the country out of its wits in the past year. The American economy of Titanic proportions is becoming like the Titanic – sinking slowly. Only a year ago, America was the land where the great boom party would never end. Our stock values were going up, and we were looked upon as the drivers of an ever-revving economic engine. Now that engine is screeching to a halt. We are at a crossroads. After the implosion of the dotcoms, several traditional industries have also begun to follow suit. Every industry is reporting gargantuan losses, and some of our largest companies are laying off people by the tens of thousands. This includes many of our cherished companies, such as Boeing, Motorola, Lucent, GE, Cisco, Oracle, Sun Microsystems and all the major airline carriers. The bloodletting and bankruptcies seem to be unceasing.

Take the telecommunications industry. It has, in the past year, laid off over half a million people and has written off billions of dollars worth of inventory as unsalable, unusable and obsolete. How did such a surreal misestimation of supply and demand occur and, puzzlingly enough, so pervasively across so many companies? Why couldn't anyone read the market signals? How could so many companies fall asleep at the wheel?

Enron, just a year ago, reported over $100 billion in revenues. It was ranked number 7 on the Fortune 500. It was lauded by media, industry, and pundits alike as an aggressive, forward-thinking company. But, overnight, this company collapsed right in front of our eyes—with its stock in tatters and its people running helter-skelter because their 401(k) money was appropriated by the company unconscionably. What were the regulatory agencies doing when Enron was whitewashing its balance sheets?

The airline industry recently asked for—and received—a multi-billion dollar bailout from the federal government. Not offering assistance would not have been politic, yet the industry's financial woes have more to do with histories of operating losses among the top players than with the September 11 attack. United and others did not instantly lose massive amounts of their revenue or take a one-time hit for updating their fleet. Capacities, prices, services, technology, mergers, and a myriad of factors that determine competitiveness were not constantly recalibrated in light of the changing habits of today's travelers.

The steel industry is begging Washington to impose heavy duties on imported steel and to take over the administration of the health care that it owes its workers.

In industry after industry, the collapse is like an entire town having a vomiting craze after drinking a potion that looked like sweet lemonade just yesterday.

The Merger Mania

Look at the rash of mergers in the last year alone. America produced more mergers than Europe and Asia combined. We have witnessed shake-ups in so many industries—banking, insurance, publishing, software, communications, automotive, oil and gas, chemicals, pharmaceuticals, et al.

The reduction in the number of players in key industries, combined with the interrelatedness of many industries and the intricate nature of financial markets, has created a negative ripple effect in our economy. Many of these industries are in a driver-dependent relationship with one another. When a dependent industry does not create its own stream of revenues and transfer its competencies to develop its own aftermarkets, there is an unhealthy web of reliance.

As an example, saturation in the personal computer market has meant that semiconductor, peripherals, and other "feeder" industries have taken painful bottom-line blows. With regard to durable goods, fortunes of companies that make steel, glass, tires, and automobiles are intrinsically linked. When one company has problems producing efficiently, selling competitively, and operating profitably, then all companies it does business with are adversely affected.

When there are only a few large companies that serve a market segment, multiple problems are created, not the least of which is inhibited innovation. When healthy competition is curtailed, incentives for creating more efficient processes and more exciting products are diminished.

Mergers, aimed at helping companies benefit from their natural synergies while reducing redundancies and overhead, do not lead management teams down the yellow brick road. When made at times of financial desperation, mergers often put two poorly performing companies together with too limited a shared vision to realistically improve prospects. Where there are technological and cultural mismatches, mergers inevitably fester and fail. A company that joins forces with another with whom it shares some market niches but not methods for managing information often sets itself up for years of daily operational struggle. Like the great houses of Europe that sought to fortify their hegemony through intermarrying but instead produced hemophiliac heirs, companies who choose the quick merger bailout strategy often never make it to adulthood. Virtually every merger of last year has had human casualties. Even the proposed merger of Compaq and Hewlett-Packard was calibrated at a layoff of 15,000 people.

What is it about the American psyche that predisposes it to slaughter people like cattle and shuffle them around like pieces of chattel? Why do we not look at problems holistically? Why are we entrapped in a cut-and-paste, all-or-nothing culture? Our corporate lives are but a musical chairs game of borrow, binge, bleed, burst, blame, and break down. Yet we have exceptions on our own soil—

companies that manage to do well, during good times and bad—companies that value and preserve their people. As an aside, is there any correlation between America's being the divorce capital of the world and our corporate affairs?

The faults in our commercial fabric are the result of our education system.

Our Poorly Planted "Learning Tree"

The business degree was created over 100 years ago. The actual value of a business degree now demands examination. Do curriculums at our business schools actually help create business leaders?

Marketing is still taught as marketing, finance is still taught as finance. The marriage between technology and business strategy occurred more than a decade ago, yet some of our best schools are unable to comprehend the fusion, let alone offer relevant courses. Even under the guise of updating curriculums, the strategic prefix "e", as in "e-business" or in "e-commerce", too often represents hollow substitutes for meaningful learning based on the relationship between information technology and business problems. The common thread of cause and effect that transcends disciplines and ties together the corporation as a whole is hardly taught in any of our schools. The intricate relationships between products, markets, customers, and value cut across several disciplines; they transcend the traditional silo thinking that afflicts our schools, our curriculums, our professors, and our graduates.

Often our professors who seek tenure for life are tethered to the past. They are merely carrying on the tradition with which they are most familiar. In approach, subject matter, and techniques, they educate the way they were educated: fragment, fragment, fragment.

The silo mentality in corporations is but an extension of silo mentalities in business schools. Our corporate managers follow the traditions of fragmentation inculcated in even our "best" schools. We are producing managers who are conceptually crippled and creatively impaired. How many marketing executives comprehend the essentials of manufacturing? How many product engineers appreciate the nuances of thoughtful market research? The chain of dysfunction extends link after link, lap after lap, and course after course into companies.

Our business education system is, in fact, in business to perpetuate itself. More than ever, business professionals are acquiring MBAs. Often under corporate-sponsored tuition reimbursement programs, they acquire degrees to gain professional advantages in a competitive job market, and rarely do they transfer knowledge to their companies.

Business education itself has been fragmented into a million pieces. We have "fast-track" MBA programs in project management, document management, web-site management, event management, etc. These programs are mushrooming like fungus. We are producing a myopic army of half-baked specialists in the marketplace.

Unless our curriculums are updated, our courses made relevant, our thinking based on cause and effect, and our perspectives made long-term, our brand-name schools will fast become bastions of absurdity and anachronism.

We Must Take Action Now

Our stock values have plummeted, our economic system has been badly shaken, and our stories are all too familiar.

This is the time for serious reflection and not semantic self-delusion. Our survival as a nation of prosperous and independent-thinking people depends on our ability to view ourselves through new lenses and make changes according to the new realities.

No European nation deals with economic ups and downs with massive, mind-numbing layoffs. Japan is also going through a recession. But was Japan's first reaction to decimate its work force? Market vicissitudes are not new. Business cycles are as old as the hills. Was it raining only on our team when we lost?

It is time to change now. We must break the yoke of dysfunctional, short-term thinking.

Focusing on core business and organizational issues, not relying on miracles, magic, or governmental manipulations, is where we must start. Trying to modulate interest rates close to a dozen times in a year is somewhat like adjusting the thermostat so people will grow more body hair for warmth.

Transforming Our Corporations

We have to restore a corporate culture that places people first. We have to rebirth as a nation that values innovation, creativity, and our individual self-expression. We have to create tangible value in terms of relevant products and satisfied customers through the contributions of a productive and motivated work force. Shakespeare said, "The fault, Dear Brutus, is not in our stars, but in ourselves that we are underlings." The fault, Dear American Business person, is not in our stocks, but in ourselves – in our own ineptitudes, inefficiencies and inebriations. To transform our economy, we must transform our behaviors, our businesses, and our bent, or we will continue to pay a dear price. The economic failures precipitated by applying fragmented solutions to regularly occurring business challenges and perpetuating these failures through our education system have had an enormous human toll. Immediately, people suffer economically through layoffs and periods of reduced buying power. On a grander scale, during difficult economic times, people feel a personal loss of value in their limited opportunities to contribute their talents.

In a multinational economy, with a maddening maze of connections, with decreasing customer loyalty, with an unending proliferation of products, with myriad variations required for each market—the critical thinking required to make responsible, holistic decisions is far beyond what our schools can now teach. We are living in a business world of multiple cultures, languages, and management styles. We are living in a world where our choices regarding technologies can spur or stifle a company. We are living in a world where, more than ever, we must value human beings. To build strong companies, we must have a strong appreciation for what a motivated work force can do. To run companies of tomorrow, we need transformational leaders, not transaction peddlers. We must groom a new generation of leaders who understand people, cultures, technologies, and the globe. We need men and women who have courage, creativity, and compassion.

We need a new civilizational consciousness. We must draw a new baseline for everyday existence. The first baseline was to learn how to drive a car. The second baseline was to learn how to work on a computer. The third baseline is to understand the fundamental nature of business. A car is basic; a computer is basic. Consciousness of business must also be basic. It has to become the next common denominator.

We must as a citizenry understand the workings of business, its causes and effects, its actions and reactions, its tight spots and its trapezes—and, yes, understand its transformations. Otherwise, we will have an intellectually crippled society and a myopic work force in which the destinies of many will be manipulated by a mindless few. Without a more holistic approach to understanding our economy and the workings of the individual corporations that comprise it, we are destined to ride on a roller coaster of accidental innovation and resignation about prospects that could be immeasurably better. We all need to know the fundamentals of the steering wheel of a business and what the tires look like and whether the windows will roll up and down.

Transforming Corporations is an action guide for turning around any company, in any industry. Transforming Corporations dissects the problems at play in today's economy, offers a new, holistic way of looking at key elements of these problems, and then provides prescriptive recommendations to improve the financial results and human experience involved in being a worker and consumer in America. The fuel for transforming our corporations is knowledge and a fierce intolerance of mediocrity. This book is a manifesto for all breathing people, not just business people. It is written in a simple, straightforward language that anyone can understand. The propulsion for results has to be driven by communalization of ideas and a collective call to action. Whether you are a CEO, housewife, student, banker, bookmaker, policy maker, or simply someone concerned with making a contribution, then this book is for you.

Our lives are at large, and humanity is at work. Let transformation be at play, because business is everybody's business.

Dan Balan

Chicago, January 2002

Section I

Thinking Trees and Unpicked Apples

Understanding Cause and Effect

Dawn breaks over a Florida orange grove. The dew combines with the scent of ripe fruit hanging in the trees. As the light grows, there is utter silence.

But that silence is short-lived. At half past five, a host of orange pickers arrives, carrying ladders, special pruning tools, and fruit crates. From that hour until late afternoon, they work deftly, rapidly, severing fruit from the branches. All day long, with the sun high overhead, pickers fill bushel boxes bound for the processing plant.

Tropicana's juice-processing plant sits on the same land as the company's headquarters in Bradenton, Florida. When the fruit-laden trucks pull into the loading docks, workers carry the bushel boxes of fruit to conveyor belts. Inside the processing plant, inspectors separate and discard the immature or rotten fruit, and machines press juice from the rest. Then the juice is pasteurized and packaged for shipment. Within hours, people at the plant are sending juice directly to the refrigerator cases of supermarkets across the country.

Just as the juice reaches supermarket shelves, the national newspaper *USA Today* runs a major story that cites a study praising the health benefits of orange juice. It's a free public relations blitz that, like its competitors, Tropicana hopes to take advantage of.

Take advantage is exactly what Tropicana does. The company's response is practiced and swift. Countless times a year, the firm reorganizes and reshuffles the harvesting in its orange groves, adjusts production schedules at its processing plant, and coordinates store-bound trucks to exploit the potential surge in demand afforded by beneficial media coverage.

From the outside looking in, an observer might think that Tropicana's trees could think for themselves, that the trees could read newspapers, forecast demand, and grow fruit accordingly. Clearly that's impossible; no one strikes such deals with Mother Nature, and not even the most advanced bioengineering comes close to achieving such a goal. But how has Tropicana built such an efficient, precise organization, from initial production to final delivery? What lessons can today's organizations—across all industry sectors—learn from Tropicana's faultless and efficient operations?

Before we answer that question, let's look at a situation in which the reverse is true. Consider a case in which superior product design, combined with brilliant creative advertising and a clear interest on the part of consumers, all converged in a sharp upswing in demand—but the company could not meet that surge and failed to capitalize on opportunity.

In 1996, after five years of struggle to maintain growth and meet shareholders' expectations, Apple Computer launched the iMac. The appealing new PC quickly became the symbol of Apple's resurgence in the PC market. The cool, translucent style, the eye-pleasing design of the chassis, the machine's functionality and blazing performance—all now unmistakable—resulted in a strongly favorable reception by the market. Later, driven by an advertising campaign that likened the machine to candy, Apple introduced pleasing new colors for the machines, which consumers loved. Suddenly, Apple had a hot new product again, iMacs began to move briskly, and the company's profits saw a sharp uptick as a result.

To follow the immensely popular iMac, Apple designed and introduced the iBook, a stylish laptop computer. Sleek and seductive, the new laptop was also very successful—except for one problem. A shortage of screens from Apple's Asian suppliers drove prices higher and limited the supply. Facing a cash crunch precipitated by the Asian economic meltdown in 1998, suppliers had to cut production and could not meet Apple's needs. That limited Apple's production of iBooks.

The result was immediate—and debilitating. Apple had pent-up demand for its laptop units, but no way to fulfill retail orders for this highly desirable, lucrative product. Sales stopped because there were no units to sell. Customers were disappointed, profits dipped, and shareholder value tumbled.

Let's compare Apples to oranges. Compare Tropicana's management of its supply to meet demand with the situation at Apple Computer at the time of the iBook launch.

At every moment, Tropicana manages every stage in the movement of fruit from its orange groves to the freezer cases of supermarkets around the country, guaranteeing its ability to respond to increased demand. Season after season, year after year, despite the vagaries of the weather and the changing demands of a capricious market, Tropicana's work force satisfies changing market demand. To respond to market expectations 365 days a year, Tropicana flash-freezes its juice and stores it for a short period. Then workers thaw the juice, package it, and ship it to retailers.

This is only one component of the orange juice production process. The other is managing supply. Just as toy makers cannot make 50 percent of their toys the day before the holiday shopping season, Tropicana cannot harvest Florida oranges year-round. If the company used only Florida orange groves, it would have to store juice for up to twelve months—using huge floor space for merchandise from which it would slowly draw for the balance of the year. The company would also need an uncanny ability to forecast changing demand for juice six to nine months in advance.

Instead, Tropicana buys oranges on the world's commodities exchanges from global locations, such as Brazil and Argentina, locking in prices with these advance purchases. The result is a continuous supply of oranges as well as the ability to better manage sales price. Tropicana sells fresh orange juice at the proper retail levels, at optimal prices, with no unwanted juice or fruit sitting unused and facing spoilage at the plant, and with no overstocks forcing price cuts or, worse, stock returns.

Apple, on the other hand, missed a chance to exploit market demand at a critical moment in the company's history. A link broke in the movement of vital components from its supplier to the original equipment manufacturer for iBooks, interrupting the flow of Apples to the consumer. An opportunity was lost.

Clearly, the fault did not lie simply with Apple. Neither can the company's suppliers be assigned all the blame. Rather, a series of miscues and breakdowns in communication and management contributed to the problem.

Had the right communication and management systems been in place at Apple, the company would have had several options to better manage the situation. First, as soon as Apple learned of a disruption in the production cycle, its marketing managers could have muted the company's marketing of iBooks so that demand did not outpace supply. Second, executives who worked with Apple's supplier companies, in concert with Apple's marketers and forecasters, could have created better sales forecasts. Third, manufacturing managers at Apple's suppliers could have implemented more cost-effective plant systems—flexible enough to respond to rapid changes in demand. Finally, Apple's financial management could have worked with suppliers during the cash crunch, creating cash-flow financing to keep production alive.

If all of these steps had been taken, perhaps the iBook could have reached its full market potential. If any one of these four management groups—marketing managers, supply managers, production managers, or financial managers—had taken the right action, Apple could have lessened the effect of the shortages. The managers' inability to make any one of these decisions illustrates a fundamental lack of connection among decision-makers in the company's supply chain. Ironically, for a company in a superb position to appreciate the opportunities of today's information-driven economy, the world-famous Cupertino-based computer maker lacked an appreciation of the critical need for the exchange of information.

For the right decisions to be made, not only should those exchanges have occurred within Apple's own production management structure, but the information exchange should also have extended across the broader constituencies of all its marketers, financial managers, suppliers, and others who contribute to the flow of products from manufacture to final consumer.

Our comparison of Apples to oranges represents only two brief vignettes of management success or failure in our global economy. But the contrast between them is telling. For while each seeks market leadership in its respective industries, one of these companies clearly appreciates the importance of corporate cause and effect.

Tropicana has developed a finely tuned sense of the importance of synchronized supply chain management. This is a state in which a company's business strategy, information technology, and production and distribution capability allow it to meet rapidly changing consumer demand and the changing effects of different events and circumstances in the marketplace. Apple apparently had not developed such a sense—at least on the strength of what we view as its struggle to bring iBooks to market. Tropicana prioritizes the exchange of information throughout its decision making structure, extending that information exchange to every link in its supply chain, both inside and outside the company. At least by the 1997 product launch, Apple had not prioritized that exchange.

Apple is not alone. The curse of the modern corporation is a conceptual disconnection: a pervasive, endemic dislocation of different corporate competencies and constituencies. This can in some cases be attributed to an organization's size. It can also arise from ongoing efforts of companies to compartmentalize different functions and focus on improving them—a worthwhile goal, certainly, but one that can lead to the loss of a connection...the organization as a whole.

But the dislocation goes further. Organizations large and small lack an essential appreciation for the importance of managing cause and effect holistically. A synchronized supply chain affects the company's products, customers, markets, and value. The management capabilities of companies such as Tropicana include

- An ability to swiftly respond to market trends—both dips and surges—and to capitalize on opportunities

- An ability to move goods and services from their supply sources to final consumers with minimal waste

- Consistent on-time order fulfillment in a world that increasingly expects it

- The commitment to innovating internally and with alliance partners

- The ability to provide specialized or customized products and services while maintaining a slim cost structure

- An information network that connects the organization to its customers, suppliers, factories, and distribution centers

- A structure that allows for efficient global transportation of goods

- The ability to energize its work force with a common understanding of shared goals, a common body of knowledge, and a shared passion about achieving its purpose

The condition for achieving all the above is the creation of an equilateral triangle with information technology, supply chain management, and business strategy as its vertices. Companies that consciously construct this geometry are setting the pace in a rapidly accelerating business world. They are leading examples of how a corporation aligns its business strategy and execution with changing conditions.

Understanding Supply Chains: Corporate Cause and Effect

When you look at an illustration by M.C. Escher, you probably appreciate the fascinating, bewildering complexity of his masterful optical illusions. Fish turn to birds and back again. Staircases upward lead only to other stairs that wind back down. Walls appear and disappear. Nothing is as it seems.

In recalling an Escher drawing, perhaps you also remember a certain frustration accompanying your fascination with the image. Few people can take only a quick look at the late Dutch artist's works because his drawings force the eye to continually seek a fixed point of reference to make sense of the conflicting perspectives. Viewers find themselves focused on the complications, wondering how they happened.

**M.C. Escher's "Pre-destination" © 2001 Cordon Art B.V. - Baarn - Holland.
All rights reserved.**

The reference to Escher is useful in assessing the fascination and the frustration of understanding the complex information environment in today's corporations. The core dysfunction of major corporations, from their leaders to rank-and-file workers, is that they do not all fully realize the whole picture or share the same perspective from a common point of reference. Their businesses lack a common landscape and a collective vocabulary. They lack a comprehensive understanding of how their organization needs to function as a synchronized whole.

The interplay of functions in the human body is another analogy to a company's struggle to balance cause and effect. Consider what would happen if a person's heart, operating independently of the resting brain, began beating 200 times a minute while he or she slept. That person would likely have a stroke or sustain serious damage to other parts of the vascular system that would shut the heart down.

The human body operates from the top down, for the brain is the source of demand and the organs are the agents of fulfillment. The stomach—with its ability to process food into energy—is the center of manufacturing, and the feet are the primary mode of transportation. But the brain cannot function capably without sufficient information and feedback from the individual organs and nerves, and it constantly adjusts its responses to changing stimuli.

How does this correlate with the way organizations are run? Imagine what would happen if a company's product development department operated autonomously, without input from sales and marketing. How often have we heard of a company with a product development "breakthrough" that ended in disappointment or even disaster because its engineers and purchasing agents barely collaborated with one another?

Our comparison underscores the need for conscious thinking about cause and effect in corporations. Without a culture prepared to connect, communicate, and collaborate across all links in the supply chain, a company will lack decision makers who know how to best leverage the strengths and compensate for the weaknesses in that chain.

Consider the following list of questions to which every executive must continuously seek answers:

1. How do we maximize our responsiveness to our customers while minimizing costs?

2. How will we track demand to understand our customers their buying patterns and constantly changing tastes?

3. Do we know, at any point in time, how to offer our customers a cost savings that no other competitor can give them and still be profitable?

4. How will our planners know which customers are the most profitable? How will they synchronize the production and delivery of materials with capacity in time, and how can they sequence products intelligently to meet customer delivery dates? How will they minimize cycle-times?

5. How frequently will the company launch new products? What are the tradeoffs between market opportunities and product features and functions? Do our marketers know the full implications of introducing new products? How will the newly introduced product affect our profit margins? Other products?

6. What is the ideal production mix to maximize profits? How will product life cycles influence operational costs?

7. Is purchasing being used as a strategic weapon in supporting the organization? Do product engineering and purchasing understand the full implications of design and process changes on supplier relationships and costs?

8. How do we know if we're using the right suppliers? Do we need as many as we presently have? Are they meeting our needs? How do we collaborate with suppliers to ship us components at the right time?

9. If we can't make all the products because of limitations in raw materials, what can we do to retain our customers? Given a barrage of order changes, how quickly can we recover and still promise delivery by the dates our customers request?

10. Has the organization accounted for transportation issues in its overall strategy? How will transportation be integrally connected with orders, inventory levels, and shipping destinations?

11. How will we plan our distribution in the face of volatile or unpredictable demand?

Ten years ago, these questions would have been discussed by a small number of planners and high-level managers. Today, to create an effective supply chain, the relevance of every function must be analyzed as to how it supports customer needs.

This shifts the paradigm away from the narrow perspective that still handicaps many companies. At certain points, some executives still respond to some questions like those above with statements such as "Well, that's a marketing question" or "I leave that to my transportation people." This view is no longer sufficient. It is time for an intellectual awakening in organizations. It is time for corporations—all institutions, actually—to realize that supply chain management is not simply a logistics function shunted off to one corner of the building, but one that dictates and deserves full institutional focus.

People at any level of an organization should be able to answer these questions. Individuals must forget their specific job title and its tasks, asking themselves instead, "What is the fundamental question for which I am the answer?" That self-query has a way of expanding awareness about what a person does within an organization. If every person can approach that question and come up with an answer that goes beyond pure job description, the corporation is bound to move forward.

What Are Supply Chains?

The supply chain of a company is the sum total of all the people and companies who touch any of the products, services, monies, and information that go into creating or using the products or services of that company. As Figure 1-1 illustrates, a supply chain includes raw materials creators, component manufacturers, OEMs (original equipment manufacturers), distributors, retailers, and end-consumers. Supply chains also include the innumerable service providers (shippers, warehousers, advertising firms, banks, consulting firms, web-hosting firms, and so on) that support the flow of products, services, monies, and information. All of these product and service providers and all of the customers of these product and service providers form the links in a supply chain.

A supply chain is defined both by its links (constituent companies and consumers) and by the multidirectional flows of products, services, information, and monies. The supply chains of many companies form vast networks that extend both on the upstream-side into a network of suppliers and on the downstream-side into a network of customer companies, final consumers, and retailers. Real supply chains can have

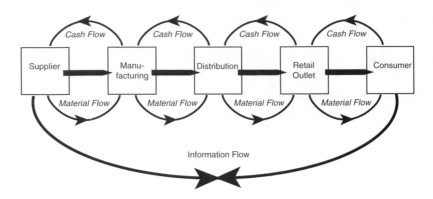

Figure 1-1   A sample supply chain flow

thousands of suppliers and millions of end-customers.

A supply chain is successful only when all the products, services, monies, and information flow smoothly to and from every part of the chain. If any link in the chain is a poorly run company, the entire chain suffers from disruptions in the flow. Disrupted flow creates myriad problems in coordination, such as late deliveries, inventory pileups, manufacturing downtime, fluctuations in supplies, empty store shelves, late payments, fluctuations in orders, and so on. In the past, when companies could not be efficient or did not face efficient global competitors, the quality of their supply chains was not so important. But now companies are highly dependent on all the members of their supply chain. Smooth-running, sophisticated supply chains are the key to successful businesses in the 21st century. This is why supply chain management is so important now.

The Organization as a Supply Chain

Logically enough, the concept of supply chains was first adopted by manufacturers; however, the concept applies to every organization that exchanges goods or services, information, and monies along a linked sequence. That organization can be a "bricks-and-mortar" company or a virtual e-business startup. It could be run for profit, or it could be a not-for-profit. If an organization exchanges monies for goods and/or services, then it has a supply chain.

To appreciate how supply chains operate across the broad range of organizational types, it is appropriate to briefly review some nontraditional examples. Following are some representative descriptions of how different organizations can view their respective supply chains.

Financial Services

Financial services firms (banks, brokerages, and insurance companies) all have very real supply chains with a downstream flow of products (such as financial instruments like stocks, bonds, and CDs), services (accounting for monies in customers' accounts), and the delivery of monies themselves (dividends, annuity checks, foreign currency, and other instruments). Financial stock exchanges are even an inspiration for e-commerce-based supply chain concepts in which large numbers of buyers and sellers convene to set prices fairly. Financial markets play a major role in traditional supply chains as manufacturers try to hedge price fluctuations related to commodities and currencies. The point is that the customers of financial services firms depend on the orderly delivery of financial services in the same way that a manufacturer depends on the orderly delivery of component parts.

Internet Services

Even companies in the virtual world of bits and bytes have supply chains. The supply chain of a pure online dotcom business would include all the service providers that support it, such as web-hosting companies, website designers, fulfillment centers, call centers, and other service providers. And even the most virtual e-business is dependent on suppliers of computers, networking hardware, and software.

The supply chain for e-commerce can also be viewed in terms of the flow of hits from one website to another. For example, the whole basis of banner advertising is to shuttle potential customers from website to website. When Barnes & Noble buys a banner ad on Yahoo, it is asking Yahoo to supply Barnes & Noble with access to customers in the form of a certain number of page views. Every time a click-through to Barnes & Noble occurs, Barnes & Noble pays Yahoo, and every time a viewer from Yahoo buys from Barnes & Noble, Yahoo gets paid.

In many ways, Yahoo (and many other "free" Internet services) could be considered a "buyer" and "seller" of page views—a distributor of page views. Clearly, Yahoo sells millions of page views to advertisers. From where does it get these page views? When

Bard Watching

web surfers go to a Yahoo web page, they give Yahoo a fully formed and "finished" page view that Yahoo distributes to one of its advertisers. Yahoo "buys" page views from consumers by giving them valuable information services. The company then closes the loop internally by converting advertisers' dollars into the information services sought by viewers.

The point is that there is a flow of page views (the product) from people sitting at their computers to Yahoo and then to Barnes & Noble and other advertisers. Consumers create page views, Barnes & Noble buys page views, and the middleman, Yahoo, distributes page views. These exchanges and activities form a supply chain, even though there is no physical product. E-commerce companies have suppliers, and they have customers. They pay supplier companies to obtain specific things, and they are paid by customers for particular things.

Local Governments
Every taxpayer is a customer to whom municipal and county governments deliver a range of products and services. These include

utilities... such as water, sewage and drainage systems, electricity, and fire and police services. They also include infrastructure... such as roads, bridges, and parks. Therefore, the business of government involves a very real supply chain, for municipalities or other agencies need to obtain everything from patrol cars and asphalt for roads to flowers for park gardens and uniforms for their firefighters. Local governments also frequently function as distributors for their supply chain partners; that is, they manage contracted services, such as specialized health, education, and welfare programs for their state government or for national programs.

Determining Objectives in a Supply Chain

The concept of supply chains suggests that all organizations participate in a network of goods, services, monies, and information and that organizations are the conduits for these flows. They can manipulate them and create them. The questions for corporations are

- How can we contribute value to these supply chain flows?

- How can we extract value from these supply chain flows?

Over time, regardless of industry and company, organizations that have built robust supply chains have embraced the following common objectives.

Minimize Total Supply Chain Costs

Traditionally, the main cost components of any product are labor, material, and overhead. However, there are several other points in supply chains at which costs accumulate to the flow of a product. It is critical to understand how these cost drivers contribute to value or negatively affect value. Some of the cost drivers are administration and order processing; others include scrap, rework, transportation, freight, storage, handling, after-sale customer care, and a host of other miscellaneous activities. Several companies are still on the age-old standard costing system and have not matriculated into the world of activity-based costing. Consequently, their computations of profits, margins, revenue, and costs are bound to be erroneous. The total cost to serve a customer should be viewed as the sum of all relevant costs across a business cycle as opposed to mere transaction costs.

Optimize Use of all Available Assets across The Network

Most companies face a bewildering array of choices in deciding which assets to use for which job. Multiple locations, multiple machines at each location, multiple people, and multiple vehicles for moving goods make it hard to decide how to deploy assets. Each customer order and every forecast for sales demands a decision about which people should be involved, which machines should make the product, which trucks should ship the product, and on and on. Optimizing the use of assets to create value includes making the following types of decisions about how and when your assets will be used:

- Allocation decisions: which assets will be used on what work activities

- Scheduling decisions: the exact timing of work activities

- Sequencing decisions: the order in which work activities will occur

Maximize Responsiveness to Customers

Companies must be able to respond swiftly to customer requests, whether they be in product development, customization, delivery, or complaint resolution. By whatever means a company chooses to segment products for its customers—by margins, profits, order patterns, or product type—it must be able to assess customer demand and fulfill it in a cost-conscious and time-sensitive manner. A company has to correctly capture all the relevant customer and order information, so that at any given moment the progression and disposition of an order are transparent. In order for companies to maximize responsiveness to their customers, they should themselves maximize the value created at three points in their supply chain: by delivering value to customers, by creating value internally, and by acquiring value from suppliers.

Optimize Time-to-Value

Time is of the essence in business, but that essence is a complex brew. Companies must constantly seek to minimize the time it takes to realize value in their overall business cycle. They must learn what impedes the flow from order to delivery and what slows a business operation. On the one hand, a company should minimize time-to-value by reducing the cycle-times in product design and development, manufacturing, distribution, and financial payment from customers. On the other hand, a company should maximize the time-to-cost by deferring expensive activities, such as buying materials and making investments. Successful companies strive to maintain a positive cash-to-cash cycle, the time between paying suppliers and being paid by customers.

The real goal is to be on time, to synchronize with suppliers and customers so that you deliver value exactly when it is needed. In an optimal supply chain, early delivery is almost as great a sin as late delivery. It demonstrates inefficiencies.

Achieving an Optimal Supply Chain

To better understand how these objectives can be achieved—and how an enhanced perception of supply chain management can improve a company's operations and its value—let's review some world-class companies whose superlative management of supply chains can serve as a touchstone for other organizations.

Minimizing Total Costs: Industrie Natuzzi SpA

In 1959, in a little village in southern Italy called Teramo, Pasquale Natuzzi began making furniture. Four decades later, his company makes over 400 models of sofas, recliners, armchairs, and sofa beds with some 430 covering choices, including seventeen varieties of leather (in 200 colors) as well as various fabrics. Natuzzi can handle everything from the penchant of German consumers for extra-firm seats to the California laws mandating use of fire-resistant foam in cushions. Industrie Natuzzi SpA now is the largest producer of leather upholstered furniture in the world. It coordinates operations in 144 countries and realizes 40 percent of its revenues in the United States, where it controls one quarter of the market for leather furniture.

What Natuzzi's rivals envy, however, is not the variety of models and styles it offers to customers, but its reputation as a low-cost manufacturer. Despite changing hundreds of models each year, Natuzzi retains its customers—retailers around the world—by consistently offering them attractive wholesale pricing. Changing tastes in furniture in New York affect Natuzzi's factories nearly half a world away, but the giant manufacturer is nimble enough to fulfill any order. How does the company maintain operational efficiency and compete profitably anywhere on the globe?

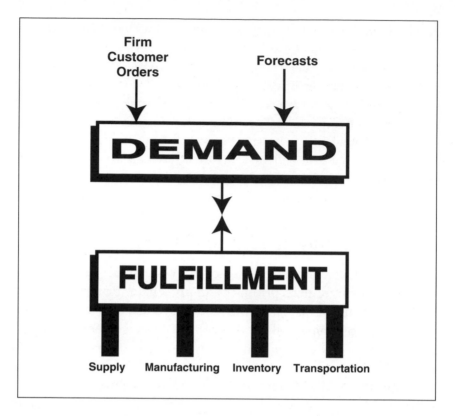

Figure 1-2 Elements of a supply chain

Natuzzi is vertically integrated and does all its manufacturing in central Italy—everything from pouring the foam for the seats to tanning the hides for the covers to figuring out how to efficiently pack the furniture for shipment. Natuzzi's trick for efficient fulfillment is a sophisticated made-to-order manufacturing operation that coordinates Natuzzi's over 4,000 workers across more than one million square feet of manufacturing space. All of Natuzzi's craftsmen use computer workstations to track orders and log progress. For example, when a worker finishes sewing a cushion, he or she enters it into a computer (and gets paid a bonus if the job is done quickly). Automated trolley systems and overhead conveyers move partially complete furniture and materials around the plant. The result is that these workers churn out over 10,000 made-to-order pieces of furniture every day.

Another reason for Natuzzi's success is its attention to detail. Natuzzi knows exactly how much material and labor is required to make every model of furniture, down to the screws, the amount of dye in the leather, and even the length of thread required for upholstering the cushions. The result is careful sourcing of materials and low waste. Because furniture is so bulky, Natuzzi even wrote its own software for packing shipping containers with furniture; it prints detailed packing and orientation instructions. The story extends all the way to collecting invoices. To ensure speedy payments from its retailers around the world, Natuzzi has a real-time link into Citibank.

Industrie Natuzzi's operational success relies on a highly effective combination of its company culture and information technology. Realizing the benefit of these continuing efficiencies in its operations, the company announced in early 1999 that it can deliver a sofa in the U.S. for 20 percent less than the price at which the same sofa was sold to Macy's in 1982. By closely auditing the manufacturing process, creating an environment for successful mass customization, and compressing both time-to-market and its accounts receivable cycle, Natuzzi doesn't simply stay abreast of change. It dominates its marketplace.

Optimizing Network Assets: John Deere & Co.

Natuzzi is not the only company realizing high-performance, flawlessly efficient operations on a worldwide scale. Deere & Company, the maker of farm and construction equipment, from transmissions and drive-trains to excavators and backhoes, has its headquarters near the Iowa border, just outside Illinois; but the company does business from Accra to Zimbabwe, from Korea to Kazakhstan.

Around the world, the needs of farmers differ according to geography and climate, soil and crop rotation, farm size and budgets. Today, when buying farm equipment, a farmer chooses from a range of features that go well beyond traditional requirements of fuel economy, horsepower, and durability. Deere has closely studied the characteristics and evolution of each market it competes in as well as the true cost to serve and satisfy its customers, and it tailors its product innovation to specific target markets. The company offers option packages that range from air-conditioned cabs with fancy upholstering to top-of-the-line models with high-end stereo equipment, lumbar supports, and other creature comforts.

Deere's commitment to on-time delivery reflects the firm's 152-year legacy of meeting promises to the customer. And management knows that profit is the key to staying around for the next 150 years. Every day, analysts pore over reports, ensuring that final assembly and delivery of their units matches orders from their more than 450 dealers worldwide. Today, as it reviews the launch of a new line of tractors, management will compare the actual number of specialized components on hand against planned deliveries. Tomorrow, it will examine cumulative reports of its customers' buying patterns, studying statistical trends to determine which features are most in demand for backhoes and transmissions. The company will try to determine how customer input can help it refocus manufacturing lines, factoring this innovation into the cost of serving its full range of customers. All this is part of Deere's effort to tailor products for each of its competitive markets.

So how is it that Deere is able to serve each of its market segments, manage the complexity of customized ordering, and still dominate the market with on-time delivery? Perhaps because the company learned the same lessons in managing its production and supply chain as Natuzzi. But where Natuzzi has chosen to maintain one centralized manufacturing operation in Teramo, Deere has different factories that specialize in building different products. Where Natuzzi cuts and stretches its own fabrics, Deere needs to source parts from multiple original equipment manufacturers and distributors around the world.

When a dealer submits a new order, Deere's challenge is to determine how to get that order made. The company must start by choosing which set of factories and suppliers it should use to manufacture components or sub-assemblies, and which factories will manage final assembly. The moment a Deere customer places an order, a database automatically matches supplies of raw materials and parts to production capacity at one of its fifteen factories around the globe. If the order includes multiple pieces (such as a tractor and multiple farm implements), Deere might use different locations and suppliers for separate parts of the order, and then merge the order at an appropriately chosen distribution center for final assembly. Deere's computer systems pass the customer's specific order through a sophisticated telecommunications network, allowing the company's 20 international warehouses to coordinate the movement of products in a timely manner.

At the same time, the firm needs to account for the related handling costs: trucks, forklifts, and even storage space have to be allocated and scheduled. Information systems monitor whether the company has products to match the orders on the day's schedule, and then plan for the demands of the succeeding day.

In the past, this process of producing a custom order to the desired specifications required two months. The company can now build a made-to-order product within sixteen hours of receiving the request. Such decisions are standard procedure. To build more products with its existing assets, Deere redesigned its manufacturing processes to improve the flow of activity on the factory floor.

Maximizing Responsiveness to Customers: Wal-Mart

Supply chain consciousness has propelled another successful global company—a retailer of mammoth proportions with an unassailable business model—to the top of the retail marketplace. That company, of course, is Wal-Mart.

The story of Sam Walton's business success, and its scale, is familiar to many managers. But that success is worth rehearsing. For as it grew from a chain of small-town variety stores into the world's largest retailer, Wal-Mart succeeded not only because of the fierce negotiating skills of its founder and his associates, but also as a result of its relentless management of how merchandise moves.

Every single customer purchase affects how Wal-Mart stocks its shelves. Knowing demand to the minute—both understanding sales volume and being able to detect sales trends—the company uses that information to drive better arrangements with its suppliers. The combination of competitive zeal and logistical savvy has allowed Walton's Arkansas company to nearly bury traditional competitors, such as the venerable icon of retailing, Sears, Roebuck and Co., and K-Mart. And Montgomery Ward is now only a memory.

Calling Wal-Mart a successful retailer defines it too narrowly. Although the company does not manufacture anything, Wal-Mart is one of the country's best examples of excellence in orchestrating the procurement, distribution, and sale of goods and services. Wal-Mart grasped early on that an unremitting focus on costs and rigorous attention to the efficient movement of goods would enable it to stock its stores at the lowest possible prices.

Responsiveness means anticipating customer demand and fulfilling it in a timely way, notwithstanding the challenges. For example, every year, during the month of August, Wal-Mart sells over 50,000 window air-conditioning units made by Whirlpool. Window air-conditioners are a "high-ticket" item; they are heavy, bulky, and fragile. They take up valuable retail space, and are costly to ship and to return. Therefore, to forecast demand for cooling units in the succeeding summer season, Wal-Mart holds discussions with Whirlpool between six months and a year in advance. As summer approaches, Wal-Mart and Whirlpool share demand forecasts and adjust them to account for changes in demographics or any alterations to the Whirlpool product lines (such as varying color schemes or new super-efficient cooling technology).

Even after the product is in the stores, supply chain strategy continues to play a role. Just because 50,000 units were sold in August does not mean that 50,000 will sell in September. Although Wal-Mart uses EPOS (electronic point of sale) data to drive replenishment on store shelves, it does not simply automate a "sell-one, restock-one" policy. Wal-Mart anticipates seasonal changes in customer demand—geographical variations, such as the difference in climate between Minneapolis and Phoenix—and plans its moves accordingly.

Optimizing Time-to-Value: Kyocera

Ceramics is older than metal as a material, dating back to the first time someone left a lump of clay in the fire and it hardened. Despite the ancient and lowly origins of this material, Kyocera Corporation can turn mud into gold by applying ceramics to the most modern and advanced of technologies. This company has brought diverse products to many different markets faster than most companies in any industry. Kyocera is a pioneer in speedy innovation in a staggering range of industries.

The value of ceramics is based on its strength to withstand adverse conditions without breaking down like metals or plastics. The value of Kyocera is based on its amazing ability to manipulate ceramics for a wide variety of high-tech markets. For example, Kyocera supplies more than two-thirds of the world's ceramic packages for semiconductor chips. Kyocera has also used its knowledge of ceramics and materials manufacturing to create over 500 very different products, including automobile turbochargers, BIOCERAM (artificial bone and ceramic for hip joints and dental applications), synthetic gemstones (emeralds, rubies, sapphires), and even ceramic kitchen knives. Creating value in each application requires both knowledge of raw materials, ceramics processing, and customer needs (for example, artificial ceramic hips are coated with a material that is in human bones).

Kyocera has also moved beyond ceramics into glass. The company has leveraged its skills for processing materials at high temperatures to the manufacture of specially-formulated optical glass for camera lenses, copier printer drums, magneto-optical disks, and solar cells. And, most recently, it became the first manufacturer to successfully incorporate the functionality of a personal digital assistant into a cellular phone.

The point is that Kyocera can deliver great value rapidly in vastly different markets by leveraging supplied materials, applying internal manufacturing prowess, and understanding customer needs, not to mention having mastery of its global supply chains.

Achieving Supply Chain Objectives

World-class companies will concentrate on four key objectives:

- Driving costs down

- Using network assets more efficiently

- Continually enhancing relationships with customers

- Optimizing use of time

Singly, each of the objectives has appeal, but if a company seeks to achieve all these objectives at once, the strategies for achieving them could contend with one another. The four goals for a well-run supply chain are impossible to simultaneously and completely satisfy. A company should understand that

- You can't be too responsive if it costs too much to serve.

- You can't cut too much cost without degrading the value.

- You can't maximize every asset without trashing the bottom line.

- You can't do things too quickly without sacrificing quality or spending too much.

Successful companies will appreciate the importance of prioritizing the objectives, emphasizing those that best fit their competitive environment.

The Role of Information

Establishing a successful supply chain strategy is far from formulaic. Executing it involves more than an investment in foundation infrastructure. Tropicana, Natuzzi, Wal-Mart, Deere, and Kyocera did not simply set up a series of computer connections to send data back and forth. Strength, efficiency, and flexibility in their supply chains demanded a change in awareness among individuals in that organization, and required the companies to define how every constituent in the supply chain interacted at every major node and in every critical process.

A supply chain strategy needs processes to support the flow of information, and it needs to arm participants with a sense of purpose. To successfully achieve what Deere, Tropicana, Wal-Mart, Kyocera, and Natuzzi have achieved means instilling three concepts in the culture of the organization:

- **Connect:** Create an information infrastructure, both internally and externally, so information can flow.

- **Communicate:** Create processes for information exchange across the supply chain to ensure that information does flow.

- **Collaborate:** Create mutually beneficial purposes across the supply chain so information flows for a reason.

In business today, problems have to be addressed at the level of cause, not effect. Developing robust supply chains across companies involves asking questions, anticipating problems, and, most important, anticipating opportunities inside and outside the organization's four walls. Let's consider what happens when companies fail to pay attention to the three Cs...

Unsynchronized Supply Chains

Nature is replete with examples of synchronized relationships. Flowers bud in May because the showers of April have prepared the soil for seeds and bulbs to germinate. Investigation of a marine ecosystem reveals a fantastic interplay between the specific needs and characteristics of the local sea life and the environment that supports it. Predators leave scraps for bottom feeders. Unencumbered streams of sunlight ensure an inviting temperature for the plant and marine life that inhabit those waters.

Unfortunately, it seems that only through aberrations in the expected flow of events do we realize the incredible importance of the cooperation that takes place in nature. Only when we have especially dry springs (and consequently less than lush summers), or when an oil spill tampers with the normal water temperature and forces an area's marine life to relocate, do we consider what it means for things to work in harmony. A similar analogy can be made with respect to commerce. In business, synchronizing events to take place in an optimal order needs to be considered in a larger context than as a short-term management achievement. It is emblematic of things being in an appropriate relationship to one another, functioning according to their core purpose. To a great extent, it is by identifying lapses in operations, by examining the symptoms of unsynchronized supply chains, that we can identify what needs to happen for things to operate in flow.

The following represent some key symptoms of unsynchronized supply chains. Each can represent a tremendous loss to a company individually. Yet to assess the actual impact of any of these conditions, one needs to recognize that they are interrelated (one operational symptom easily affects performance in other areas) and that any individual symptom can have repercussions on other companies throughout the chain.

Poor On-Time Performance

On-time performance is a general term that encompasses timely delivery of any product or service within the fulfillment process. When a delivery to a customer is late, it's not the occasion to simply lament a delivery failure. Instead, it is an opportunity to identify lapses in performing well along the entire supply chain: the causal relationships between actions along the supply chain predict that a negative outcome is the result of a failure anywhere within it. And the consequences for poor on-time performance are significant. The inability to deliver product on time negatively impacts cash position, as money invested in production cannot be recouped in revenues for an extended time. This may, in the short term, force customers to choose alternative sources, or it may inhibit a company's ability to take advantage of current publicity, promotions, or unusual market conditions. It can even have a long-term impact on a company's reputation and image, affecting customer trust, employee morale, and shareholder value.

Miscoordinations

When you twirl a forkful of spaghetti, you cannot trace a single strand from one end to the other. Each strand has become intertwined with so many others. Similarly, it is often difficult, within the production fulfillment cycle, to isolate one miscue or error because each one naturally is intertwined with other aspects of operations. Inaccurate forecasts and frequent back-order situations are two of the most common examples of miscoordination. Inaccurate forecasts occur when all relevant gauges of demand are not consulted. The impact of such a situation can result in minor adjustments in production or an unbearable overstock of products that cannot be quickly exchanged for cash. A related symptom is chronic back-order situations, resulting from poor coordination between production activities and fulfillment requirements and from incorrectly estimating material and capacity needs throughout the supply chain. Both situations introduce special challenges for managing cash and can literally ruin a business—driving customers to competitors who can supply the desired goods on time.

Difficulty in Meeting Obligations

A business needs a dynamic mechanism to determine what can be promised, based on what is on hand, what stock has been previously allocated, demand for other products, scheduled production and available capacity, and other criteria. When a business lacks a system to accurately maintain information on product availability and subsequently to communicate that information to customers, it creates multiple challenges for itself. Lacking such a system, a company can lose not only at the transactional level—missing out on sales where customers' sole purchasing criteria is availability—but can also fail at the relationship level as well. Each inquiry made about product availability that cannot be answered immediately and accurately is a battle lost in the longer-term engagement for the chance to meet or exceed expectations.

Bloated Cost Structure

If the cost to service a customer is going up when all other aspects of the business are staying the same, the company has an uncontrollable leak in profitability. A situation in which increased sales could be considered a detriment to a company seems absurd, but this certainly would be the case if the cost of providing goods or services goes unchecked. An old business adage pokes fun at this potential paradox: "If a company is selling cans of tuna fish at a five-cent loss per can, then it will have to sell ten thousand cans to make up the difference." An operational symptom of an unsynchronized supply chain would be the absence of systems to monitor costs of raw materials, labor (including overtime), rush shipments to meet promises, or carrying inventory on slow cycling products.

Poor Supplier Performance

Educational systems can produce skilled and civic-minded adults only when students, schools, and families all do their part. Similarly, a lack of standards shared by a business and its suppliers naturally degrades into a lack of accountability and a systemic failure to perform. The efficacy of any process that involves cooperative interaction between parties requires standards. Inoperative or poorly functioning communications or linkages in certain areas—such as providing order status and shipping information, product availability, and disposition on product quality concerns—can have monumental consequences throughout the chain.

Loose or Unaligned Functional Metrics

Poor supplier performance, while often seen as a failure in communication, actually begins with poorly conceived methods for setting and monitoring standards and compliance. If, for example, goals established for one area of operations are not aligned with other strategic objectives, overall performance will be affected. For example, if production is focused only on attaining volume objectives regardless of sequencing the order mix, profitability could easily suffer.

Lack of Velocity

Velocity is defined as the degree of swiftness with which activities are carried out, either internally or externally. Velocity is becoming an increasingly important factor in contemporary business models. Lack of velocity, as demonstrated by slow inventory turns, is just one obvious danger to profitability. Speed in planning and adjusting (re-planning) to take advantage of windows of opportunity and quickly build new revenue streams is just as important as speed in plugging leaks. In an unsynchronized supply chain, a company may suffer from cumbersome and slow product design processes, lack of plans for secondary sourcing on primary components, and lack of timely information systems that furnish useful customer purchasing information in time to affect production.

No Value Stratification

The qualifying expression "all things being equal" certainly does not apply to profitable business operations. All things are not equal. All customers are not equal. All orders are not equal. All special requests are not equally "special." Different customers have different values in terms of how they may contribute to the business potential of an enterprise. Time, product, and other resources need to be applied in direct proportion to the value individual customers can be expected to bring to a business. The 80/20 rule, so often used in intelligently managing sales efforts, poses that since 20 percent of a company's customers constitute 80 percent of its overall business, that population deserves 80 percent of its attention. This is just one example of value stratification. If a company lacks routine systems to determine priorities for investing time and attention—systems to identify top customers, which orders to ship first, and which customer or supplier situations require the most urgent attention—it will not be able to perform to its potential.

The following example of Procter & Gamble's struggle to market a product after a competitor got to customers first illustrates the problems that result when different domains in a company do not coordinate with one another or with suppliers and customers.

P&G's Gummed-Up Toothpaste

Procter & Gamble is the maker of that venerable cavity fighter, Crest toothpaste. But when Colgate introduced a new competing toothpaste, Total, the company took the lead because the toothpaste was said to whiten teeth while also protecting against plaque and gum disease (not just fight cavities). P&G should not have been surprised that a toothpaste of this type would be a hit in the marketplace. That aging baby boomers would want to protect their smiles should have been predicted more than 40 years ago. Although P&G was working on such a smile-protecting toothpaste, it had frittered away six years and was still just testing the product. Colgate smiled—and pounced.

At P&G, either of two groups could have prevented this snafu. First, its brand managers could have been more proactive in highlighting the latent demand for new product features. Second, its product development group could have moved faster to fill the gap in their line of offerings. The internal coordination and communication among the various groups—market research, product development, and manufacturing divisions—could have greatly shortened the response time of P&G.

Spotting Supply Chain Defects

Like Apple's failure to deliver iBooks to customers, P&G's failure to counter Total toothpaste was an internal supply chain failure. However, supply chain issues do not often present themselves so clearly. The operational symptoms of a poorly organized supply chain—and of a lack of sufficient synchronization of its elements with a company's strategy—can be spotted in a number of ways. The observant eye can note many everyday issues that contribute to the problem:

- End-of-the month sales campaigns that seem to indicate poor marketing management and inaccurate demand forecasts

- Late or erroneous deliveries to customers that suggest poor fulfillment management

- Backorders, shortages, or late or defective supplies that imply poor supply management

- Clogged loading docks that signal poor transportation management

- Empty shelves, overflowing shelves, or misplaced stock, suggesting poor inventory management

- Idle machines and idle workers that show poor manufacturing management

The point of these examples is to show that an unsynchronized supply chain leads to problems that could be easily prevented if only companies connected, communicated, and collaborated more—the 3 C's. A poorly managed supply chain or one in which any one link is not operating with the efficiency of the whole starts to affect companies anywhere along the chain. Then, too, minor problems tend to amplify themselves—a phenomenon that supply chain strategists refer to as the bullwhip effect.

The Bullwhip Effect

The bullwhip effect is particularly helpful in explaining how supply chain problems affect an entire business. Imagine a situation in which a new video-game console starts flying off the shelves because a certain CD-ROM has captured the attention of eleven-year-old girls. Suddenly, in response to a changed market for the consoles, retailers order more volume from their distributors. Some distributors, however, take extra time to fill the orders. Perhaps the requests for additional product sit on a salesperson's desk and wait in the order queue. At the warehouse, perhaps the ordered products sit on the loading dock until a truck hauls them to the retailers. Small delays can add up to an appreciable length of time.

What are you nursing?

Meanwhile, demand at retail outlets continues to be high. Retailers see the systems moving off the shelf and fear that they will soon be out of stock, yet their first restock order has yet to arrive. Frustrated, retailers place even larger orders, feeling they must cope both with the extra demand and make up for lost inventory.

Unfortunately, the same process repeats itself between distributors and the manufacturer. Distributors see a second round of orders from retailers and think that demand is growing rapidly. In reality, demand has been relatively consistent, even if higher than previously. But the second order effects a huge shift in the equation. To compensate, the distributors crack the whip, placing massive initial orders with the manufacturer. Since the consoles require time to produce, the distributors end up repeating the nervous error of the retailers and place an escalating series of orders as well.

Then the bullwhip cracks again. The manufacturer produces consoles to cover what it sees as an exponential growth in demand. But once the product makes its way through the unsynchronized supply chain—once orders are filled and inventory is replenished—the retailers stop ordering in volume. Since the distributors believed the orders reflected actual demand, they perceive a reversal of previous growth and not a normal correction. As the retailers and distributors start canceling orders, the factory must cut production. Somewhere in the process, one or more of the supply chain participants suffers from massive overstocks.

Of course, it's not over. In an unsynchronized supply chain, the whip cracks once more when inventories eventually decrease. Then retailers and distributors start ordering once more. One can imagine the disgruntled phone calls up and down the chain. Clearly, this phenomenon reflects a lack of timely communication. It is also important to note that this lack of communication applies both internally and externally. All parties overreact because they see the demand and fulfillment needs so poorly. The result is that the constituents in a supply chain swing from feast to famine. When every small variation in orders is amplified, the resulting volatility in a supply chain is much larger than the changes that started the whole problem.

The Benefits of a Synchronized Supply Chain

When it comes to gauging the overall performance of a business, Return on Assets is one of the most common metrics. With an ROA analysis, a company measures its success by subtracting its expenses from revenues and dividing the remainder by its assets. A synchronized supply chain supports each aspect of this equation. When information and processes interact in timely and appropriate ways within a company, and between a company and its business partners, revenues are increased, costs are reduced, and use of assets is optimized. Following are some specific benefits a company may experience from synchronizing its supply chain.

Short Order-to-Ship Time

The velocity of commerce among a company, its customers, and its suppliers is often the truest reflection of that relationship's health and viability. A short order-to-ship cycle is a concrete demonstration of what occurs when information, planning processes, and execution of tasks take place in a timely and well-integrated manner. The synchronization of supply chain is the essence of the proverbial win-win situation. Everyone involved benefits when orders can be shipped at the precise time the customer wants them. When this happens, the customers can turn around and sell goods more quickly and can more readily initiate reordering. When the order-to-ship process flows quickly and smoothly into a reorder process, it benefits a company's suppliers as well. They share in the benefits of this new business. In addition, the pressure to meet this kind of performance forces a company and its suppliers to exercise efficiencies throughout their operations.

Short order-to-ship cycles require effectively integrating information, such as projections of customer demand with planning processes, production scheduling, purchasing raw materials, delivery arrangements, and so on. When companies are attentive about gathering demand information and have systems in place to efficiently share this information with relevant participants in the supply chain, then everyone can work together proactively. Anticipating needs and the resulting brief order-to-ship cycle become standard operating procedure and not accidental boons. Being able to maintain a short order-to-ship time is an operational benefit that can translate into a major business advantage: a positive cash-to-cash cycle.

Positive Cash-to-Cash Cycles

Everyone benefits from the synchronization of information, manufacturing, and distribution systems. A positive cash flow allows them to allocate assets for other elements that will help grow the business. A company that benefits from positive cash-to-cash cycles simply has more working capital to invest in a wide range of opportunities.

Positive cash-to-cash cycles, which occur in tandem with short order-to-ship cycles, are only possible when a company is committed to synchronized supply chain practices.

Reduced Costs

Cost containment is one of the primary goals of almost any business model. Reducing the cost to serve customers relative to revenues generated is a key element in the equation for return on assets. In the context of synchronized supply chains, reducing costs takes on an even larger meaning, and is achieved not merely by eliminating unnecessary overhead or streamlining business processes. To a large extent, it comes from improving coordination among information, planning, and activity. Companies today cannot hope to build inventory in hopes of a commensurate demand; they must have information on what demand will be, and rely on that information's being communicated through the organization. Information must precede the instinct to build inventories. Cost containment begins when costs are monitored and that information is funneled back into planning as frequently as needed for appropriate adjustments. Critically, a company has to be able to gauge real demand and understand the constraints it operates within in order to make midstream adjustments. Reducing costs, as a business benefit, is largely the result of designing processes that enable a company to keep current.

Improved Positioning for Growth

A short order-to-ship cycle contributes to a positive cash cycle. A positive cash cycle, coupled with reduced costs, helps a company achieve growth. The interrelated nature of systems within a supply chain model and the benefits they generate provide immediate benefits to a company. Cumulatively, they help position an enterprise to achieve long-term objectives. The goal of a business should not be survival today, but success at least a few years from now. When a company provides goods and services on a timely basis, it attains competitive advantages over companies that don't. Further, when that same company succeeds in cutting costs, it improves its cash positioning and range of choices in planning its growth.

The ultimate benefit of operating within a synchronized supply chain is both highly functional and loaded with significance for the individuals who participate in it. To make the supply chain work smoothly, customers and suppliers must think of each other as partners. Departments within a company need to operate in collaboration with each other. And individuals in any position within the system need to offer their full commitment and participation.

Managing Cause and Effect

By promoting an understanding of cause and effect, everyone can become increasingly aware of the role others play in the supply chain and the role they play themselves. Supply chain consciousness means increasing everyone's awareness of others in the company. In particular, each constituent of the supply chain must understand

- The goals, needs, and dislikes of others
- The capacities and constraints of others
- The current operating state of others
- The plans of others

Connection, communication, and collaboration are the means of coming to these understandings. The resulting joint consciousness of the supply chain leads to

- Creating mutually agreeable goals
- Working within everyone's capacities and constraints while trying to enhance them
- Mutually modulating plans to fit current operating situations
- Synchronizing all plans into one coordinated flow of activity

In the best scenario, everyone in the supply chain, from suppliers to the people in the company to its customers, would understand the whole supply chain. Improved information flow and information transparency would lead to greater reliability. The company would be able to reliably fulfill demand because it would have

- Fewer surprise orders from sales (because better demand forecasts and awareness of capacity create reliable and realistic order streams)

- Fewer surprise delays from suppliers (because the company would know the capacities and constraints of its suppliers)

- Fewer surprise delays in manufacturing (because the company would have far better flows of raw materials to finished goods)

- Fewer surprise stock-outs from inventory (because the company would know the quantities and dispositions of all inventories)

- Fewer surprise delays from transportation (because the company would know the capacities and availabilities of trucks)

The point is that fewer surprises means greater reliability. It means fulfilling your promises to your customers because you can make promises that you can fulfill.

Conceptually Connecting the Enterprise

Those who most need to develop a consciousness of how supply chains work are those who participate directly with the products, services, customers, and suppliers of a company. But the highest echelon of corporate leadership must appreciate the extent to which causal relationships within a corporation affect the success of the entire business. No longer can a CEO delegate ultimate responsibility for sharing information and knowledge to executives lower down the corporate hierarchy. While the mechanics of supply chain execution will always be a team effort, moral leadership must remain with the CEO. Without the support of this leadership, a company will stay stuck in a morass of unmanaged demand, opaque operations, and unfulfilled expectations.

Supply chain consciousness means effecting major changes in both skills and attitudes. Narrow skills or backgrounds will no longer work for a financial wizard, marketing genius, manufacturing maven, or self-styled strategy guru who may not have the breadth of knowledge and insight to make sound supply chain decisions. Executives must now understand the junctures that make or break their companies. These break points are often between demand and fulfillment, where only a coordinated change in several domains of the company can create the desired results. This requires multidisciplinary backgrounds, career job rotations, and open, inquisitive minds.

It's time to cave in to the caveman

Because all the domains of a company must now work in concert, the executives who oversee these domains must collaborate with each other. Selfish attitudes, the hoarding of information, and interruptions in internal communications can stunt a company's growth or kill it. Silos must be shattered so that everyone in the organization can connect, communicate, and collaborate. The orchestration of clear thinking among all levels of a company calls for nothing less than an intellectual cataclysm. To win the supply chain battles and hence the market wars, understanding cause and effect must become part of the DNA of tomorrow's companies.

For today's corporations the challenge of managing business transformation stems from the interrelated nature of cause and effect throughout the corporation. Companies compete within their own organizations to achieve efficiencies, create the right products, manage production, and serve their key markets. All these objectives interfere with one another, and all must be resolved. The means of resolving them is a business transformation, an intellectual framework for which I introduce in Chapter 2.

The Carpenter's Creed

A Model of Business Transformation

Companies make products. And some companies fail. The connection is simple. A company's failure fundamentally depends on a collection of product and product-related failures that have been brought about by bad decision making. And there are a slew of reasons why bad decisions are made and therefore why companies decay, disintegrate, and die.

When Companies Fail Once

Some companies fail once, but only once. They somehow manage to figure out what went wrong, they are able to correct their mistakes, and then they move on, in many instances to a level of success that no one—given these companies' initial collapse—could have imagined. The key idea is that they have both the skill and the will to face up to their problems, diagnose them, and implement the appropriate solutions.

Of course, the kinds of mistakes that can lead an otherwise well-managed company down the path of ruin are many and varied. Let us look at these banana peels:

Too Many Low-Margin Products/ Too Many Me-Too Products

The first problem that can victimize an organization is having too many low-margin products. A company in this situation frequently operates on a high-volume business model that too often embroils the company in price wars.

Another permutation of the problem is having too many products that are simply imitations of other, successful products—a scenario in which a company concentrates on developing too many "me-too" products with no differentiation in the marketplace. Always playing follow-the-leader, the company never catches up to its competitors and ultimately—though sometimes slowly (but always painfully)—fades out of the marketplace.

Irrational Proliferation of Products and Services

A proliferation of products may compete for resources, in which case the products cannibalize each other and confuse customers in key markets. This is symptomatic of trying to be everything to everybody.

No True Visibility into Cost Structure

Of course some corporate failures have more to do with lapses in self-knowledge than with product imitation or proliferation.One such problem arises when a company has no clear awareness of the true cost structure for each of its products—i.e., no way to understand, audit, and control the cost of creating, developing, refining, marketing, and supporting its individual products. A company may lack tight standards for the performance of its suppliers. It may have serpentine processes in its business operations: too much duplication, double entries, and the related diminished efforts of personnel who see redundancies, trammeled decision making, stupidity, and waste.

Dysfunctional Information Systems

Some companies suffer from a global breakdown in internal communication, a result of dysfunctional information systems in which the flow of information is disjointed or delayed. The problem of having sufficient data but poor access to it yields the familiar paradox of being data-rich, but information-poor.

Unsynchronized Supply Chain

There may be other fundamental problems. A company may have a flawed process for assessing and orchestrating demand and supply. In such a situation, the suffering company is perpetually bullwhipped—at the mercy of the domino effect, in which errors at one end of the information chain multiply all along the circuit. For example, a company may not capably manage its order-to-cash cycle and its cash-to-cash cycle. In this situation, adequate working capital is not available for expansion projects, and this hampers forward propulsion, for every strategic initiative is burdened with a management that is cash-poor and gun-shy—unable to spend the necessary dollars simply because they just aren't there.

Unfriendliness to Customers

Other problems extend outside to customer service. A company may be unfriendly towards customers, and may have processes or policies that make doing business with it frustrating, unnecessarily complex, and annoyingly convoluted.

Constipated Corporate Culture

A company may be forgoing the opportunity to leverage its current competencies into creating or conquering new markets. Instead it continues to muddle its way forward in a world of minimal differentiation and in the vain hope that advertising or extra promotion will solve its problem. The company may fear innovation and thereby fail to alter its market position.

Every one of these problems has deep root causes. Sometimes the causes are multiple, and they are frequently intertwined with one another. Every one of these challenges ultimately affects all the products a company offers, thereby affecting that company's bottom line. Every one can cripple a company's opportunity for success.

A company fails once when its products fail and its people fail to take notice. The result is a company without passion, purpose, and propulsion. It is a company that has lost its spirit and seems to ride on stock market fortunes instead of intrinsic vision. Of course, every one of these problems has a solution, and each must be in place for a company to succeed over time. Success can be fleeting, however, and some companies seem either destined never to achieve it or committed to failing again and again.

When Companies Fail Twice

In Shakespeare's *Merchant of Venice*, one of the characters says, "Mercy is twice blessed...." To twist the Bard's quotation, "Mercy may be twice blessed, but the medication of management ills will be twice cursed if they are not understood." Some companies fail once, recover, and then thrive. But others seem to fail not once, but twice, and in some cases continue to stagger from failure to failure. Why does this happen?

Companies fail twice either because they are unaware of or deliberately ignore the problems summarized above or because they try too hard to solve them. The first mistake is incurable if the company persists in ignorance or fear. If you don't see the problem, you can't fix it. But even if a company is aware of, concerned about, and prepared to solve the problem that could potentially destroy it, caution is necessary. The simple reason is that doing too much may be as bad as doing too little.

Companies that pursue the course of fast, aggressive, and comprehensive reform run the risk of dissipation, particularly if they have a big idea but fail to implement it with adequate coordination and consistency. Such companies suffer from the curse of too many initiatives with no common umbrella, no connective tissue, and no conceptual unity. Too many problem-solving projects are running concurrently, and all are running helter-skelter, with little attention to the need for integration. Such initiatives breed functional disintegration, create fragmented views of the organization, and create factionalism in the company's personnel and among its divisions. Company managers lack a fundamental understanding of cause and effect, and they lack a common denominator for understanding one another's initiatives. Not only is there a philosophical disagreement over ideas and goals; even the dialogue is divisive. This is when companies fail twice.

Consider the following broad-based panaceas, which turn out to be little more than semantic band-aids.

- *"Let us be innovative."* Companies crow constantly about the need for innovation. But what about the case of a company with too many products that have no market charter? What if all the company's innovation amounts to is a series of customer-forced incremental changes? What if all the innovation that occurs is a knee-jerk reaction to market tumult? And what if the revenue from new products is a minuscule portion of the overall revenue stream?

- *"Let us reduce cycle-time."* A common refrain in so-called business transformations is that cycle-times must be reduced to improve efficiencies and realize revenues more quickly. But what if cycle-time is understood to be only manufacturing times and not administrative lead-times? What if the product itself has reached a point at which there is no more blood to be squeezed from the turnip? What if the product in question is becoming irrelevant to the marketplace or is in the last stages of its life cycle, screaming for a transition?

- *"We must be more customer-focused."* No company will willingly and forthrightly ignore its good customers. But that means knowing what a good customer is. What if the cost to serve a customer is so high that the company is losing money? What if the customer is not profitable to start with, because of the relative slimness of his or her purchases, or the sporadic nature of those purchases? Is this a customer that deserves focus? Is this a customer whose behavior should drive decision making? The point is that a blind devotion to customer needs, bereft of sensitivity to cost, can affect a company's profitability. A lopsided customer intimacy will bring fiscal halitosis, and the claim to be "customer-focused" will become, in this instance, a classic case of semantic self-injury.

- *"We will pursue product leadership."* What if the company makes great products but without synchronizing its supply chains? What if the complexity of making and supporting these products creates an invisible drain from projected revenue streams?

- *"We are operationally excellent."* What if, instead of having in place a holistic gauge for success, the company has established measures of operational excellence that are so skewed that only local measures are lauded. What if operational excellence is equated with manufacturing activities alone? What about all the nonmanufacturing activities, especially post-sales?

- *"We have a lot of e-initiatives."* The continued thoughtless priority given to initiatives for e-commerce is maddening. Certainly, the drone of e-this and e-that has abated somewhat, but the reality is not reassuring. Too many businesses continue to make decisions about web-based tools that offer little or no attraction to their core users. The result is a cacophony of e-business initiatives that actually thwart, rather than foster, a mature dialogue about management priorities and a meaningful dissection of business issues.

When companies embark on transformation initiatives driven by senseless semantic band-aids, they invariably end up injuring themselves. Often these injuries are internal and insidious, and the result is death by a thousand cuts.

M.C. Escher's "Relativity" © 2001 Cordon Art B.V. - Baarn - Holland.
All rights reserved.

What correlation does the drawing by the great Dutch master M.C. Escher bear to the dynamics of corporations? There are too many frames of reference–individually possible, but collectively impossible. The multi-gravitational contention in the drawing is emblematic of what happens in corporations–conflicting projects, colliding purposes, and confused people. Well-intentioned but ill-conceived efforts are often doomed to become ill-fated because of a lack of common ground. Ironically, even changes that increase the longevity of individual domains can short circuit the life span of a company. The relevant question is, where is the center of gravity?

The Anatomy of Business Transformation

It is time to radically redefine what business transformation is all about. A business transformation is not an e-expedition. It is time to exorcise the e-epithet (of course, pun intended) from our language. It is time to change the course and content of our corporate dialogue. The Internet is only a medium. To transform companies, we need conceptual clarity and a common denominator in our dialogue.

A company's profitability is directly proportional to the profitability of its products. Therefore, it behooves us to look at corporate transformation as the management of individual product destinies. These destinies, however, must be examined collectively and in relation to every other aspect of the entire business operation. Business is multidimensional and so are its cause-and-effect relationships. This means that corporate strategy as we know it is dead—for we must now focus on the interconnectedness among different aspects, divisions, levels, and functions of the company. Without due consideration of—that is, *absolute attention to*—this interconnectedness, a business strategy is worthless. It is like playing with a deck of cards that are numbered, but not identified by suit. You can play some games, but Hearts, Bridge, Pinochle, and Gin Rummy are out of reach. Without an understanding and exploitation of this interconnectedness, all corporate initiatives will produce local and lopsided results.

What is needed, then, is a holistic vision that takes all the variables into account. What is needed, as well, is a common vocabulary that binds strategy to execution. But what is the umbrella that will amalgamate all corporate transformation initiatives? What is the magnet that will unite all the scattered filings? The answer is QRIIO, which stands for *Quest for Rationalization, Innovation, Integration, and Orchestration*. It is a framework for analyzing products and services. It is a foundation for conducting a *coherent* transformation of the destinies of products and services. It is an umbrella under which unification of all corporate activities can occur because it organizes strategy and execution contextually and comprehensively.

Consider a family of five children—all with different aptitudes;

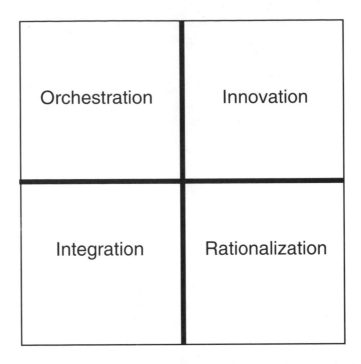

Figure 2-1   QRIIO - Quest for Rationalization, Innovation, Integration, and Orchestration

different circles of friends; different learning styles; and different preferences in food, clothing, and entertainment. Each child will evolve differently in academic performance, extracurricular activities, social adaptation, and individual talents. An across-the-board parental style, however, can hinder individual development. To maximize each child's potential, good parenting requires a clear understanding of each one's unique attributes and characteristics. In short, a good parent will respect these children's differences, read their signals carefully, and respond appropriately to each child's evolution.

Corporations have a lesson to learn from families. Like a child with his or her own abilities, interests, and friends, every product has its own web of customers, suppliers, transporters, and others who are affiliated with the product. Every product has its own markets, its unique life cycle, and its fruit-bearing abilities in different stages of its life cycle. That's why, just as every child in a family has to be nurtured differently, when a company manages multiple products, each product has to be understood correctly, appreciated differently, and analyzed specifically.

QRIIO is the lens through which the different shades of a product's destiny can be beheld. The destiny of a product is fourfold. It is the *innovation* during the life cycle of the product; it is the *rationalization* of its markets, customers, and value; it is the *integration* with its ecosystem of suppliers and customers; and finally it is the daily *orchestration* of demand and fulfillment. Let us look at each one of these components.

Innovation

Urging companies to innovate is not new; what is new is exhorting companies to innovate thoughtfully, with a clear sense of the relationships among products, markets, customers, and values. Innovation is not proliferation, and proliferation is not innovation. A company's commitment to innovation is always a choice between improving old products and creating entirely new ones and between expanding existing markets and opening new ones. Here are the questions to ask. Is the innovation a change in feature or function, or is it a fundamental value shift? Is the innovation intended to generate new revenue streams, get new customers, or both? What are the relative merits of making incremental changes for small margins or radical changes (and sometimes risky ones) for potentially higher profits? Are we tying up our development resources in delivering promises made to the customer during the sale of the product?

On one hand, the problem is too little innovation, as a result of which a company has too many mature products on the market, with too many competitors, and therefore both low profits and the prospect of even lower returns in the future. On the other hand, the problem is misaligned, excessive innovation, as a result of which a company has too many products, some bumping into each other (i.e., competing with each other for the same market share and internal resources) and some languishing for want of attention (i.e., remaining unsold because they are not being promoted).

The revered Xerox PARC, Xerox's Palo Alto Research Center, was the home of groundbreaking inventions. Yet how many products did Xerox actually bring to market? If every corporate life is either an example of what companies should do or what they should not do, Xerox became a cautionary tale: specifically, that investment in R&D is a sunk cost unless the inventions can be translated into successful products in a timely manner. Hewlett-Packard has piled up patent after patent. Mere collection of patents, however, is a misleading metric of innovation. The questions to ask are, how many of these patents will turn into market-worthy products? In the past five years what percentage of revenues came from new products? What percentage of revenues will come from new products this year? Next year?

Cisco, on the strength of its market capitalization, acquired company after company. It went on a purchasing spree, acquiring innovation in the open market. Although the basic router still remains Cisco's bread and butter, yet to deepen its penetration into the marketplace the company has moved into the realm of algorithm driven software that can be used to create complex networks.

Adopting a nontraditional way to build its creative armor, Cisco somehow managed to blend and baptize its acquired companies into a working mélange to broaden its position, given the very short market windows. Yet what Cisco suffers from is a pronounced lack of innovational continuity and an ethos of sewing instead of sowing.

Innovation is either an integral part of the corporate culture or it is not. Just as the human body cannot always depend on pharmacological stimulation to sustain itself in the long run, but has to muster its own natural resources to fight off infection and disease, so must a company rely on its own creativity and organized effort to maintain its well-being in the face of declining product life cycles and the challenges of competition.

Ultimately it is not innovation per se, but how timely and relevant the innovation is during the life cycle of the product, and what impact it has on a market segment.

In this context, innovation is not the prerogative of product development alone. Indeed, it is primarily a concerted effort that requires input from every position on the supply chain, especially suppliers, manufacturers, sales force, and transporters. R&D may be the life-blood of computer companies and pharmaceuticals, but the leaders in these industries know that innovation must also be a byword company-wide. They understand, as well, that not even the most revolutionary concepts can be turned into successful products without the materials to make the product, adequate means of getting it to markets, and customers to buy it for a price that covers the cost of the product and includes a profit sufficient to make the whole complicated process worthwhile.

Rationalization

What is missing in many companies that pride themselves on their commitment to innovation is *rationalization*, which simply means thinking through every decision and making sure there are reasons for every action. The assumption here is that every action involves a decision, every decision involves a choice, and every choice requires some exercise of rational thought—from small to large, depending on the importance of the action.

Rationalization is simply

- Mapping the right combination of products to markets, drawing the right customers, and delivering the right value

- Managing the life cycle of every product while being ever vigilant regarding the dual forces of irrelevance on the one hand and interference on the other

- Responding to revenue fluctuations due to life-cycle variations so that revenue targets and revenue structure from different products are continually calibrated and corrected

A company must monitor its product portfolio regularly and systematically. Sometimes the portfolio must be cleansed of products that have passed their prime, and sometimes it must be expanded by the introduction of new products that will either appeal to a new market or recover the market that might have been lost with the retirement of its old product.

Two companies that have recently cut a large piece out of their product mix are Mattel and Toshiba. Mattel streamlined its product line by eliminating virtually 25% of the products it was planning to roll out. It disbanded its money-losing learning company-computer game division, ended a pricey movie-licensing agreement with Disney, and began to focus on its supply chains: getting products out on time and staying close to customers to gauge market demand and synchronize its fulfillment.

Toshiba decided to exit from the commodity DRAM business when it realized that the cost of producing the chips was almost twice the market price. The commodity chip industry was suffering under the falling demand in the PC market. Thus, Toshiba sold off its unnecessary assets to focus on custom-designed chips, where profit margins are higher. The company was suffocating with a low-margin, high-volume product, dispensed with it, turned to a new product, and moved on.

Take the case of Intel. In late 2001, it shut down its web-hosting unit and its digital consumer electronics business, saying that these businesses "disrupted" its profits. Well, one wonders what had "erupted" in Intel's mind to even get into web hosting, of all things?

General Motors shut down its Oldsmobile unit, a classic case of a product line that had run its course and one that interfered with other products in the GM portfolio. The Cutlass Supreme had become so market-blunt that it "cut less" and was no longer "supreme." The product had become so old that it was no longer mobile. At the beginning of 2002, Ford eliminated four models— Escort, Mercury Cougar, Mercury Villager, and Lincoln Continental. The Escort was at one time Ford's best-selling car, but has been bested by the subcompact Focus, which has now become one of the top sellers in the world. With no growth in sight, inadequate sales volumes, minimal margins, and mounting costs, Ford had no choice but to escort these models to the door. The name of its grace-saving subcompact, "Focus," was perhaps the epiphany for Ford. How revealing!

Long Overdue...

The fact of life is, no matter how creative and culinary you are, you cannot offer 77 different gourmet dinners to five customers. Aristotle said 2,500 years ago: "All virtue is a golden mean between two vices." In the world of business, virtue is the middle ground between irrelevance and interference. Sometimes less is more, and more is less.

Integration

Every product has its own unique needs in terms of bills of materials, processing procedures, packaging, labeling, shipping requirements, delivery modes, and invoicing. Furthermore, in a global economy every product has its own market-specific requirements.

Every product also has its own ecosystem of suppliers, customers, distributors, and product handlers. Hence, the requirements for connection, communication, and collaboration are also unique to each product. And every constituent in the supply chain has its own unique topology of hardware, software, databases, and other technological paraphernalia. To connect, communicate, and collaborate, given the vast array of every product's linkages to patterns, processes, and personnel both inside and outside the company, it is necessary to integrate these disparate elements and make them work consistently and collaboratively.

The real battle in integration is, of course, informational: maximizing input received from the outside, especially regarding markets, and making sure that everyone who is in any way involved with the product—inside or outside— knows what he or she needs to know. By nature, every part of the organization is tempted to compete rather than cooperate. And every division has its own way of seeing things—observing, interpreting, and evaluating. Even though every decision at every level in one way or another affects the overall corporate commitment to align products to markets to customers to value (that is, everyone, at least theoretically, shares common goals and expectations), this commitment is viewed through different lenses not only from person to person, but from time to time.

To align all the constituencies for every product, the following questions must be answered affirmatively:

- Is all the information relevant to a product available at the right time and to the right people?

- Is the movement of the product, both internally and externally, transparent?

- Do the people who touch the product, either physically or informationally, understand the fundamental planning cycle, the product life cycle, the customer life cycle, and the order life cycle of that particular product?

Orchestration

However, one question cannot be answered yes merely because a company has successfully fulfilled the requirements of innovation, rationalization, and integration: Is the supply-demand relationship for the product visible, verifiable, and viable? In other words, a product may be innovative, it may be adequately matched to a market, and its support network may be in place. Yet even under these ideal circumstances, a company runs the risk of squandering all these accomplishments if it fails to orchestrate demand and fulfillment.

The daily act of fulfilling customer demand is where the rubber hits the road, which means that the acid test of any organization's success is its supply chain orchestration. Dell is not a classic product innovator like Hewlett-Packard or Sun, but it is an incredibly efficient merchant thanks to its supply chain synchronization. It is this virtue that helps the company squeeze out blood from stones in the PC business of razor-thin margins.

After all, a company's cash position is tied to its order-to-cash cycle and its cash-to-cash cycle. And both of these cycles have a unique profile for each product, which must be attended to on a daily basis. Even though you live near a dentist, you must brush your teeth every day. That is, everything in the company may be functioning smoothly and operating successfully, but that edifice is in danger of crumbling if customers fail to receive delivery, payment is not made, and the customer satisfaction and confidence that generate reorders or return visits to the store are not sustained. Great products die in the daily delivery wars.

Understanding Interrelationships

The right half of QRIIO embodies growth and leadership, and the left half embodies efficiency and enablement. All four quadrants are indispensable, and all of them influence each other. For those reasons, a company must have competencies in every quadrant for every product it makes or service it delivers.

Let us examine how incompetencies in one or more quadrants

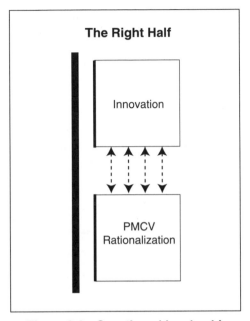

Figure 2-2   Growth and Leadership

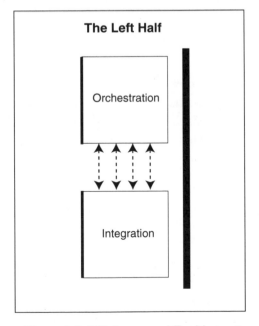

Figure 2-3 Efficiency and Enablement

can cripple a company. Perhaps the most notable contemporary illustration is Motorola. That the company's problems are serious is best demonstrated by its decision to reduce employee head count by approximately 45,000 through a combination of voluntary and involuntary layoffs, not filling newly approved positions, not filling positions of people who retired or left on their own, and selling off business units and the people in them in 2001. The question is, what led to this dire situation? As most observers have noted, Motorola has had a history of higher-than-industry-average manufacturing costs because the company has always led with its mastery of innovation and engineering, not lowest cost. That is partly why the company's margins have traditionally been near 30%, whereas Nokia's margins have been closer to 40%. Success leaves clues just as failure leaves footprints. What went wrong at Motorola? Let us look at the genealogy:

1. Motorola invented the cellular industry and offered the first cellular handset, a basic telephone with limited features,that sold well for several years. Its competitor Nokia offered interesting options and features that expanded the marketplace. It overtook Motorola in sales and variety.

2. Motorola realized that it could also offer plenty of feature-rich phones to the market, but realized that it was late to the game. So in order to compensate for its lateness, it authorized several engineering groups to design multiple products for multiple market segments that it saw as lucrative.

3. These were all different groups, and each group had its own idea of what the products would do. The groups did not share a common vision as to how the product families should evolve. There was little attention paid to compatibility, co-groupings, cross-platform matching, and a cohesive evolution plan.

4. Motorola failed to have its teams validate whether all the designs could be made in the first place, could be made profitably, and could be made in the amounts forecasted for the market opportunity– all in the time frame that was considered appropriate, and at a price point that the market would bear. Not only did these validations not occur, but there were no real contingency plans just in case the planned scenarios did not pan out.

5. What resulted was innovational incontinence for Motorola: a proliferation of products, platforms, protocols–not to mention, a dizzying dispersion of features and functions—without *concurrent validation from multiple points along the supply chain*. With no ironclad checks for producibility, profitability, promotability, or end-to-end supply chain synchronization, its designs drained its dollars. Motorola's virtue–its power to create—became its undoing.

6. Managers assumed the best in each other, and instead–in the absence of deliberate cross-pollination and mutual validation–were shocked by the number of blind spots that collectively derailed the teams.

7. In a bizarre twist in the style of a Greek play, the independent IT group at Motorola was saddled with not only having to support global IT operations, but also having to generate its own revenues by offering its services elsewhere.

What is the effect of proliferation at the design level? It is suffocation at the supply chain level and simply confusion at the customer level. When too many products compete for manufacturing and marketing resources, they drive up expenditures in an erratic manner, thereby bloating the overall cost to serve customers. Detailed costs become invisible because of the magnitude and complexity of products and processes– not just production costs, but also promotion and post-sales costs. Cost fluctuations and overruns, in particular, come to light belatedly or too late to allow corrections and adjustments. In an industry with shifting economics, intense price pressure, and unceasing competition, Motorola could ill afford not to compete on price, irrespective of its other attributes. After all, the cellular business is roughly one-fourth of Motorola's revenue streams. To aggravate the situation, without any conceptual integration, the company was unable to create synergies in its product design, production, promotion, and profit structures. In the absence of a web-based nervous system that monitors costs, volumes, profits, and revenues *by product*, the battle gets worse. Is it any wonder that its manufacturing margins were below par?

In short, Motorola has suffered terribly in all four quadrants of QRIIO, compounding the malefic effects of faltering in one quadrant after another. And, in this context, it is easy to see that the company has used massive layoffs as a temporary fix. In a depressed market, prices are likely to decline even further, and Motorola will continue to face fundamental challenges unless it ferociously addresses its faltering in all four quadrants of QRIIO simultaneously. A sad corollary to this story is that these wounds were inflicted not by Nokia, its arch enemy, but by Motorola upon itself. Sun-Tzu observes in The *Art of War*, "The biggest threat is not the ill-will of the enemy, but the ignorance of self."

If Motorola is, like Xerox, a warning, then Colgate-Palmolive is, like Mattel, an example. Colgate has perfected its mastery of swift product development and mass-market delivery. In the final five years of the last millennium, the company developed far more products than any of its competitors, with stunning agility. In 2000, Colgate garnered $3.6 billion, roughly 38% of its total sales, from those new products. Colgate dwarfed Procter & Gamble, Gillette, and its other competitors at a time when everyone was hit by global recession. What lessons can we draw from Colgate's example?

- The company clearly saw the white spaces in multiple markets and invaded them with relevant products very quickly and aggressively.

- It emptied its portfolio of old, obsolete, obtrusive products. In short, it matched its products to the right markets while delivering the right value and message.

- On a global scale, it was able to synchronize its supply chains, validate supply and demand for its products, and coordinate all of its resources because of its integrated information systems, which in turn provided the company with accuracy and quickness of insights.

- It created a culture of company-wide supply chain consciousness to move the company beyond the old model of functional views and operational separatism.

As the recent experience of these two companies attests, it is necessary to pay attention to all of the quadrants. On the one hand, companies must innovate, and, on the other, they must rationalize their portfolio. At one extreme they will suffer because of proliferation, and, on the other, they will fight price wars because their products are too mature. The navigating act between the Homeric Scylla and Charybdis is what managing the right half

O scary company that hath such people in it, everyone conceiveth a strategy, yet none loveth its execution.

Bard to Balan - B2B

of QRIIO is all about.

The left half is critical to sustain the right half. No matter how innovative a company is, profits can be elusive if fulfillment is inefficient. Likewise, good integration with suppliers and customers does not automatically guarantee a good supply chain. The cause and effect of multiple decisions along the supply chain must be first of all understood conceptually by all stakeholders. While it is not possible to have good supply chain synchronization without good integration, the converse is not necessarily true.

Organizing for Business Transformation

The success or failure of each product ultimately depends on whether the customers buy it. What are the factors that drive the success of a product and therefore the success of a company? Looking at Figure 2-

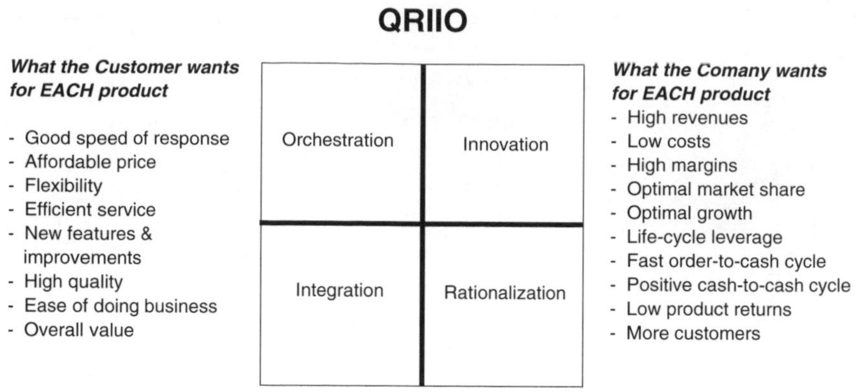

QRIIO

**What the Customer wants
for EACH product**

- Good speed of response
- Affordable price
- Flexibility
- Efficient service
- New features &
  improvements
- High quality
- Ease of doing business
- Overall value

Orchestration	Innovation
Integration	Rationalization

**What the Comany wants
for EACH product**
- High revenues
- Low costs
- High margins
- Optimal market share
- Optimal growth
- Life-cycle leverage
- Fast order-to-cash cycle
- Positive cash-to-cash cycle
- Low product returns
- More customers

Figure 2-4 The Anatomy of Business Transformation

4, it is clear that customers seek a set of virtues, and so does the company. To ensure the success of every product, to transform any product destiny, we must understand how to bridge the gap between what the customer wants and what the company is willing to live with–for that market segment. There is an optimum point at which market virtues from the customer's standpoint mesh with achievable results from the company's perspective. To compete on any or all of the virtues requires distinct competencies in various quadrants. While the set of virtues varies from product to product, and from market to market, the success or failure trajectories can be traced to the degree of health or sickness in the four quadrants. For example:

- Quality depends on good processes, including checks and balances.

- Value depends on understanding the life-cycle relationships to the customer.

- Ease of doing business depends on the transparency of transactions and the degree of commitment to the customer.

- Competitive pricing depends on being able to see and tally every item in a product's cost structure, whether material, processual, or informational.

- Speed of delivery depends on supply chain excellence.

Every product will compete in its market segment on one or more of its residual virtues. Yet it is critical for a company to be good in the virtues from the customers' point of view. Companies that pride themselves on service cannot succeed if their prices are too high. Correspondingly, companies that charge competitive prices but are tardy in their fulfillment cannot fare well either. *That is why the virtues that companies tout in the marketplace will have to be congruently back-mapped to concrete competencies in all the four quadrants.*

In other words, corporate strategy cannot sit on a one- or two- or even three-legged stool. Rather, it has to rest seurely on a four-legged table. Whether it is a product or a service, a medication for treating terminal cancer, a contraption for binding buildings, food dye, or fine cologne, it must be supported by the four legs of its destiny. Corporate strategy, to put it another way, is based on the Carpenter's Creed:

The Carpenter's Creed

Good working is woodworking the tables.
Oh! Those legs and surfaces:
Some broken, some bent,
Some spindly, some wobbly,
Some long, some short,
Some creaky, some angled,
Some scratched, some wretched.
I fix them all with glue, nails, and hammer.
I always know
How much to hammer and where.
If the table is beyond repair,
I'll pitch it without a care.

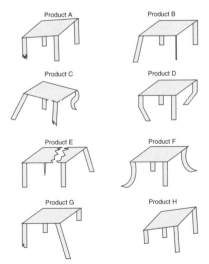

Figure 2-5 Turning the Tables on Tradition— QRIIOusly

QRIIO is a cognitive compass for raising the holistic value of a product. It is the playbook for street fights, the diagram for corporate success, and the denominator for benchmarking with your competitors. It is applicable to any industry. The success of a company depends on how it bolsters its competencies and balances interrelationships in the four quadrants–for every product it makes or every service it delivers. The rest of this book is about shaping up on all fours.

Section II

Assembling the Street Quartet

Rationalizing Products, Markets, Customers, and Value

A company is relevant only when what it produces or provides meets customer needs, in a meaningful manner that is, when its business relationships benefit both itself and those it serves. Relevant companies' products and services resonate with the times and tenure of evolution. With the confluence of globalization, the Internet, and the continuing shift to a service economy, the probability of some companies being left behind can only increase. All companies face the threat of becoming irrelevant, especially the traditional Titans of industry.

Irrelevancy occurs when a company is no longer current, when it has fallen out of touch with its marketplace and, consequently, has less value to provide. The risible stereotype for an irrelevant company is that of the clueless dinosaur, unimpressed by the nimble mammals at its feet, but nonetheless doomed to extinction because it lacks the mammalian qualities that would enable it to thrive in the existing environment.

Many factors contribute to a company's becoming irrelevant. A company runs the risk of becoming irrelevant when it

- Forgets or misunderstands the core nature of its business and the benefits it provides its customers

- Becomes focused on product features instead of understanding problems and creating meaningful solutions

- Fails to maintain a long-range focus and misses the big picture, as when its corporate mindset is based on transactions instead of relationships

- Fails to develop abilities to both create and adapt to change (internally and in the marketplace)

- Is not proactive in identifying interrelationships (among products, processes, markets, and customers) and consequently does not make developing synergies a major focus of planning

- Fails to innovate, develop, and dominate its chosen market segments

When the marketplace ceases to care about a company, that company has become irrelevant. In some ways, irrelevancy is worse than competition, for at least competition provides a clear enemy to attack. Irrelevancy, which can begin simply when a company is slow to adapt to change, leads to being spurned and ignored—a situation in which no one cares about your products or services. The longevity of companies that have collapsed into this diminished state is further threatened by the nature of contemporary commerce and communications. As everyone connects to everyone else via the Internet and other low-cost means of communication, it is easy for customers and suppliers to discern which business partners have become irrelevant and to cut them out of the value chain entirely.

History shows countless examples of businesses that became irrelevant, industries that have been replaced by fundamentally new approaches for serving similar needs, and products and skills that became outmoded because of technological change or simply natural evolution. Everyone can point to the irrelevancy of the sword in modern combat or to the eclipse of the typewriter. Who wouldn't recognize the invention of the automobile as the reason why the horse-drawn carriage became totally useless and is now but a charming anachronism that appeals to tourists in New York's Central Park or in the streets of downtown Chicago?

Change affects companies in every sector, all at the same time. Especially in established industries, companies can find themselves their own worst enemy. We suggested in the first chapter that Procter & Gamble moved too slowly to market with its whitening toothpaste, and was beaten to the punch by Total from Colgate. We also implied that Procter & Gamble's internal divisions—the managers at a company lauded worldwide for the integrity and thoroughness of its management training—could have done a far better job of communicating with one another. It's almost too easy to pick on Procter & Gamble in this case because its major competitor in the toothpaste marketplace introduced a desirable product before the Cincinnati company did.

This type of competition occurs all the time. But let's go one step further. Let's suggest that Procter & Gamble, a company that goes to the consumer market with a portfolio of over 400 products, can easily end up competing against itself, in effect cannibalizing itself, by having multiple similar products and derivations of branded products in the same market at the same time.

This leads to a series of questions about managing a portfolio of products. Does it make sense, for example, for P&G to have two different brands of laundry detergent on the shelf in one store? Does it best serve the management of profit margins to be micromanaging sales strategies—coupons, offers, rebates, direct marketing, samples, advertising, in-store displays—*within* a category instead of *across* it? Does it make sense to develop multiple variations of the same product—the endless variants of "New and Improved" product—at the risk of confusing consumers or even alienating them, for minor incremental gains? A more fundamental question revolves around internal operations and resources management. Is a company best served when it makes its own brand managers compete with one another for internal resources, whether those resources are in sales and marketing, in product research, or in industrial production and distribution?

It is a truism that a company can be better than the sum of its parts. But it can also be worse. The hierarchical nature of many companies, so long the accepted model, too often prevents holistic analysis and optimization of their aggregate corporate performance. What exacerbates this is that each manager must demonstrate the innate value and profitability of his or her slice of the pie with little regard for the other slices. In effect, a company can be in conflict with itself.

Why Portfolios?

Truth is, companies don't manage individual products; they manage portfolios of products, portfolios of markets, and portfolios of customers. These combinations cannot be managed in isolation. They must be viewed holistically. If the slices or elements of the portfolio disrupt, compete with, or degrade each other, then managers face *interference* in their portfolio.

The increasing intensity of commerce forces businesses to tightly integrate their supply chains and their internal operations, creating a synchronized, smoothly run enterprise. As coordination tightens, interactions between the elements of a company play an even larger role in its success. Portfolio management helps companies understand and manage all these interactions, enabling them to make decisions about what products or services to keep and what to discard.

The purpose of portfolio management is to maximize synergies and minimize interference. Synergy among items in a portfolio makes the portfolio better than the sum of the individual items. In its simplest form, synergy is easy to spot. If two customers of a mail-order company are physically close to each other, delivery costs can be shared. Portfolio analysis would reveal such synergy. It would also reveal other opportunities, such as manufacturing and grouping of similar products, re-useable product design, modular part assemblies, and so on. When a synergy is discovered, companies can bias their decisions toward keeping all items of the synergistic group.

The opposite of synergy in a portfolio is interference. When interference occurs, the portfolio, taken as a whole, is worse than the sum of the individual items. For example, two products, each profitable in their own right, might both require the use of the same specialized machine tool. Although each product may not require the full capacity of the tool, the combined load may lead to resource contention and poor lead-times for both products. A portfolio analysis of products would alert the company to this interference. The company could then make a sound decision as to which product to produce, when to schedule production, or how to boost capacity.

Internal competition for resources, such as production time, can also undermine the order-fulfillment process. Moreover, a company's products may cannibalize each other when they compete in the same marketplace. Diluting the significance of brand by presenting a product as all things to all people can confuse the consumer. Consumer behavior and the specific qualities of important relations can itself be a source of interference. For example, interference occurs when customers or competition for resources pull a company in different directions and force it to lose focus.

In a competitive marketplace, companies must continually determine how they can create the greatest value from their portfolio of products and services.

The PMCV Framework

Only by examining the interactions between all segments of a business, from multiple perspectives, can a company's executives make sound decisions about what practices to nurture—and what to drop. The framework we propose is called *PMCV*. It addresses which *products* you make, what *markets* you serve, which *customers* you sell to, and what *value* you provide. Before a company can synchronize its supply chains and enhance business performance, there is a set of even more fundamental questions to ask:

- How are we making the **products** we're making?

- Are we using the right **practices**?

- Should we even be making **these** products?

- Are we going after the right **markets**?

- Are we courting and serving the appropriate **customers**?

- How can we **beat** our competitors?

- Are we creating the right *value* for our customers—and can it last?

PMCV provides a set of interlocking perspectives for moving a company towards finding and staying in the "sweet spot"—a position where it can dominate its market and have the greatest potential for growth. The portfolio concept forces companies to look at the whole pie—across product categories, market boundaries, and customer segments—to understand what drives aggregate performance. If all the elements of a portfolio mutually complement and reinforce each other, then the PMCV equation is in a state of synergy, and the portfolio is more valuable than the sum of the parts.

Understanding the PMCV framework is reasonably simple, though it does require asking a series of questions across several disciplines and formulating clear answers. In business, for instance, nothing could be simpler than to rely on the value of a product or service that has historically provided a reasonable return on investment. The expectation is that it will provide a continuing return. However, what if that product or service intereferes with one of your other products or services or with a potentially more profitable product or service you could offer? How do you manage the interrelationships between customers, markets, and your products and services to ensure the greatest return on investment? At what point can you decide which direction to take? PMCV invites this type of critical examination, forcing a company to continually reassess and review its portfolio of products, markets, and customers to ensure their relevance and value.

Understanding Products

Consider the following challenges most companies face when it comes to managing products:

- Not fully understanding customer needs

- Making products that are very difficult to use

- Making too many competitive products in one development area

- Creating unnecessary product complexity that does not translate into commensurate profits

- Creating unnecessary product complexity that does not translate into customer benefits

- Fumbling product transitions from one line to the next

- Allowing slow time-to-market and costly delays

- Allowing too quick time-to-market and concomitant expenditure

- Facing too high a cost for product at the time of fulfillment

- Not having a clear project charter for success

- Facing rising costs to support the product after the sale and falling victim to the law of diminishing returns

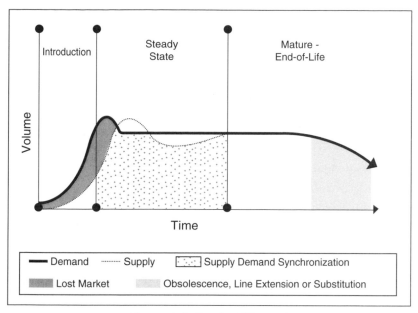

Figure 3-1 Product life cycle

What often aggravates these problems is the lack of a collective, holistic corporate prism through which the journey and success of a product are viewed by the individuals in a company.

As the first step to performance, companies must understand which of their products or services are profitable. More important, they must know how each product impacts the profitability of every other product or service they offer—a judgment that relies on understanding the internal interactions in their portfolios.

The Life Cycle of Products

Every product has a life cycle analogous to that of a living creature. Development can be thought of as gestation. The product is "born," in a sense, when it is introduced, and grows as sales grow. Maturity is the point where sales are stable and fulfillment processes operate smoothly. Thereafter, the product reaches a plateau, which for an established product means flat or seasonal sales. After this point, sales decline until the product becomes obsolete and it is withdrawn from the market.

In different industries, product life cycles can be of dramatically different duration, and the amount of time spent in gestation, growth, or maturity can also vary significantly from product to product. Products in the computer industry, for instance, have very short life cycles. A company like Toshiba, which builds laptops, has built its entire design, marketing, and production plans on the premise that new technology will rapidly and continually become available. When Toshiba introduces new models with improved features every few months, it fully expects their rate of obsolescence to be high.

So whatever Toshiba produces must be quickly sold before it becomes obsolete, for two reasons. First, unsold inventory—whether held by Toshiba or any of its channel partners—suffers dramatic devaluation if it is not sold on time. Second, the total cost of carrying obsolete inventory erodes the already razor-thin profit margins of everyone. It is a classic double whammy, for products that do not make the market window provide meager residual value. In the technology industry, moreover, immediate worldwide roll-out of products is required. Consequently, supply chains must be geared to launch new products globally within and between short time frames.

The sheer enormity of the effort needed to synchronize myriad constituents—from several hundred suppliers, manufacturing plants, product designers, and transportation providers to thousands of retailers—leaves Toshiba, like others in this industry, virtually no room for error. With maddening competition and daily "deal wars," Toshiba recognizes that failure to execute with flawless timing will adversely impact not only its individual product lines, but also its aggregate profitability. In the computer industry, most channel partners and value-adding resellers (who have polygamous loyalties) enjoy some form of price protection, making it incumbent upon the OEM to supply the right product at the right quantity at the right time. Market share is directly related to availability of the "right product wrapped in the right deal." Planned obsolescence is a fact of life, where one generation of products is rapidly bested by the next. This tightrope situation is worsened because investment in new products in the technology sector often depreciates at the rate of 25-50 percent annually. The service cycle of design-produce-sell is most complex in the technology sector.

Products in the consumer goods industry, on the other hand, enjoy much longer life cycles. Manufacturers such as Kraft spend much more time at the beginning of a product's life conducting elaborate market research to understand demographic issues. These companies plan sales volumes and profit streams based on the expectation that a product will maintain popularity longer.

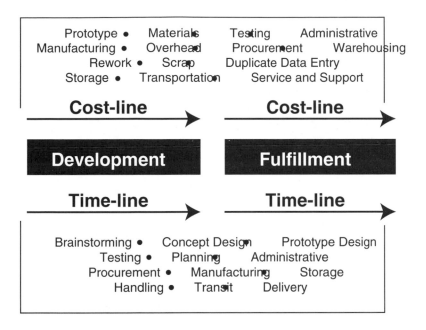

Figure 3-2 Sample cost and time-lines

Branding, advertising, and product-line extensions often prolong the life cycle of consumer packaged goods. The challenges this industry faces are much different from those in the high technology industry. A musical analogy would be the difference between staccato notes and lingering rhythms.

Why must companies understand the life-cycle stages of products? Sales volumes, costs, constraints, and profits at different stages of the life-cycle are all different. Illumination in these areas is as important as innovation itself. A clear strategy for managing the trajectory of a product is critical.

In general, having a balanced portfolio of products at different stages of their life cycle is the ideal. The birth of a new product, just like that of a newborn child, is an inherently stressful and risky time. Too many new products demand extra resources both in marketing and in ramping up error-free fulfillment. Conversely, too many obsolete products are a death sentence, as declining sales inevitably lead to overall decline in revenues. Too many obsolete, low-margin products suffocate a company's supply chain. The ideal portfolio includes growing and mature offerings along with an orderly stream of products *in vitro*, as it were, to replace what's outgoing.

Development vs. Fulfillment

The PMCV framework allows companies to analyze the time and costs associated with both product development and fulfillment. Development focuses on creating something new. Fulfillment delivers a copy of a product or service, focusing on routine and repeated execution of a predefined process. Development and fulfillment therefore represent opposite ends of the spectrum of business practices, although it can be beneficial to view them in tandem. By reviewing time and cost, companies can determine how they can best achieve synergies. Every product creation has an independent sequence of activities, which we can call the time-line, and its own sources of costs, the *cost-line*. Companies need to optimize both.

The time-line of development and fulfillment is subject to a complex set of precepts as well. Smart managers know they can increase profits by minimizing time-to-value—that is, reducing delivery cycle-times—and by maximizing time-to-cost, which means deferring costs. Managing the time-line also involves synchronizing supply with demand, which means delivering value exactly when needed—not before and not after.

Satisfying customer demands by developing products and producing them consumes time and cost, but the relationship between time and cost is not simple. Ideally, companies want to minimize both, but this is not always possible. There is no single formula or direct relationship between time and cost that can be used universally to optimize the development and fulfillment cycle. Adding time to a process can increase costs, but it can also decrease them. In some circumstances, adding time will not affect costs at all. The following precepts can apply in different situations:

- *Cost buys time:* Expediting saves time but adds cost.

- *Time is cost:* Inventory costs and working capital requirements scale upward over time.

- *Time is money:* Customers may value quick fulfillment and pay more for it.

- *Time and cost can be independent:* Tighter coordination or concurrent activities can save time while adding little cost.

The complex interplay of cost and time implies that both win-win and tradeoff scenarios are possible. Smarter planning or executing activities concurrently is a win-win scenario, reducing time without adding direct costs and subtracting indirect costs, such as inventory and working capital. A tradeoff occurs when these win-win improvement measures reach their limit. Further improvement requires adding resources to reduce resource contention or using expedited handling. While both of these additional attempts will reduce time, they will also increase costs correspondingly.

Development Time-line

Product development traces the gestation of an idea until a product is introduced. The first step is to understand market demands, for example, Colgate's customers' desire for a whitening toothpaste. Then product developers must answer a sequence of questions: What do customers want? What problem does the product solve? What features should the product design have? What are the means available to designing and manufacturing the product? What volume can we realistically manufacture to meet demand? Managers must answer such key questions and gather relevant background data.

In the second phase, the company designs a product that effectively sits at the intersection of the market's needs, its own technological potential, and its capacity to fulfill orders. In the third phase, the company prepares for volume sales and production by implementing demand generation mechanisms, preparing for a product's introduction to the market and its subsequent sales, and implementing fulfillment systems—ramping up for product fulfillment and delivery to customers. All these activities must be completed coherently in order to launch a successful new product or service.

Reducing product and service development times is more important than most companies realize. The benefits of a shorter development cycle-time arise from all sides of the supply chain. Upstream, they include a reduction in the technological obsolescence of components, because a supplier's latest innovations are incorporated into the developed product or service. A shorter cycle-time also increases a supplier's willingness to collaborate and invest with the company, because the supplier itself will benefit from the faster orders.

There are also benefits downstream, since shorter cycle-times reduce the risk of intervening technological or economic market shifts and allow companies to beat competitors to market. Because development incurs serious costs and risks, the faster a product is brought to market, the sooner it can create value that offsets those costs and resolves the risks. Internal benefits of reduced development cycle-time include lower costs for the accumulated capital that is carrying the costs of development, and a reduction in the volume of sales required for an acceptable return on investment (ROI) or net present value (NPV).

Development Cost-line

New product development can be expensive and risky. Companies can spend vast sums to develop and launch a new product. Gillette spent millions to develop the Mach 3 razor. Airbus is considering whether to spend $12 billion to create a super-jumbo jet. Because minimizing cost is a major goal of supply chain management, and forgoing new product development is not advisable, companies must manage development costs intelligently. The key is neither stinginess nor paralysis by analysis, but a strategy of justifiable risk taking that creates value in excess of incurred costs.

Development costs fall into three categories: design costs, fulfillment implementation costs, and market development costs. When professionals are working to define a product or service without creating salable examples, they incur design costs. In the manufacturing world, engineers perform this work, but even financial services firms have design costs, such as when lawyers or financial professionals create new contracts or financial products. New products and services usually require special assets or one-time adjustments to existing assets before the product or service can be produced in volume. Purchasing new machine tools, building fixtures, and adjusting the existing manufacturing assets often precede the manufacturing of a new product. Both manufacturing and service firms face de facto product asset costs in the form of training their people to produce the new product or fulfill demand for a new service.

Each new product also requires marketing and advertising. Product announcements, demonstrations, review copies, and catalogs are all necessary to inform potential customers. The intent is to achieve mind share, but to also delay customers' purchase decisions until the new offering is available, and create demand for something that customers did not know about.

Coordinating Development and Fulfillment

Synchronizing development with creating demand is a multidirectional assessment companies must make, obeying eight key imperatives:

- Can the design be produced? Fulfillment capabilities (supplier identification and component support, and manufacturing) must drive the selection of feasible design features.

- Can the product be sold? Market and customer needs must drive the choice of desirable features.

- How much can we sell? Assessments of market demand will drive the scale of production.

- Is marketing ready to sell the product? Have all the sales channels been identified, and are they prepared to fully support the product?

- How much demand can we meet? Production capacity determines the scale of marketing efforts.

- Are our fulfillment processes ready to produce it? Actual design features should drive the addition or adjustment of fulfillment assets.

- Do we have a solid, sustainable supply chain design? Are the elements of demand, supply, manufacturing, and distribution aligned to support the product?

- Can we service the product and nurture post-sales relationships with our customers?

Resolving these multidirectional interactions between design creation, fulfillment implementation, and market development is often challenging because each of the respective three groups must communicate its respective constraints, capabilities, and recommendations to the others. Breakdowns in communications occur when each constituency fails to see beyond its role within the context of the big picture, when each one holds a myopic view of its business and focus only on its area's immediate needs.

Product design and development represent only a fraction of the battle of winning in the marketplace. Look at the rash of recent failures in the dotcom world. Many of these companies either did not understand or grossly underestimated the mathematics of fulfillment. They found, much to their shock, that being a glorified cyber-order taker with a cool web site in hot colors was not what the world was coming to. Much to their chagrin, these companies discovered too late that timely fulfillment is the unchanging name of the game. In 2000, even the venerable Sony, a world leader in consumer electronics and a master in branding and design, was forced to halve its Play Station 2 console roll-out—from one million units to a half-million—because of a dramatic, unexpected fulfillment challenge. Because of the remarkable complexity of the chips needed, Sony failed to correctly anticipate how long it would take to produce the chips it needed to meet the surge in demand for the Christmas season. The company's first mistake was in choosing to produce the chip on its own, knowing full well that its core competence was not in manufacturing; its second was promising to deliver one million units to market in a short time frame—setting the company up not just for fulfillment failure, but for a damaging blow to the reputation of its brand.

3M, on the other hand, has a world-class reputation not only for designing products that serve real needs and function effectively within their designed purpose, but also for swift, high-volume fulfillment. In the days to come, innovation will matter even more, but fulfillment that is both time-sensitive and cost-sensitive will eventually dictate market success.

Fulfillment Time-line

Though, perhaps, a lesser factor than the development process, making copies of the designed product also consumes time and cost. The time-line for replicating product and fulfilling customer demand is called *lead-time* or the *order-to-ship* cycle-time. This time-line includes all the activities between a customer's decision to order the product and its final delivery. These activities fall into seven categories:

- Administrative order handling
- Planning time
- Procurement lead-time
- Manufacturing
- Storage
- Transit and delivery
- Service and support

The time-line for a product often includes a large number of steps and multiple operations in each of the preceding categories.

For example, making a single tractor involves procuring hundreds of raw material parts and components, numerous manufacturing operations, a good deal of internal transportation, and a potential need for interim storage locations.

Within the fulfillment process, numerous approaches shorten cycle-time. First, a company can reduce the time of each activity or eliminate unnecessary steps. Second, it can relocate where activities take place to reduce travel distances. Third, it can improve planning and coordination of activities—so that such activities take place concurrently, or the idle time between steps is minimized. Compressing the fulfillment time-line through improved planning and coordination requires well-conceived and efficient information linkages throughout the supply chain. For instance, quickly integrating changed sales projections into production schedules or giving shipping departments access to account and order information or personalizing the order-entry process by customer can all compress order-to-ship time significantly.

Fulfillment Cost-line

While companies can concentrate on filling orders more quickly, that achievement is useless if fulfillment costs are too high. The cost-line must be broken down to identify all the elements that result in higher costs. Costs accumulate in four principal areas: at the unit, at the order, at product variation, and at indirect levels.

Unit costs increase with every unit produced. These costs include the labor of all those who touch the product, such as machinists. They include the use of assets, such as equipment, facilities, and working capital. They also include the supplied materials that go into the product.

Similarly, order costs will increase with each customer order, regardless of the number of units ordered. These will include labor, as well, in the form of sales, administrative, and setup costs. They also incorporate use of assets and materials—principally in the form of waste from warming up to produce an order.

Product costs increase with each product variant, regardless of the number of orders. Again, this means labor costs—in engineering and marketing. It involves the use of assets: dedicated equipment and facilities, and capital for product development. And it necessitates some use of materials, for prototypes and demonstration models. Last, indirect costs include general administration and management, training, support, documentation, facilities, and working capital, along with certain materials, i.e., office supplies.

Each of these costs can be further categorized in terms of the seven fulfillment activities in the fulfillment time-line. Depending upon the product, costs emerge in all these areas. The challenge for companies is how to minimize or at least defer these costs for as long as possible.

Minimizing fulfillment costs usually focuses on direct costs, the goal being to reduce the resources expended in making another unit in response to another order. Approaches include seeking increased productivity by providing greater incentives, better tools, and more efficient management; improving asset utilization, chiefly in resource management and intelligent scheduling; and lowering material costs by prudently sourcing materials, minimizing waste, and better order lot sizing both in manufacturing and procurement.

As with minimizing the time-line, minimizing the cost-line should focus on the non-value added activities. Inefficiencies, duplicated efforts, waste, defects, and scrap are all sources of cost that lend themselves to trimming.

Where is the food for thought?

Achieving Synergy and Avoiding Interference

Few companies subsist on a single product. Most have multiple products or product variants, even if they are confined to a narrow product category. Thus, most companies have a portfolio of products, often divided into product lines. The product lines provide a range of options for customers or help the company cover different markets. But with a portfolio of products come questions about how to manage the portfolio and each of the products in the portfolio. Companies have numerous options for deciding what to do with each product and also with the overall portfolio. In making these decisions, they must look beyond the narrow assessment of individual products to consider the impact of each product on the entire portfolio. There are six possible answers:

- *Make no change:* Make no design or marketing changes and continue to sell the product as is.

- *Change marketing:* Adjust marketing and promotions to modulate sales.

- *Change price:* Increase or decrease the price to modulate demand and profit margins.

- *Change design:* Make a change in features, services, performance, or styling, or else combine two or more products into one.

- *Change processes:* Improve fulfillment processes for quality, efficiency, or time-lines.

- *Drop the product:* Discontinue the product because of insufficient value to customers or the company.

The middle four options can be applied in combination. Still, the decision of what to do with each product affects every other product in the portfolio. Synergy occurs when products are beneficially coupled in the marketplace, including situations in which one product induces sales of another (such as consumables, upgrades, or follow-on services). Hewlett-Packard is a perfect example: the company sells printers, but makes the bulk of its associated profits on the ink cartridges. Two products can share costs, in joint or overlapping technologies or equipment investments. When a company has product-to-product synergy, though, the removal of one product can potentially damage sales or profitability of another product or of the whole company.

There is another synergy in the consumer and business-to-business markets. When customers prefer one-stop shopping, they won't buy any of a company's products unless the company offers a full line. In these circumstances, the seller must adjust product offerings to achieve synergy. For example, grocery stores may sell Thanksgiving turkeys at a loss, knowing that customers who buy the turkey will probably buy all of their other dinner items at the same time. Competing on the price of turkeys might not improve the profitability of that one item, but would improve overall profitability across the portfolio.

Products in a portfolio can also interfere with each other. Sometimes, products are unfavorably coupled in the marketplace. In such a case, removing one product can potentially increase sales or profitability of another product or of the whole company. Types of interference include

- *Self-competition*—products that are so close to each other that they compete for shelf space and customers. Many consumer goods companies, such as Kraft, Nabisco, and P&G, have a proliferating range of products that can actually poach markets from one another.

- *Operational and support complexity*—Mercedes has elasticized its brand strength into multiple market segments. It has created so many models whose names resemble an unappetizing alphanumeric soup that consumers cannot easily appreciate the differences. Too many models create complexities that arise on several fronts—from part number proliferation, supplier miscoordination, a bewildering array of product and sub-assembly configurations, problems in tracking and/or tracing myriad engineering changes, and mismanaging spare parts, not to mention the confusion within the company. Every model has its own serpentine supply chain. The question for the "Silver Moustache" is— what is the true cost and "price" of market share? Is it a case of mass customization gone too far and insidiously awry?

- *Resource contention*—production or supply capacity limitations, which cause companies to effect a tradeoff between producing one or another product. This is very often the case when a production planner has to decide which products to schedule and sequence first—a low-margin product that was promised to a customer, or a higher-margin one that needs to be shipped as soon as possible. Interfering products also compete for capital, for research and development resources, and for advertising. Under such circumstances, supply chain optimization is critical.

Companies must ask themselves, "How congruent and connected are our products to our markets?" No longer can they make product-related decisions in isolation. They must, for instance, ask: "If we change or drop product X, what will happen to sales and profits of product Y? Will they go up or down?" Individual product-line managers must connect, communicate, and collaborate to make jointly optimal product and product portfolio decisions.

Decisions to change a product or to change a product portfolio must also consider holistic effects. All products in a company are connected to each other by the customers who buy them and by the corporate infrastructure that makes them. In a well-run company with a tightly integrated supply chain, there is little slack—a small change in one product can influence the machinery or customers of another product.

The goals of holistic product management are to eliminate obsolete, irrelevant, or unprofitable products; to enhance product synergies and eliminate interference; to adjust in order for products to close gaps in the portfolio; and to create new products to extend the portfolio. Companies can do this by carefully examining and optimizing the interactions between products in terms of

- Mapping the relevance of every product to its market

- Stimulating demand for complementary products that include bundled additions

- Managing a portfolio of product lines

- Coordinating a portfolio of product development time-lines

- Sharing costs across a portfolio of product development

- Coordinating a portfolio of product fulfillment time-lines

- Clearly mapping current revenue streams and future revenue potential to the portfolio of products

The result is a product portfolio that congruently and powerfully addresses the markets in which the company operates.

Understanding Markets: The Mosaic

Markets are where customers live. The unique culture of each market niche affects the products and services offered, and affects the value propositions and marketing messages used by a company. But markets are neither monolithic nor isolated from each other. There is a multidimensional space that defines all the markets that a company can target—and this multidimensional space we can call the *market mosaic.*

A market mosaic can be thought of as a tool for analyzing a company's business potential. Market mosaics are multidimensional models a company can use to consider the attributes, dimensions, and criteria of factors that will enable it to diagnose its situation and set strategies to improve its position. This market mosaic captures the intersections and the opportunities within a given company's market place.

Figure 3-3 shows an example of a hypothetical company's market mosaic, segmented by combinations of categories along several dimensions. Such dimensions might include customers' location by geographic segment, and customer sales volume, including volume segments or low-end to luxury price points.

The goal of a business is to dominate its market. Within a market

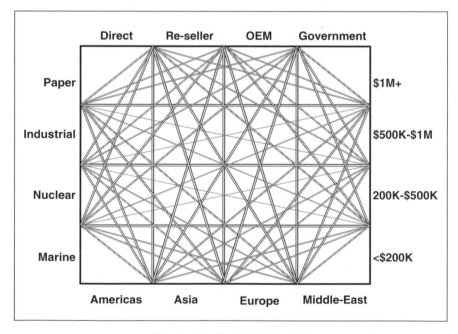

Figure 3-3 A market mosaic

mosaic, this would be synonymous with extending one's market space. Extending dominion requires looking for ways to leverage technology, talent, and timing across the complete range of market factors. Any company can create a figure of its own market mosaic, which will identify its sales channels, such as original equipment manufacturers, industrial distributors, consumer retail outlets, etc., and its typical customers' industry affiliation—whether it be in the automotive, chemicals, government, and/or financial services industries. Any thorough market mosaic will also address product segments or technology application segments (such as industrial pumps for water, hydraulics, or corrosive fluids), and will address the customers' capabilities or service needs.

Just as a mosaic is made up of hundreds of individual tiles, each combination in the market mosaic represents a potentially unique micromarket with its own special needs. And some tiles of the mosaic may be empty—having neither customers nor potential customers for that slice. For example, say a company does business across Europe and sells a range of products from low-end to luxury. Arguably, that company's market mosaic will depict all the market opportunities, by geography, product category, sales volumes, and customer type. But it's easy to imagine that the company's "Eastern European Government Luxury Products" segment will be empty because these governments are highly cost-conscious and Eastern Europe struggles to maintain high standards of living. Therefore, this segment is not a legitimate market.

Other tiles may have less distinct boundaries because multiple companies may be actively selling to that market. In reviewing opportunities on a mosaic, companies must consider four types of market spaces:

- In an *empty* niche, no company has customers in the space.

- In a *captive* niche, your company has customers, and no other company serves them.

- In an *occupied* niche, other companies have customers in the space, but your company doesn't.

- In a *competitive* niche, you have customers, but you vie for those customers with other companies who compete with you.

Companies must evaluate who occupies a particular tile and

what aspirations drive them. They must look at what is above, to the side, and below each tile in the mosaic in order to understand how they can extend their space. Since markets exist across multiple dimensions, it can be invaluable to consider your customers' and competitors' mosaics, in addition to your own. Each company must decide where its best opportunities lie and whether it should enter, stay in, or get out of each of the niches in the market mosaic. The truth is that a company seldom has every niche in a market mosaic all to itself. The co-occupants are potential competitors.

Are co-occupants of a market segment always competitors? The answer is no. The degree to which co-occupants in a market segment compete is defined by the extent to which they actually overlap in terms of products, services, performance, and messages, and by how they ultimately overlap in customers' minds. Whether your co-occupants truly are competitors depends on how well the market mosaic represents the real boundaries in the marketplace. For example, if the customers of a supposed competitor never seriously considered your products, and your customers never seriously considered theirs, then there is no real competition. Mercedes does not compete with Yugo, though both make cars. For you to consider a relevant company as a competitor, there must be some further market segmentation (brand image, product features, price range, performance element, etc.) that consistently splits the market between you and your competitors.

Creating Opportunities

Market mosaics are multidimensional spaces, but that does not mean that all the spaces are filled. The boundaries in the mosaic represent presumed discontinuities and distinct differences between market segments. These discontinuities actually represent opportunities— white spaces—in part, because the boundaries were arbitrary to begin with, and also because of the dynamic nature of the marketplace. Mosaic boundaries are associated with three types of opportunities: exploiting gaps, breaking boundaries, and creating new spaces. Each one involves a bid to increase the size and scope of a company's "solution footprint"—thereby increasing growth and profits.

Opportunity One: Exploiting Gaps
Gaps or crevices in the market mosaic are unfilled opportunities.

And some segments of the mosaic are likely to be empty. These white spaces represent markets that are not being served, and this may be the simplest way to explore opportunities in a market mosaic. Even though a company may have had good reason for eschewing a market segment in the past, it should periodically review that decision because that segment may have expanded in economic importance, making it worth pursuing.

Also, a segment previously disregarded may now overlap with another segment that the company does serve, making it easy to add the new niche market to the existing portfolio. Perhaps the company has developed new products or skills that suit a particular niche that had been overlooked in the past. Or, because of greater efficiencies in production, it can now make profits selling to lower-volume markets or extremely high-volume/low-margin market segments.

Since change is a constant, it is important to regularly reconsider a market mosaic. The opportunity to exploit a gap can present itself at any time. Whatever the circumstances, if the market situation has suitably changed, then the company can enter the gap and gain new customers. Consider the market for sport utility vehicles in the U.S. In the last ten years, automakers have seen a revolution in car buyers' tastes. At some point in the late-1980s, they saw the potential of evolving the light-truck category by combining characteristics of several different categories of vehicle—the carrying capacity of trucks or station wagons, the comfort of sedans, and the versatility and sportiness of Jeeps. Today, everybody is buying SUVs; half the suburban mothers in America drive these hybrid vehicles. This market has become so desirable that even carmakers who once focused solely on the luxury buyer—such as Mercedes and BMW and Lexus—are selling high-end vehicles that are stylish and fun, sporty yet utilitarian, and still appointed with luxury amenities. The automakers are using the historical power of their brands to bolster marketing these vehicles.

In this instance, the market mosaic for these companies has evolved. Mercedes, BMW, and Lexus are transcending the boundaries of their brand. Now, the SUV market is beginning to mature, and soon these companies will again be forced to review their market mosaic.

Opportunity Two: Breaking Boundaries
Companies must not get too fixated on the artificial boundaries

that they have placed between different market segments. The way a company slices its markets into a mosaic is arbitrary to some degree. As customers change and products change, markets will also change, and companies should constantly consider if they should stretch the boundaries between segments. They should ask, "What is outside each segment in the mosaic?"

For example, a company might offer special services to its high-end market segment, but not to its low-end market. But as the cost-to-serve drops, the company might consider changing the service level at which customers reach the high-end category. The point is that companies need to constantly reexamine the boundaries between market segments to see if those segments are still relevant. Consider the speed of change at technology hardware companies. These companies are realizing that developing technology and selling hardware are not sufficient to sustain growth. As the cost of developing new technology increases and profit margins continue to drop, the challenge for such companies is figuring out how to generate new revenues.

The answer is by providing services that add value. IBM spent the 1990s transitioning itself from being primarily a hardware company to being a business systems consulting firm. Not only was Big Blue selling high-end servers and mainframes; now it was offering the expertise to build complete solutions for business challenges as well. This meant bringing hardware, software, architecture, and business knowledge together to solve day-to-day business problems. Today, other hardware companies are beginning to follow suit and are acquiring consulting outfits that specialize in implementing technology. In 1998, for instance, Cisco Systems, the "Grand Plumber of the Internet," bought 20% of KPMG's consulting business for $1.2 billion. And, in 2000, Hewlett-Packard began wooing PriceWaterhouseCoopers (PwC)—only to drop the bid after realizing the complexity of the proposed merger and after appreciating that absorbing the giant professional services firm would be a Herculean task. Compaq, after realizing that selling computers is, after all, a razor-thin-margin business, has recently begun to build a services unit to gain greater margins and add to its revenue stream. Hewlett-Packard is now trying to wed Compaq.

Why this sudden surge of interest in consulting companies? Because that's where hardware companies have to go in order to secure and sustain new revenues—through ongoing consulting services and implementation of solutions that customers need. Today's hardware companies know it—and that's why they're breaking the boundaries in their market mosaics, to create new opportunities and greater profits.

Opportunity Three: Creating New Spaces

Revolutionary corporations do more than incrementally expand in existing mosaics—they create whole new ones. Companies that create new market spaces—segments in nobody else's mosaic—have unfettered opportunities. Before Sony created the Walkman, a portable cassette player was a clunky box because the market was defined by indoor, tabletop applications. The Walkman created an entirely new realm of portable products, adding new vistas in the mosaic of consumer audio equipment. That raises the question: "What if you can completely change the mosaic?"

Sometimes new spaces are created by the most unexpected sources. Companies from outside an industry may often perform the freshest analysis of where a new space can be created. Hewlett-Packard, a leading manufacturer of personal computers and peripherals, was the first company to introduce a personal-use digital camera, and this innovation took the photography industry giant, Kodak, completely by surprise. But HP foresaw what Kodak missed: the growth, promise, flexibility, and lowered cost of digitalization. HP saw unfulfilled needs for digital photography equipment at a time when Kodak obviously missed the big picture. And a whole new market emerged.

Knowing Your Competitors

A successful depiction of the market mosaic for your company, then, depends on an accurate assessment of competitors and other occupants of your markets. Who is close to you and what are they doing? Companies must actively seek out information about market segments and about co-occupants via market intelligence and competitor intelligence. The relevant questions are

- Why do people buy your product instead of your competitor's?

- What are the marketed features of your competitor's products and services?

- What are the actual features of your competitor's products and services?

- How do those features differ from those of your own product?

- How will you make the flaws in competitors' products an advantage in your own?

- Who would care about those differences between competing products and services?

- Who are your current and potential competitors?

- What are your competitors moving towards? Moving away from?

The most insidious type of competitor is the one that is not even in your market mosaic. Some competitors are invisible: products and services that compete for mind share and market share without being anything like your products and services. For example, Intuit's Quicken competes with more than just other personal finance software packages. Intuit considers the pencil to be a competitor—because some potential customers of Quicken still prefer pencil and paper for tallying their expenses. By seeing pencil and paper as the principal alternative to using its financial software, Intuit made its product easier to use (even getting rid of features and accounting terminology that other more complex packages were touting). The result was new white space, because new customers appeared who would never previously have bought this type of software.

Likewise, Southwest Airlines views the car to be a competitor—the airline tries to replicate the convenience and low cost of automobile travel, while reducing people's travel time. Southwest Airlines is a low-cost air carrier. But when it opens a new route or adds service to a new airport, it does so not just to compete with other airlines, but to actually increase the total air traffic on that route and to that location. Southwest thus gears its service to be as convenient as and yet faster than travel by personal automobile.

These examples highlight what smart companies do—they compete not just within their industry, but between industries. These companies create new white spaces, built to suit their own competencies.

Achieving Synergy and Avoiding Interference

Most companies occupy many segments of a market mosaic, having a portfolio of markets that they serve. This portfolio will usually be a subset of the total market mosaic because few companies serve every niche market in their industry.

But with a portfolio of markets come questions about how to manage the portfolio and each of the markets in the portfolio. Global competition, deregulation, convergence, and cross-industry collisions all conspire to change the market mosaic around a company. Companies have numerous options for what to do with each market and what to do with the overall portfolio. In making these decisions, they must look beyond the narrow assessment of individual markets to consider the impact of each market on the entire portfolio.

Each market is the subject of individual management efforts—leading to decisions about how best to handle the market. Each of these markets is different, with a slightly different culture, different demands, and different products. Thus, it may not be desirable for the company to invest in them equally. Just as a company needs to evaluate products for a portfolio, it needs to choose different courses of action with each of the different markets it occupies:

- *No change*—Leave the market untouched and continue the same sales approach.

- *Change the product portfolio*—Change the products and improve front-end and back-end services that are marketed to that niche.

- *Re-mark the boundaries*—Adjust the definition of some market segments and reposition the products (changing geographic groupings, product-line or solution groupings, or feature stratification).

- *Merge multiple market segments*—Create a single market segment from several niche segments.

- *Create new mosaic space*—Create entirely new markets with a revolutionary product or service concept.

- *Leave the market*—Discontinue sales to the market because of insufficient value to its customers or to the company.

The second, third, and fourth options can be applied in combination. The direct effects of these decision options are confined to a single market segment, but not the indirect effects. Although a company could choose among these options with no consideration of the other markets it is in, that would be a mistake.

Market-to-market synergy occurs when markets are beneficially coupled with each other. In such a case, the removal of one product can actually damage sales or profitability of another product or of the whole company. Types of synergies include

- *Leading-edge markets*—demanding markets that spur innovation that is later sold to more mundane markets (such as defense contractors undergoing economic conversion to commercialize certain products)

- *Reinforcing a brand image*—markets that overlap in the optimum brand-image category (such as two allied or aligned markets that value high performance)

- *Leveraging a technology or asset base*—markets that combine to help amortize investments in product development or capital equipment

- *Inter-market customer migration*—markets in which customers in one market become customers in the other (such as marketing credit cards to college students because they later become affluent professionals)

The markets in a mosaic can also interfere with each other in many ways. In such cases, entering a new market can potentially decrease the sales or profitability of another market or of the whole company. Types of possible interference include

- *Brand confusion or dilution*—Confusion or dilution occur when a company tries to market both low-end and luxury versions under the same brand name. We've already spoken of Mercedes-Benz's flirtation with mid-range automobile markets. This is a classic case where, by trying to serve too many markets, a company may interfere with its brand image and dilute the perception of its value in the marketplace— trying to be everything to everybody.

- *Channel conflict*—The computer industry is a classic example of how one market—such as the direct-to-consumer market— can put a company in direct competition with its own customers in another market, such as in the traditional retail market. For manufacturers like Dell and Gateway, channel conflict has been a major challenge with regard to their substantial mail-order business; they have had to reevaluate their sales strategies as new retail channels, such as discount appliance centers, have started to support computers. Moreover, companies face a confusion of means in managing the sale and the post-sale relationship with the customer. Consider the example of buying a Sony laptop from CompUSA, where Sony's own policy does not allow the retailer to service and support the customer during his or her first year of purchase. Instead, customers are forced to ship the defective product to Sony's central location in Fremont, California, to get it repaired—an unnecessary inconvenience that can only reflect badly on both parties to the original sale.

- *Resource contention*—Special tooling, frequent changes in machine setups, labeling, packaging, and country-specific and market-specific compliance, are potential areas where serving one market may interfere with serving another, especially when those markets are overseas.

- *Antitrust*—There is an additional risk of interference, this time from an outside perspective. Filling too much of the market mosaic—such as Microsoft's dominance of operating systems, applications, and browsers—can bring unfavorable attention from government regulators.

Companies can no longer make market-related decisions in isolation. If a company changes or exits market X, will sales and profits from market Y go up or go down? To make jointly optimal product and market portfolio decisions, the managers from different constituencies must connect, communicate, and collaborate. Decisions to exit or change a market segment or change a market portfolio must also consider holistic effects on purchasing, advertising, costing, pricing, fulfillment, shipping and so on.

Although the notion of looking at sales and profitability in individual markets is valid, it is only a start. Companies must consider how all the markets interact with each other to estimate the impact of a given market on the aggregate performance of the company. Rather than consider whether a market is innately profitable or not, the company must determine how that market contributes to the entire span of its operations.

Managing Brands

Now we come to brands, which are of growing significance in modern marketing. Companies that are reviewing their portfolio—seeking to make the adjustments that lead to synergy between products, increased dominion over areas in the market mosaic, and a greater share of profits in market segments—must also recognize that when they begin such review, they have an opportunity to strengthen their relationship with customers and therefore to strengthen their brand. And, in an era of globalization, swiftly changing markets, and increasing price competition, a company's brand can be one of the most important aspects of its success with customers.

In short, a company's brand is a key asset for several reasons, which can be summed up in three short statements. First, Dom Perignon really doesn't compete with Veuve Cliquot on price. Second, Dell does not make the computers it sells. Third, Ford fought tooth and nail to dissociate itself from Firestone. Let's look briefly at what each of these statements implies.

The claim that Dom Perignon doesn't compete with Veuve Cliquot on price is a sweeping one. Perhaps some qualification is in order. Sometimes, perhaps, a buyer will choose a magnum of Veuve Cliquot over Dom Perignon because he or she thinks the Veuve Cliquot is a better deal. But, usually, customers are responding to characteristics of these champagnes that they associate with the differences between the two brands. Both are perceived as having high quality; both have an established pedigree. Too, each has the allure of French authenticity and has become a status symbol. Each is enjoyed by the rich and established, and by those who want to be seen as such. But there are differences between the two. Dom Perignon is the champagne of celebration: of weddings, anniversaries, parties—the King of Champagnes. Veuve Cliquot brands depend on an image of romance, of *La Grande Dame,* of early Art Deco design and the Paris of the 1920s.

Once consumers of one of these fine wines elect to buy, it's important to recognize that they are paying only a portion of the purchase price for the champagne *as a beverage.* Anyone can buy a cheaper brand of champagne; none of the wines much differs in alcoholic content; and taste is famously difficult to quantify. It's far more important to the buyer that a fine appellation champagne has the nameplate of a luxury brand—and all the promise of quality, reliability, and status that the nameplate implies. In short, the customer of Veuve Cliquot or Dom Perignon is paying for the integrity of the brand and trusts that brand. Even buyers of a Korbel champagne from California will tacitly acknowledge the same thing. To distinguish a product and its maker from others, the first filter is the evocation of a certain image in the mind of the buyer and the invitation to share in the qualities of an alluring brand.

The other lesson in the example of these two champagnes is that *product proliferation*—the competition within categories or market segments for the same customer—is only increasing. With the likelihood that any severe disparities in quality between two luxury champagnes will be close to nil, the brand, again, is crucial. The winemakers are selling the *experience* of style, of romance, of celebration—and that's exactly what customers want.

The importance of Dell to the argument about branding is also obvious: Dell doesn't make computers. What Dell does—better than anyone else—is take orders for computers, configured just as customers want them, and then ensure delivery. And what Dell did better than any other computer manufacturer during the 1990s was

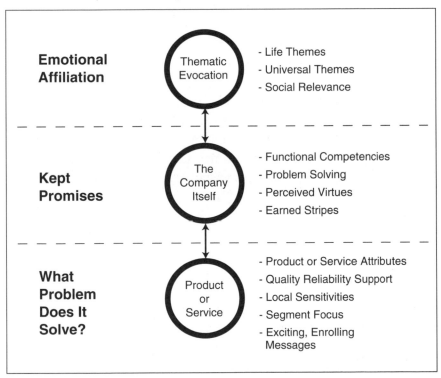

Figure 3-4   The anatomy of a brand

to offer better product customization. Customers flocked to a company that offered them fully customizable computer units, at the front edge of technological innovation, at competitive prices, and with reasonable speed. The key to Dell's success is being the coordinator of all the services that ensured delivery to customers, from just-in-time component purchase and tightly managed inventory to order processing, build-to-order assembly, and transportation of completed units.

Because Dell has focused so well on outsourcing services to its many providers, the company never actually needs to physically assemble computers in order to sell them. The value of the company is the reliability and efficiency of how it manages the necessary processes for getting a product with its nameplate in front of the customer. Dell is selling integrity—the sureness of a customer's getting what he or she asked for. That's the promise of the Dell brand. And the company's experience in managing its brand shows something else, too: customers see the name *on* the box, but they rarely, if ever, remember who *delivered* the box, and they likely do not know who made the motherboard or the silicon chips *inside* the box. IBM is fashioning a similar mythology for its own new servers that subtly acknowledges this reality: the new servers are marketed as "the Magic Box."

A company's brand is not simply a name or an icon or a logo or a colored design. Instead, a brand is an abstraction, an impalpable quality, a constantly evolving relationship between the company and its audience. That audience includes customers, potential customers, and non-customers. In some ways, a brand is a myth. It conjures up a favorable impression of a company; it is a mental image. Brand is a story with a constant refrain, a story that people are subtly reminded of every time they hear or see it. It bears a meaning that audiences unconsciously accept or reject. A brand evokes feelings, favorable associations, affiliations with positive things; it opens, enchants, energizes, stirs its audience. Even after a customer makes a purchase, the brand reassures, reminds, and reaffirms the customer's choice.

Brands can also suffer irreparable harm, which brings us to our third example—catastrophic damage to the integrity of a brand. Whatever the favorable qualities of a brand might be, they can be sacrificed or destroyed if a company takes actions that can provoke and/or alienate its customers and potential customers. Ford Motor Company tried to distance itself from Firestone because it knows that its alliance with the Japanese tire maker can represent almost insurmountable harm to its own future. The quality problems that plagued Firestone's tires for large SUV's—particularly the Ford Explorers—seem to have been ignored or overlooked by the manufacturer, and the tire tread separations that resulted in fatal and damaging accidents have become a catastrophe for the Firestone brand.

It is difficult to conceive of the company's recovering from this disaster; but it could, and there are strategies for recovering from a fatal blow to a brand. One strategy is to kill the old brand and create a new one. Remember that when a Valu-Jet plane went down over the Florida Keys in the mid-1990s because of a fire caused by cargo that should never have been carried on a passenger aircraft, the company disappeared for three years before taking off again as a newly named company.

Brands in a Portfolio

A company reviewing its portfolio is managing the future of its brand. Therefore, every executive—from purchasing and operations to human resources and strategy—is by default a brand manager. And every company's brand is composed of three fundamental components. For the sake of argument, let's call them *reason, quality,* and *commitment.*

The first aspect, the *reason* of the brand, derives from the company's reason for existing: that is, its fundamental skills in product or service design, engineering, manufacture, delivery. These skills enable the company to satisfy a need, and they are why the company has customers. This is the set of core capabilities that the market identifies the company with.

Second is the *quality* that the company achieves in providing products and services. By that, we mean the attributes of its products or services, which include the quality of a company's business processes, in operations or product management. It is what enables the company to satisfy its customers' needs well.

Third is something larger. By *commitment*, we mean the image or impression of what a company stands for—what differentiates the brand in the minds of audiences everywhere. This image is what companies often try to create through advertising—i.e., something that establishes an emotional relationship with a brand. Often, it depends on the evolution of a company: its founding, its history, and the successful extension of its competencies and the product or service attributes into the public sphere. It means a reputation that has been earned; it implies promises kept; it evokes standing for something larger than the product or the company itself—a larger humanitarian or universal theme, a greater calling.

This favorable image is ineffable. It is not built overnight—and it almost always depends on the integrity of the company. One example of a company that has successfully promoted a strong brand image is the climbing-gear manufacturer, Black Diamond, founded by the passionate climber and environmentalist, Yvon Chouinard, in Ventura, California, and the company which also gave birth to the active-wear clothing company, Patagonia. Black Diamond contributes a significant percentage of its profits to environmental protection programs and actively supports environment-friendly procedures at its manufacturing facilities. Another example is Paul Newman, the actor and race-car driver, who founded a food products company, Newman's Own, which donates all its profits to charity.

A powerful brand, then, is not built simply by the ubiquitous drumbeat of advertising and the constant drone of key messages in the media. Neither does visibility always equal durability. Though repetition will help enforce belief, it will not always overcome skepticism or allay a lack of trust. Brands are not as much a function of the right colors or font sizes or taglines as they are about integrity and earned trust. Products and services must deliver on the promise of the brand; business processes must contribute to the brand's success; management decision making is reviewed in the court of public opinion; and a meaningful, successful strategy is judged by Wall Street. Longevity is certainly a factor, but the emotional relation with the customer is based on those "moments of truth" when a brand is in play—the moment when a brand is challenged to live up to its promise.

Brands do face constant challenges. Perversely, a brand is always most visible when it is in danger, when there is some doubt—if you like, a cognitive dissonance—between what the brand purports to stand for and what the company actually delivers. This happened to Coca-Cola in 1999 and 2000. The company's brand suffered damage on three counts in three different spheres. First came news that the company's returns to shareholders were falling (i.e., Wall Street made a judgment). Second was the news that some employees had filed suit, claiming discrimination (i.e., a perceived lack of fairness in its business philosophy). Third, complaints arose that Coca-Cola's flagship product was contaminated in shipments made in Belgium and France (i.e., a lack of quality in a business process)—complaints that the company at first sought to dismiss.

Favorable management of a brand can lead to extraordinary success, such as in the extension of the Oprah Winfrey brand to her new magazine, *O*. The magazine, providing ordinary women with a forum for exploring their lives and expressing their creativity, had the most successful debut of any magazine in history and continued to outpace all expectations. But the real lesson of Oprah's success is that she succeeds in all three core elements of her brand: reason, quality, and commitment. She has created a wonderful product that fills a need. She delivers that product consistently and properly in every program, day after day. And she manifestly cares about the lives of the people on her show—and it shows.

On the other hand, poor product management can lead to market confusion and disarray, which can negatively affect the brand. This is the problem faced by Motorola. A leader in technological development, this company offers an astonishing diffusion in the number and variety of its products. Motorola actually employs some of the world's finest engineers; but, much like Texas Instruments in the 1980s, the company throws off technical marvel after marvel with no clear market charter. Motorola lacks a cohesive brand profile. Consequently the company lacks a loyal customer base on which to evolve and grow.

The lesson of a brand is that the customers and key stakeholders—even more than the company itself—will make the most important judgments of the strength and promise of a brand. Fortunately for Motorola, and for other companies that need to overcome an indistinct or negative brand image, brands are elastic. They can bend, stretch, and return to their former shape. British Petroleum, in rebranding BP after the purchase of Amoco, is trying to convince people that it goes "Beyond petroleum." The jury is still out, but the effort to capture the attention of American consumers is underway, and BP will have to deliver. Volkswagen, after two decades of desultory sales in the American car market, cleaned up its lackluster image in the 1990s, improving quality, smartening up its designs, providing more powerful cars, and launching a frank, engaging, slightly edgy ad campaign aimed at its target market of young buyers.

The key to success for Volkswagen? The young minds this company appealed to likely didn't remember the stodginess of Volkswagen's cars from the 1970s and 1980s. It's also true that the quality improved, and so did the appeal of the brand.

In the context of our discussion of PMCV, the key lesson in branding is that fulfilled promises and integrity in dealing with the public are the greatest possible opportunities for market success. The lack of either can be fatal. Furthermore, the brand must be relevant to the times and the sensitivities of the targeted customer base, and a company must deliberately shape the role it wishes to play in the marketplace. For that, companies must better understand their markets, which means knowing what customers buy, what they want to buy, and why they buy from particular providers and not others. That is the next topic of our discussion.

Understanding Customers

It is important that while a company prepares to do battle in a marketplace, it does not lose touch with the customers it serves, both as purchasers with their own unique matrix of concerns and as people with their own set of perceptions and needs.

Markets are convenient abstractions. Not everyone in a market is a buyer, and some buyers are not exclusive—i.e., they buy the competitor's goods and services as well. Customer relationships are complex. In addition, for any single product, there may actually be multiple customers, each customer with his or her own set of requirements and standards. For example, in the toy industry, the customer could be either the parents who buy the toy or the child who plays with it. For industrial components, the customer could be the engineer who specified the component, the manager who approved the selection, the purchasing agent who negotiated the purchase, the manufacturing personnel who inspected the component, or the service personnel who have to replace the component when it breaks.

All of these parties influence the decision to buy; therefore, all their needs and perceptions need to be considered. Any one of them could steer the decision towards or away from your company. Customers are those who affect the buying decision, either directly or indirectly, initially or eventually.

So a company's customers are a subset of its market. Accurately integrating customer information into a company's planning and operations is further complicated because a customer's perceptions and needs will likely change over time. Effectively managing these relationships then requires different approaches at different times.

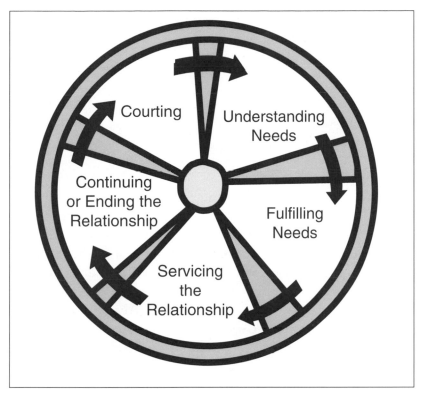

Figure 3-5 The Customer Life Cycle

Like products, customer relationships have a life cycle that parallels the birth, growth, maturity, and death of a living creature. The termination of the relationship could represent the final stage. Throughout the life cycle of a customer relationship, the following phases take place on a continual basis. They do not follow a one-time, linear sequence but are stages in a long-term, cyclical process. As with product life cycles, it is healthy for a company not to be at the same relationship stage with all its customers at the same time. These are the stages of the customer relationship life cycle:

- *Courtship*—wooing potential customers

- *Understanding Needs*—engaging in meaningful dialogue about current and future needs

- *Fulfilling Needs*—satisfying customers' needs and solving their problems

- *Servicing the Relationship*—continuing to satisfy customers and creating loyalty

- *Continuing or Ending the Relationship*—gauging the value of the customer relationship

The five stages of the customer life cycle must be executed to perfection, or the customer will be lost. Although an occasional mistake can be overcome and forgiven, it is far better and far cheaper to do it right in the first place. Serving customers in all phases of their life cycle requires impeccable customer-facing actions. Customers judge companies by the quality and integrity built into these actions.

During the courtship phase, it is important for a company to create and deliver suitable marketing messages. The emphasis needs to be on conveying value and building strong impressions of the brand. When focusing on understanding needs, the company must make it easy for the customer to ask questions and then answer them responsively. Helping customers understand their own needs while showing them how those needs can be satisfied is a compelling way to guide them to select your products and services. Integrity is an implicit need of customers. Demonstrating the ability to keep promises—and to return calls as promised—is essential.

In fulfilling customer needs, a company needs to demonstrate the ability to process orders accurately and efficiently; to provide answers, as needed, to questions about product features, availability, and shipping; and to deliver products that function as designed, are defect-free, and are reasonably priced. Being proactive in helping customers manage the business they conduct with you may point to other appropriate actions. Examples include partnering on issues related to the order/re-order process or exploring new ways to facilitate better interfacing of information systems. In other words, when fulfilling needs, the company should live up to the value propositions and brand image touted by its marketing messages.

When servicing the relationship, the company must deliver continued support for products that have already been purchased and track patterns of customer behavior that better enable the company to understand customers' needs. A commitment to a relationship is similar to meeting straightforward needs, but the former requires a more proactive approach to communications. Rather than merely responding to questions, announcing new products or policies, or sending letters of thanks for past business, etc., the company should demonstrate a commitment to the relationship and to continual improvement. This gives customers a better experience with the company and shows its interest in earning their business.

How do you create consistency along such a broad front of interaction? In the past, many companies appeared to be very poorly run and disorganized. The right hand did not seem to know what the left was doing. Phone-tag and bureaucratic runarounds meant that customers could not get simple answers to simple questions. But the notion of presenting one face to the customer means creating a single point of contact where customers get *all* of their questions answered and *all* their needs fulfilled. Instead of having to call sales to place an order, accounting to discuss an invoice, and manufacturing to check the status of an order, the customer should be able to call only one person.

Having to maintain contacts in several different products or service divisions is a frustrating waste of time for customers. The whole point of one face to the customer is to make it easy for your customers to do business with your company.

Poor Supply Chain Synchronization

Deciding to present just one face to the customer also unifies different product divisions. It means revolutionizing the front office, reorganizing it into a customer-facing organization, and putting customers first. But the change requires more than just altering how the sales offices operate. "One face to the customer" is an empty phrase if customer-facing people are disconnected from the back office. If disconnected, these people cannot promise shipments, check status, or help customers. They must connect, communicate, and collaborate with the people that actually fulfill customers' orders.

Thus, one face to the customer will not work if the company has poor supply chain synchronization, which makes a hash of all of a company's customer-facing actions. The symptoms of poor supply chain synchronization appear in breaking promises to customers and in troublesome interactions with them. These disappointments can take place when the company

- Promises a special promotional deal and then runs out of the product

- Claims that the product is in stock and then sends a back-order notice

- Promises a certain lead-time and then delivers late

- Protests that the order was shipped when it was not

- Delivers the wrong items—twice in a row

- Charges full price on promotional products and then claims it wasn't paid for those products

Customers will not continue doing business with a company that makes these mistakes. All these problems arise from poor supply chain synchronization and lack of informational visibility. It is worthwhile to see the correlation of these mishaps:

- Customers going away unsatisfied means bad demand forecasting or planning.

- Salespeople can't reliably promise anything—for there is no inventory or capacity visibility.

- Bad handoffs between sales and manufacturing mean orders get delayed and garbled.

- Parts are ordered late, tasks sit in long queues, work-in-process piles up, amounting to poor fulfillment planning.

- Stock-outs and delays are routine, for there is no collaboration between manufacturing and distribution.

- Administrative processes are sloppy and orders are lost or bungled.

The point is that although the front office sees the customer, collaboration in the back office satisfies the customer. Clear, reliable, and timely collaboration across the entire organization is the key to good service. The only way to create an image of integrity is to give the customer-facing people in the company the tools and the informational access to tell customers the truth and to implement customers' directives. Only when there is supply chain synchronization will the promises made to customers be fulfilled.

The Moment of Truth

A customer is a human being with whom your company has a relationship of mutual benefit. A customer is not an object or an extensive profile record in a database. Customers are human beings seeking human experiences; and they must feel that their own core expectations—the motivation to serve, an understanding of their needs, and a commitment to meeting those needs are acknowledged.

In understanding customers as individuals or as enterprises composed of individuals, the value of having bright and well-trained front-line personnel cannot be underestimated. The thinking processes and actions of the customer-facing representative greatly impact the quality of the relationship at every stage in the customer relationship cycle. Every point of contact with a customer is a moment of truth. In these moments, a company is defined as either a problemsolver or merely a source of information. At these moments, a company can differentiate itself by caring about its customers. The moment of truth is an interaction at first between individuals and only afterward between companies or entities. Front-line personnel must be equipped with information so that they can provide the basic components of service. They must be skilled in the art of establishing and maintaining rapport. This is an important, yet underestimated aspect, of demonstrating sensitivity and understanding to customers. Lapses in creating and maintaining rapport can undermine the entire relationship.

Choice for Customers

Rather than foist a set of "take-it-or-leave-it" standard products, today's business is about giving customers exactly what they want, meaning more choice for the customer. This orientation has certainly been embraced by the computer and automobile industries.

Despite the benefits that increased customization provides, however, new problems can arise. With a wider variety of products and services comes an added responsibility to both explain the options to customers and take legitimately configured orders. For example, in buying a mail-order computer, the customer is faced with an enormous number of highly technical buying decisions—which processor, how much RAM, how big a hard disk, etc. With every component of the computer, the customer must decide between the cheapest, the fastest, or something in the middle, while the total bill climbs skyward. Front-line personnel must understand all the product variants, all the options, and all the interactions (because some pieces may be incompatible with certain other pieces). As choice becomes important in an industry, a company must be able to respond with the quality of people and training to support this way of doing business.

Well, we have mocha, we have loca, we have pica, we have ice grande, we have low calorie, we can give you whipped cream, we can give you skimmed milk, frothy or saucy, or we can just give you water.

Coffee for headache? Or headache for coffee.

Customer Revenue and Cost Streams

Every customer creates both revenue and costs, and these revenues and costs do not end with a sale. Support costs, warranty costs, and legal liabilities also occur. Cost-to-serve encompasses all of the costs associated with a customer. A company's course of action with a customer will strongly influence both the cost stream and the revenue stream for that customer. Ideally, each incremental increase in the cost stream will create a greater (profitable) increase in the revenue stream.

The ugly secret of business is that some customers are unprofitable because they use more free services and buy fewer goods and services than others. Determining customer profitability entails more than just totaling up the sales and multiplying by an aggregate profit margin number. Companies need to consider the total time-series of interactions with that customer, and the costs and revenues associated with each interaction. This includes all past interactions as well as future predicted interactions based on some model of the customer's behavior.

The method for computing the real profitability of a customer has two steps. The first is to identify all of the interactions between the company and that customer. The second is to accurately model the cost and the revenue associated with each interaction. This is where software tools come into the picture.

Customers do not exist in isolation. They talk to other customers and potential customers. They know who else is using your product. Their actions or their very presence in your portfolio can increase the sales or profitability of other customers. For example, some customers want to buy from the same supplier who services the quality leader or standard-bearer in their marketplace. (Once several computer manufacturers chose to advertise "Intel Inside," this became an important feature for competitors.) And through these interactions comes the potential for customer-to-customer synergies. The mechanisms for synergy are threefold:

- Cost sharing, as when collocated customers share delivery and/or transportation cost

- Influencing customers, as when satisfied customers favorably impact the buying decisions of other customers by

    - *giving referrals (that is, one customer tells another customer about your product)*

    - *seeking publicity (that is, a customer highlights his or her success and your contribution to it)*

    - *co-marketing (that is, a retailer advertises your product, or you make celebrity customers your spokespeople)*

- Knowledge sharing, as when one customer helps another customer use your product

These synergistic customers are more valuable than might be estimated from analyzing their individual profitability, even their long-term profitability.

Customers can also interact in unfavorable ways—poisoning your relationship with other existing or potential customers. This can occur because influential customers become unsatisfied and communicate their dissatisfactions to the marketplace by

- Creating a "complaints web site" where they collect and publish stories about poor customer service

- Telling stories about problems to personal friends in informal conversations

- Blaming your company for their troubles

Achieving Synergies and Avoiding Interference

Companies make decisions about the importance of particular customers every day, paying them more or less attention as befits the company's impression of their worth. These actions may include giving price breaks to some customers or putting their orders ahead of those of other customers. These are direct applications of value stratification. Deciding what to do about any given customer is a function of evaluating two issues. One is the long-term profitability of that customer (Net Present Value of the revenue stream and cost stream); the other is the long-term interactions of that customer with other customers (holistic portfolio effects, i.e., how this customer will affect your position in a market). Whether a company makes money on an individual sale is less relevant than whether it makes money on a long-term customer relationship. Companies must carefully consider the following:

- *Consumables and lifetime service*—creating the basis for revenue streams

- *Retention and continued sales*—creating a stable revenue stream from each customer

- *Up-selling and cross-selling*—growing the revenue stream from each customer

- *Co-innovation and co-creation*—inventing new revenue streams and new sources of value with the aid of customers

Just like managing product and market portfolios, a company keeps a customer portfolio in which actions with one company can be looked at individually or together. When making a decision about each customer, companies have six courses of action:

- *No change*—Continue to serve the customer as he or she is.

- *Change price*—Increase or decrease the price to modulate the customer's purchases or profitability.

- *Change marketing*—Adjust marketing frequency or messages to that customer.

- *Change service levels*—Improve the quality of fulfillment and support services.

- *Change relationship closeness*—Adjust the closeness of the relationship (such as adding a special portal to enable all transactions to occur in one place, in-plant personnel, key account managers, joint projects, and so on).

- *"Fire" the customer*—Stop doing business with the customer because of insufficient profit.

Before a final decision can be made about an individual customer, it is important to understand that one cannot view the relationship in a vacuum. Failure to see key relationships between factors in a market can be damaging. So can be the relationships of one customer with others.

Changing prices for one customer will likely affect other customers' perceptions and expectations of you. Changing service levels for a customer or group of customers, without changing available resources, may mean cutting back services to other customers. Making changes with customers must be thought out carefully to avoid loss of business with other customers. Potential synergies need to be evaluated as well. If a company improves service to customer X, will sales and profits from customer Y go up? Examining revenue and cost streams, customer-to-customer synergies, and customer-to-customer interference is fundamental to managing a customer portfolio.

What is the basis for investing effort in any given customer relationship? It is to build value. Companies must systematically understand how the delivery of value to each customer drives revenues.

Understanding Value: The Eye of the Beholder

Many companies mistakenly believe that they deliver products and services—a holdover from the bad old days of arms-length, anonymous transactions. What companies really deliver is value—fulfilling some combination of the demands or the desires of their customers.

Value will always finally be judged by a company's customers.

Products and services are only the means for realizing that value. To an Eskimo, the only intrinsic worth of a sealskin blanket is in its immediate ability to keep a person warm. But in a world where a blanket is purchased for its design, for its brand name, or for what buyers believe the blanket's design or brand name says about them, then the intrinsic value of the blanket is a negotiation in the marketplace that transcends utilitarian value.

In a dynamic business environment, companies continuously create new forms of value—and that means understanding all the characteristics of a product or service that can determine value. Also, as whole sectors of the economic landscape change, the old forms of value may become irrelevant; companies must consciously question the value they provide, understand the role which value plays in customers' lives, and realize opportunities to create new value for the future.

Although customers expect a supplier to deliver the purchased product or service, they want much more than that. They really want a combination of three things. First, they want to be confident that suppliers will deliver what they promised—when they promised it. Second, they want the use of the product or service, such as a high-quality raw material or component part, a productive piece of equipment, or a useful change in process because of a key service. They want the results that come from that product or service. Third, they want long-term support—the confidence that suppliers will be there in the future with additional products and services that they need.

These three wants define the value of a company's products and services as perceived and received by the customer. That definition of value is up to the customer, although companies can help to sway customers toward certain value propositions. Each of these three wants can be further defined in terms of the minute features of the company's products and services. For example, customers' definitions of "productive piece of equipment" depend contextually on the exact details of what they are doing, where they are doing it, and how they are doing it.

Value is a holistic concept—based not on any one feature, but on the sum total of all product features and all interactions with customers. A company that has feature-packed, high-quality products but terrible customer service will sooner or later become irrelevant.

Value Creation

Emphasizing value means adopting change. Good companies create new forms of value for four reasons:

- To fulfill customers' changing needs (synchronize with customers)

- To address entirely new needs (innovate into new markets)

- To differentiate themselves from their competitors (compete)

- To escape low-value or irrelevant markets

The following subsections describe three prominent types of value creation.

Moving to Finished Goods Manufacturing

The raw materials and industrial components business is a commodity business. The perceived value of yet another pump maker is low because so many companies operate in that market. Companies that make such parts can create value by building on the parts that surround their "core" business, or by creating entire finished goods products that incorporate their raw materials. For example, Kyocera, a Japanese ceramics and coatings maker, has moved beyond making photocopier drums to making the whole photocopier.

High-Grade Versions of Existing Products

Where can you add performance and quality? Having mastered the basic components of quality, companies can turn to creating new products and services that leverage their skills in quality. Rather than produce commodity goods at commodity prices, companies can move into a more valuable market niche by producing ultraquality, noncommodity versions.

But this migration to the high end also shows just how intense and dangerous business is becoming. For example, in the past, only luxury cars had anti-lock brakes, passenger-side air bags, built-in CD players, power windows, etc. But the increasing efficiency and value-creation activities of mid-market carmakers has stolen this source of value, as mid-priced sedans now come with a host of "luxury" amenities. High-end carmakers have fewer and fewer tangible product features with which to differentiate themselves. The point is that value creation leads to crucial, but temporary, competitive advantage—forcing companies to relentlessly innovate or face irrelevance.

Service-Oriented and Lifetime Support

Most customers do not really want the product itself—they want the benefits of the product. When someone buys a computer, they do not want a big beige box; they want to perform work, access information, and/or play games. Computer companies must understand that their products are really a means to an end, not an end in themselves.

So companies can also add value by adding service. Extended service plans, 7x24 support, on-site technical service, upgrades and repairs are all services that reflect the fact that customers do not want the box—they want what the box lets them do. The entire concept of outsourcing and of application service providers is based on the notion of wanting the results of a product or service, not the actual product or service itself.

Four Categories for Value Creation

Value creation can also be viewed from the perspective of process—by reviewing how value was created, instead of what type of value was created. Methods for creating value fall into four categories.

The classic approach to adding value—innovation—of course remains popular. Innovative products and services will always be a source of value. Innovations in development can include adding new features, or new combinations of features, to existing products and services; enhancing performance or quality; and finding ways to combine performance features that smash assumed separations, such as selling high quality at a low price. Innovations in fulfillment can also be a tremendous source of value because each customer's business depends on reliable delivery. These can include shorter cycle-times; reduced costs-per-unit, per-order, per-product, and per-customer; and increased consistency in lead-times and product quality. Innovation applied to improving customer interfaces, such as new systems to enable faster order-entry or provide instant information on the status of an order, also represents an especially important area for new value creation.

Second, value is achieved through improved coordination of repetitive processes. The value created here is reliability. Improved coordination often results from streamlining steps in the process. It can also be the by-product of repetition itself. Even the best product design in the world is worthless if the company cannot reliably and profitably reproduce a product or service and deliver it. The greater a company's experience is with on-time delivery, the greater its opportunity to offer reliability. Systems that enable a company to produce and ship on a just-in-time basis or support low costs and inventory levels improve through repetition.

Third, enforcing standards over other participants in the supply chain creates value. The value that a company delivers is built upon the value that the company acquires from its suppliers. Therefore, companies can look to their suppliers for new sources of value. Better raw materials, new component technologies, and streamlined supply chain processes all create value that can be delivered to end-customers. Supplier-related sources of value creation include

- Finding better suppliers (synchronizing supplier portfolios)

- Co-innovating with suppliers (synchronizing supply with true need)

- Coordinating with suppliers (synchronizing work activities)

Fourth, acquiring knowledge is a key method for creating value. While knowledge and expertise are generally valued by customers, companies sometimes forget that their customers are a tremendous source of knowledge. Customer knowledge can help a company improve its internal systems, lead to more interdependent partnerships (which in turn creates new value), and enable a company to be a greater informational resource for other customers.

Few companies appreciate how valuable their customers can be to them in this way. Knowing how a customer uses and experiences a product or service can lead to opportunities to better fulfill their real needs (i.e., provide value). Being attentive to learning this paves the way for other processes that help create value, such as co-innovation. Collaborating with customers can be instrumental in improving products and processes. It can

- Define which product features are valuable and which are irrelevant

- Offer new options for defraying or sharing development costs, allowing customers to help design the product for you

- Set quality standards, which in turn will better enable you to guarantee satisfaction

- Improve supply chain protocols and synchronization to aid the flow of business

This kind of collaboration benefits customers as well. It may provide

- An increased potential to get more tailored and customized product

- A greater assurance of the long-term profitability and sustained existence of the supplier. Although the process of evaluating suppliers can be costly, it can represent a tremendous benefit.

- Special access to or pricing on the new product

Co-innovation is win-win because the company gets a new product or service at both lower cost and lower risk. Assuming that the co-innovating customer is appropriately representative of the market, the co-developed product will enjoy a higher chance of sales and higher market share. The effort exerted by the customer will mean lower development costs, which means less risk.

Co-innovation is becoming common in the automotive industry because big automakers need uniquely customized parts—and suppliers, acting outside of a partnership, may face greater challenges in delivering such parts at costs that they can live with. But only when the automaker and the supplier collaborate can they create the best possible component part that both suits the automobile manufacturer's design application and is cost-effective to the supplier. Because suppliers have the means and customers have the needs, it makes sense for everyone to connect, communicate, and collaborate to create new value.

Extracted value is generally improved on through product innovation and all the activities (such as market research or collaboration) that might contribute to some kind of improvement in product design or quality. As one travels up the pyramid, service becomes a greater determinant in perceived value. A good product is no longer enough. Customers evaluate value based on how a supplier's level of service better enables them to operate their own business. When considering a customer's overall perception of value, one must consider the personal experiences between customer and supplier personnel at every point of contact. Courteous communications and sincerity in maintaining rapport are key. More important, value grows in concert with the level at which customer and supplier personnel recognize their interdependence.

Portfolios of PMCV

Should you emphasize products, markets, customers, or value? No single perspective guarantees success. The days when a company could simply be the lowest-cost producer or the highest-quality producer are over. Now, companies must offer low cost and high quality while fulfilling the unique demands of each customer with speed and reliability. To survive and thrive in a competitive global marketplace, companies must understand products, markets, customers, and value. Those who do not understand PMCV will likely become irrelevant—like fish in a drying pond.

Engineering your supply chain comes down to taking particular actions in PMCV space and maintaining a holistic perspective. The goal is to find that "sweet spot" of synergies between products, customers, and markets—delivering maximum value for minimum cost. Finding your place in the market mosaic means navigating the PMCV space—taking particular courses of action with each of your products, your markets, and your customers.

A company needs to ask which products, markets, and customers it should invest in. Existing products, markets, and

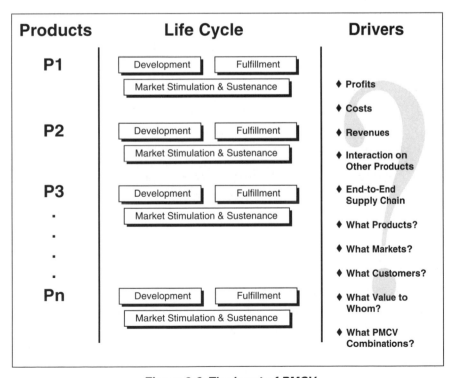

Figure 3-6 The heart of PMCV

customers are all a continued source of value and profits. Incremental adjustments and investments in these areas help a company to maximize the long-term return from its products, markets, customers, and the value that the company delivers. As follow-up, a company must ask if the incremental benefits (of an investment) are greater than the incremental cost? Companies must both understand the cost/benefit ratio for any incremental move into PMCV space, and they must reduce all costs on incremental activities to increase the PMCV space that can be profitably filled.

Determining where it would be most beneficial to allocate resources raises questions about current investments. Some such investments may have to be abandoned because resources can be better allocated. For example, it would be reasonable to abandon

- Products that have become obsolete or cost-prohibitive to produce

- Markets that have become unprofitable because of declining size or increasing competition

- Customers that have changed their business focus, away from your core value

- Old forms of value that have become irrelevant (or less valued) by customers in the markets you serve

The point is that customers' definitions of value are fickle and profits are always fleeting. This does not mean that a company should discontinue a product, exit a market, or abandon a customer at the first sign of low profits. Rather, the criteria for vacating a part of PMCV space are

- *Low innate value:* The long-term expected financial performance from the product, market, or customer is low.

- *Limited synergies:* The product, market, or customer does not favorably increase the performance of some other products, markets, or customers.

- *Significant interference:* The product, market, or customer unfavorably decreases the performance of some other products, markets, or customers.

Sometimes a seemingly unprofitable item should be kept; sometimes a seemingly profitable item should be eliminated. The combined effects of these three criteria define the holistic impact of the product, market, or customer on your entire enterprise.

Incrementalism is a severely limited approach because it eliminates the possibility of innovation. Extending existing product lines is also an inadequate strategy because it cannot delay markets from saturating. How can you create entirely new products, markets, and customers? Companies must look to new technologies and new fulfillment processes. They must create combinations of performance and cost previously unrealized. These innovations let a company create entirely new white space in the market mosaic and create new customers.

For each product or service you offer, ask yourself:

- What value does that product or service provide?

- What is the cost to fulfill demand for it?

- How does it impact the rest of your products and services?

- Should you keep, change, or discontinue it?

For each market you target, ask yourself:

- What value should you promise?

- Do your products and services actually provide that value?

- What is the cost to serve that market?

- Does that market affect the rest of your markets?

- Should you stay, adjust tactics, or exit that market?

For each customer you serve, ask yourself:

- What value should you provide?

- Do your products and services actually provide that value?

- What is the cost to serve that customer?

- How does that customer influence the rest of your customers?

- Should you keep or adjust the relationship, or fire that customer?

And one final question:

- How will you create the value that you should promise but don't yet provide?

These questions are aimed at making your current infrastructure relevant while maintaining a long-range perspective. They will also train your management team to think holistically and strategically, and to avoid irrelevancy. Then the challenge becomes building robust information systems that link suppliers, customers, and other constituents in the value chain so that your company can align congruently its products, its markets, and its customers while delivering value. That is the focus in the succeeding chapter.

Nerves and Twitches

Building Robust Information Systems

The fundamental role of the business manager is to make decisions that affect the future effectiveness and performance of the organization—and to make those decisions operational. Simply put, the central issue is how to add value to the greatest extent possible with available resources and assets. A deliberate effort must be made by these managers to understand the current state of the organization, to evalutate the impact of their decisions, and to maximize value creation across the business organization.

Vital to this informed, conscientious effort is a robust information system that links together all the key functional processes and business groups to ascertain its current state and how decisions will impact the organization.

In this chapter, I examine the basic processes and common impediments associated with good decision making, introduce a powerful framework for rationalizing the choices made by business organizations, and apply this framework to a series of corporate examples to further illuminate its components and universal applicability. Then I build the case that a well-designed information system is vital to business success for a variety of reasons, and conclude this chapter by providing specific guidance for building robust information systems to effectively support corporate decision making.

Understanding Decision Making

Figure 4-1 illustrates a company with its basic departments and decision structures. Each of these departments has a specific purpose. The arrows represent the multitude of transactions that flow between departments. For example, manufacturing is expressly dedicated to physically making products in an efficient manner and shipping them to the customer on time. Purchasing is focused on procuring materials in a cost-effective and timely manner to feed manufacturing. Engineering has the responsibility of designing products that are market-worthy and feasible for manufacturing.

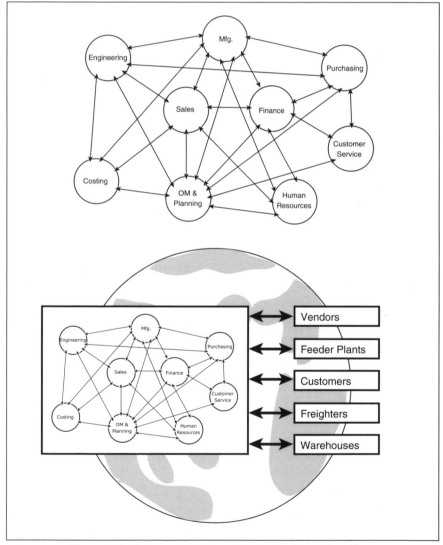

Figure 4-1   Intra- and inter-company information flows

The number of interactions between these departments for an individual company may vary, depending on the complexity of the products and the composition of its processes. Thus, the manufacture of an aircraft is far more interaction-intensive than making blue ribbons. These interactions are both internal and external, and every such interaction is nothing but an answer to a question. Let us look at some of the questions posed by different people in an organization:

- What resources do we commit to the current portfolio of new products?

- What is the optimal sequence of activities? When is the appropriate time to launch, given the current market conditions?

- Where do we make our products? How many do we make? How much raw material do we buy? How much do we store? How much do we transport? When do we transport?

- What products do we promote? At what prices do we promote?

- Who are our profitable customers? At what levels should we serve these customers?

- What is the projected profit from the current plan? How much and what should we sell to realize our revenue and profit targets?

Often, business managers ask questions and make decisions based on their own functional view of the world. But every major decision made in a company is invariably connected at its roots with many functional areas—not just one. Often this interconnectedness is either lost or simply not acknowledged, or is even misunderstood because of deficient information systems, delayed information flow, or a diminished perception of the business.

A design decision, for example, is influenced by marketing, sales, finance, manufacturing, and services. The product has to be feasible, marketable, sold profitably, and capable of being supported. A simple component change to an existing design impacts procurement, manufacturing, and bills of material records. A price change for a specific part or product not only requires recalibrating the revenue stream but also has potential impact on other products, with respect to volumes and capacities they demand. A product launch, with all its promotional advertising, will be worthless unless holistically supported by manufacturing capabilities and logistical alignment. A late delivery to a customer is perceived first as a logistical problem, and only later as having an impact on product cost structure, customer relations, and the revenue calculus.

Corporations suffer when the reaction and coordination of any one department to an unplanned event is not collectivized until too late. We assert that full visibility of a product's progression—from design to manufacture to delivery to a customer—is mandatory for meaningful business decisions.

Impediments to Effective Decision Making

Perhaps the single biggest impediment to swift decision making is a *functionally disconnected organization.* Among its many symptoms are

- Managers in the organization lack cross-functional competencies and coordination.

- Functional managers attempt to run the company in several directions at the same time.

- Senior management cannot conceive or implement strategy past a PowerPoint deck; many employees may actually believe that their job is completed when the PowerPoint presentation is done.

- IT makes monolithic decisions and sets requirements based on recycled RFPs, as opposed to real analysis and operational relevance, and spends millions of dollars only to accumulate acronym-driven software in place of an effective IT strategy.

The second impediment to swift decision making is what I call the *madness of multiplicities.* By that, I mean to describe a situation in which there are multiple conflicting priorities, multiple decision paths with no clear accountability, multiple basic hardware platforms, multiple unconnected databases, multiple software application architectures, etc. Often, an unsustainable anarchy of loosely cobbled systems proliferates from unofficial information sources—mostly in the form of individuals pursuing their own needs, using local systems that are not aligned with the rest of the organization. The problems these systems spawn are not only technical but also operational. A lack of integration creates endless paths into the company, but no consistent mosaic for anyone to stand on.

The third impediment is the *inertia of indifference.* This describes the condition when a company suffers such a lack of resolve that its employees will not embrace change, and will instead persist in outdated ways of doing business. This inertia can manifest itself in stifled innovation, lack of passion about the business, and a management team unwilling to initiate programs for making their employees information-savvy.

The early warning sign of these impediments is a *diminished velocity of corporate response.* Critical domains remain uninformed, careful decisions are not crafted, and consistent actions are not taken in time to make a difference. A company will forfeit its opportunities when all it can see are patchy, piecemeal pictorials of its performance.

It is time to think about and execute businesses and business processes differently so these impediments are eliminated at their source. It is time to turn the attention of management to those areas

It is system-attic

of the business most critical to driving success in real time, and to align internal structures and investments with the key components of corporate strategy. It is time to rationalize the business around the critical determinants of competitive success.

The Business Alignment Model

To provide a fundamental structure for building robust information systems, I have created a Business Alignment Model. It can be used by personnel at all levels of a company to illuminate root causes of poor decision making in organizations, supporting the type of decision making that leads to success. Adopting this model is the first construct for the future. It unifies businesses externally and internally, but most importantly it unifies a business philosophically, operationally, and in terms of its information architecture. In short, the Business Alignment Model is a *holistic construct for bonding business strategy to operational execution, supported by appropriate technology.*

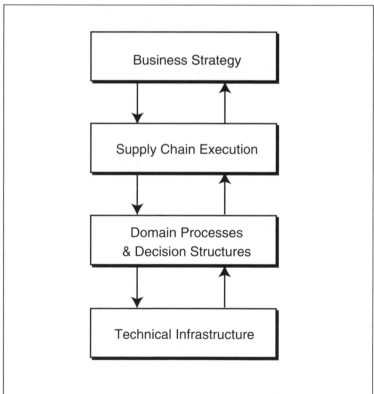

Figure 4-2 The Business Alignment Model

Elements of the Model

The Business Alignment Model provides us with key insights into the inner workings of the business and the subtle influences that impact the drivers of success. One of the more controversial aspects of this model that flies in the face of contemporary business thinking is the idea that customers should not be the central concern and the focus of your business decisions. Nor should your shareholders. Nor should your employees, and certainly not your competition.

Rather, I submit that the central concern for any business today is its *supply chain*.

"Supply chain?" you ask. "Not customers? Not shareholders? Not competitors or employees?"

"No," I'll say. "Supply chain."

"But," you insist, "How can this be? How can we survive as a business if we don't address our customers' needs?"

"That's not what I said," I will reply.

Note that I said "the central concern of your business." I'm not telling anyone to ignore customers; for whom you choose to serve and choose not to serve is a highly important and relevant exercise. But increasing market share alone is the booby prize of corporate success. All the talk about "markets of one" and "mass customization" ignores the economic realities of business fulfillment: you have to be able to *deliver* what you've sold and *deliver at a profit!* Without an efficient, responsive, economical supply chain at the core of your business, there won't *be* a business to serve your customers. Reality dictates that as the production run size of a product decreases, total per-unit costs must necessarily increase. It doesn't matter if the product is an automobile, an airplane, a bag of corn chips, a sweater, or a consulting engagement. The fixed costs of running the business and managing production changes are necessarily spread out across a smaller base of units.

One of the principal contributing factors to the unfortunate but most impressive implosion of the "new" dotcom economy, even beyond some highly questionable business models, was the almost total lack of understanding and attention paid to the fulfillment side of the business—i.e., supply chain, production, and distribution. The dotcom craze was all about demand generation and sometimes just about collecting "eyeballs." The key lesson was that astute business people recognize the impact that increasing choices on the customer side of the business has on the supply side. Well-intentioned customized offerings can wreak havoc on the supply chain, driving costs and complexity up, while eroding or destroying margin altogether.

The Business Alignment Model provides a powerful tool for ensuring that decisions made on the customer side of the business can be profitably delivered on the production and supply side, and that the constraints inherent in any business are known and observed *before* poor decisions are made.

We'll return to this concept later in this chapter. Now let's begin our construction of the Business Alignment Model by identifying and discussing its four components: strategy, supply chain execution, domain processes and decision structures, and IT infrastructure.

Strategy

The first layer of the Business Alignment Model, *strategy*, fundamentally addresses a company's blueprint for achieving its growth, revenue, and profitability goals in the face of competitive threats and resource constraints. It defines answers to key questions, such as

- Where are the markets for our products and services? The revenue streams?

- What products or services will the company take to market?

- Which customers should we sell to?

- What is our value proposition to the customer?

- What are the potential profits, now and in the future?

- Who are our competitors, and how should we fend them off?

- How should the company differentiate itself and its offerings?

- What are the known risks? How will these risks be mitigated?

- How will our strategy be communicated across the enterprise?

- How will the strategy be revalidated over time?

- What are our contingency plans should the overall strategy prove to be invalid once it is implemented?

Often has it been said that the best laid plans of mice and men go awry. So it is with strategy. Successful companies analyze and understand the answers to these questions on a continual basis, for the extent to which a company is nimble in recalibrating its well-laid strategy with respect to its market conditions is a key determinant of its success.

In many companies, the underpinnings of strategy are not even understood, much less analyzed. Such companies incorrectly assume that a strategy session means sharing sales forecasts, as opposed to rationalizing its portfolio of products, markets, customers, and value. It is not enough for a company's leaders to just declare that they will be a customer-focused company without knowing what that means, without understanding how the daily contentions along the supply chain will be resolved, and how the day-to-day aberrations and abnormalities will be addressed and by whom. Instead, they must ask themselves how supportive their processes are and how functional their current information systems are.

And they must ask what role everyone plays. Strategy can succeed only when it is aligned and affiliated with execution, and that means people in the company must clearly understand their responsibilities as they relate to realizing the business strategy. Hence, strategy must have supply chain equivalence, informational equivalence, and infrastructural equivalence. Companies that do not understand these inviolable axioms will be doomed to failure because they will become their own worst enemies.

Supply Chain Execution

The second layer of the Business Alignment Model is *supply chain execution*, and it poses a very fundamental question: "For every product that we decide to make, or a service that we decide to deliver, is there a solid supply chain to support it?"

Supply chain execution is simply managing day-to-day contentions among cost, time, and value. Focusing on customers without attending to costs and time is a lost cause. Many companies fall easily into this quagmire. Some of the conflicts among cost, time, and value are visible, but many are not. They are invisible in the daily hustle of getting customer orders out the door. The sad corollary is that profit margins are often eroded and are neither noticed nor captured until it is too late. What are these ever-present conflicts?

- Managing inventory levels vs. meeting customer service demands

- Balancing customer satisfaction with the costs of such structure and services

- Upholding profit margins vs. prioritization

- Choosing investments against maintaining the status quo

- Allocating resources for one product vs. another

- Choosing to build now or electing to build later

Executing the supply chain then becomes the efficient marshalling of resources in desired time frames, driven by congruent processes and guided by correct metrics. It is intelligently managing daily contentions so that revenues, costs, and profits form an optimal relationship for every product and for every customer. It is ferociously focusing, *with every product*, on minimizing order-to-ship cycle-time, compressing cash-to-cash cycle-times, shipping the entire order on time, and optimizing the use of resources.

Effective supply chain execution depends on the ability to align *supply* and *demand* so that *concurrent planning* can occur for all resources—materials, machine capacity, labor, and transportation—against actual demand.

For supply chains to work, a company must follow these core steps:

- Correctly predict and manage demand

- Align fulfillment resources with expected demand throughout the operating year

- Plan, schedule, and sequence production optimally in the face of constraints

- Efficiently manage distribution and delivery

For these steps to be accomplished, the operational data must be accurate, and there must be total visibility of the supply and demand relationship for every product across the whole supply chain. This requirement dictates that all underlying processes be straightforward and streamlined to support the progression of a product.

Domain Processes and Decision Structures

The third layer of the Business Alignment Model is *domain processes and decision structures*. In the flow of products or services from demand generation to delivery, many functional units within and across the company will "touch" the product or service, or will need to make informed decisions about it. The processes by which this flow occurs are uniquely determined by a combination of practices within the company's internal decision structures. This layer encompasses the individual core processes of the business, such as the order life cycle, billing cycle, payment cycle, product life cycle, customer life cycle, inventory receipts and reconciliation, release cycles and the final arithmetic for revenues, costs, and profits for each product sold or service rendered.

Various transactions take place among the stakeholders of these processes. In some cases, there may be simple information flows; in others, there are complex "handoffs" of physical components or manufactured goods. These processes and decision structures must be in place so that the nature of these transactions and the flow of information can be understood. Without them, decisions are made without sufficient information to make intelligent choices.

These processes must define what decisions need to be made. They must answer questions such as "At what points?" "By whom?" "When?" "How are they related to each other?" The processes must also take into account the consequence of each decision along the supply chain: for example, how do marketing decisions at one point affect the supply chain, manufacturing processes, and distribution? How does delayed billing or pricing a certain customer at an abnormal discount affect the current cash position? What is the effect of replacing a certain component with another when the new one has different machining, service, and installation standards?

A decision structure is an arrangement of who makes what decisions, and in what manner, regarding what issues, based on what criteria, and in what frequency. The interrelatedness of a company's processes and business functions underscores the importance of comprehending all the steps that are necessary to make a decision. What are these steps? It is defining the problem or the situation to be resolved, gathering and analyzing all relevant data, weighing different courses of action, understanding the cause and effect of different decisions, and making an appropriate decision.

On one hand, the decision making processes in a company are pre-determined by the quality and functional worthiness of its information systems. On the other, they are also influenced by how quickly the company gets things done. The arrangement of how decisions are made within a company and within departments or across them will either spell success in decision making or will delay the response.

Managers can therefore ask: Does our company have an intrinsic culture for quick resolution of matters—for quick, sensible, informed decision making? No strategy can survive if it takes the company two days before it can locate the details of transactions on its key account. A billing process in a company that cannot combine multiple invoices into a "comprehensible" single invoice to a customer is far from being customer-focused, no matter what the company's marketing slogan says. Likewise, a company that professes to compete on time, but takes four hours to process a basic customer order, or has a serpentine procedure for a product refund, will be perceived as having semantic schizophrenia unless it can behave congruently.

Domain processes are the spices that add taste and flavor to a meal. No matter how farm fresh or organically grown the strategy is, domain processes will determine how the meal will taste. The unique map of a company's processes and its decision structures will either make a company's strategy work or will work insidiously to break it.

IT Infrastructure

The fourth layer of the Business Alignment Model, *IT infrastructure*, is akin to the structural components of a house: foundation, framing, plumbing, wiring, and the supply of utilities. In the world of IT, the analogs to these components require answering these questions:

- What is the overall composition of the total IT infrastructure?

- What hardware platforms does information have to traverse during a full business cycle?

- What software applications does the information have to traverse during a full business cycle?

- Are the software applications portable across the necessary hardware platforms?

- Are the software applications scalable as the business grows?

- Can the current combinations of hardware and software co-exist within a workable topology?

- What security measures exist to protect company assets within and outside the company?

- What are the protocols for connecting the networks both within the company and with customers, suppliers, and other partners?

- How is the Internet being utilized for moving information to multiple supply chain constituents?

- Where and how will the data be stored and managed?

- How will knowledge and learning be captured and disseminated so that the corporation can learn and continually improve?

To move information across a complex web of suppliers, retailers, manufacturers, and transporters, a company must understand the issues above for all its business partners. Like railroad tracks that enable movement of goods by train, IT infrastructure is the track on which information flows. Managers of information technology must focus on understanding and delivering the *informational equivalence* of the business strategies, processes, and physical flow of orders and products across the organization.

As described, these four layers very much depend on one another. A well-considered business strategy is incomplete unless it can align the support structure of supply chains, processes, and technical infrastructure.

Application of the Business Alignment Model

The Business Alignment Model is applicable to virtually all businesses and across all industries because it is based on fundamental concepts that transcend the unique domain specializations and jargon of any industry. In the next several sections, we will apply the model to a variety of businesses that would seem to have little in common: Frito-Lay, Polo Ralph Lauren, and Steelcase. We then discuss in detail what the model reveals is common to all three of these businesses.

Case Analysis: Frito-Lay

Frito-Lay, a subsidiary of PepsiCo, is the largest snack-food maker in the world. The company owns some of the best-known, bestselling

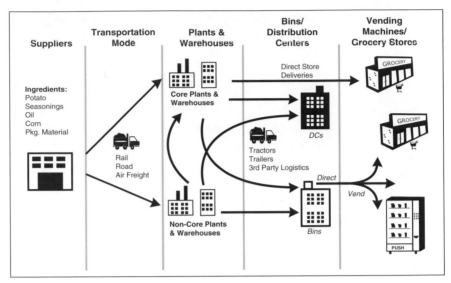

Figure 4-3 Frito-Lay's retail supply chain

snack-food brands in the world, including Cheetos, Cracker Jack, Doritos, Fritos, Lay's, Munchos, Rold Gold, Ruffles, and Tostitos. Frito Lay holds a 60% share of the U.S salt-snack foods market and a 40% share of the global market, and sells products in more than 120 countries.

A global player, Frito-Lay succeeds in the face of literally hundreds of competitors (other major national brands, specialty, niche players in specific geographic areas) in its markets. The company has learned how to masterfully create and manage all manner of variations in its products, sizing, and packaging, not to mention scores of languages.

Strategy

At the strategy level, Frito-Lay's fundamental issues revolve around what it is going to do to maintain and build its already successful global business. Obviously, it already has several different brands of snack foods, but it will constantly be considering if it should add more. Should the company develop new varieties—say, new flavors—of its old standbys, such as Fritos or Doritos? Should it retire marginally performing brands to make room for introducing new ones? Are there any brands that would add strategically to the existing portfolio if they were to be acquired?

Frito-Lay will consider many more factors. It will ask sales managers to indicate what markets the company should pay particular attention to, either because they are performing very well or because they are not performing as well as expected. It will assess whether any of the brands are particularly strong in regional U.S. markets, say the South or Midwest—and strive to learn why. It will seek to use that knowledge to increase sales in other regions and other markets around the world. It will constantly ask brand managers if there are movies, sports, or music tie-ins that would boost sales, particularly in hard-to-dominate markets.

Supply Chain Execution

In managing its supply chain, Frito-Lay must be able to correctly assess demand across all of its products. Point-of-sale data must be readily available to planners, so they can discern selling trends and can plan production accordingly. The company must take full advantage of bulk purchasing—but without building up excess inventories of ingredients or finished products. Manufacturing and distribution networks must work together to correctly match fulfillment with demand. Spoilage must be factored into replenishment cycles, as must be the cost implications of making a product in one factory and shipping it from that one location, compared with producing in another factory and shipping from there.

There are other questions to resolve—and continually to monitor. When is direct store delivery meaningful, as opposed to shipping to warehouses? How are resource contentions dealt with— in factories, in trucks, in suppliers' capabilities? Are Frito-Lay's cash-to-cash cycles for each product fully compressed, ensuring that the company is achieving the highest degree of working capital efficiency possible? Are orders of Cheetos, Doritos, and so forth, properly consolidated into delivery trucks to ensure the lowest cost in transportation? Answering the above questions is a daily ritual and a differentiating religion at Frito-Lay.

Domain Processes & Decision Structures

This layer simply asks two questions. First, "Are we easy to do business with internally?" Second, "Are we easy to do business with externally?" From purchase requisition to shipments, from invoices to receipts and returns, from store assortments to electronic fund transfers, from adjustments to exchange, from brand promotion to managing the retail theater, from budget revisions to product launches, innumerable processes occur in the transformation of a spud to a crispy dinner bud.

For Frito-Lay, perhaps the two most important business drivers are customer loyalty and ensuring the right mix of products to maximize the customer share of wallet in the snack-food category. From the customers' perspective, Frito-Lay must ensure that it has timely business processes that monitor and report in near real-time any changes in customer buying patterns and preferences, and link these changes directly to the supply chain for adjustments. This means that core processes must be fully integrated upward and downward to pass along and act upon vital business information without bottlenecks or disruptions. Key event and alert notification systems must be integrated into day-to-day management activities to signal changes in the business environment. Good domain processes must support orchestrated responses from all affected organizational functions faster than the competition.

So ask of your own organization: Who are the people who touch the product, either physically or through accessing information about it, or both? What are the underlying steps in each transaction? Are they all smoothly aligned? Are they handled with a minimum number of touches? Are they conducted without delay and "informational distance" from the customer and from the constituents within the company itself?

IT Infrastructure

To support the complex real-time and near real-time information needs of the organization, management for Frito-Lay's IT infrastructure must constantly monitor and evaluate how well its IT systems are supporting Frito-Lay's ecosystem. Critical choices must be made and revisited around hardware platforms, software applications, network topologies, and industry standards. In short, every aspect associated with modern IT must be aligned with the unique business needs of the global Frito-Lay organization.

Frito-Lay's need to capture and process huge amounts of market, sales, and production data places particular importance on decisions around considerations such as database structures, security, and scalability. It is also critical that the company be able to interoperate not only across its own far-flung operations, but with those of its suppliers and distributors. Its supplier network encompasses potato farmers, corn suppliers, seasonings manufacturers, packaging material providers, transporters that include rail, trucking, and air freight, and third-party logistics to move in and out of forty-five plants.

In this ecosystem, everyone should be connected. Upper management has to constantly address—and facilitate—the movement of information, so that data flows to whoever needs it, where and when they need it. Meeting these challenges is the very essence of the IT infrastructure.

To effectively compete in its global markets, Frito-Lay must decide what to promote in each market, how to plan and achieve its growth objectives, and how to reenergize or kill products that are not meeting expectations. The company must also be meticulous in managing supply issues, such as freshness and inventory levels. Frito-Lay operates in a high-volume, low-price sector; it is a complex distribution business with inventory and stock management issues that durable products companies don't face—not the least of which is shelf life. And while buyers manifest some degree of preference, the marketplace is characterized by low customer loyalty: if a bag of chips from one brand is not on the shelf, consumers will buy the next most similar item.

Recognizing the facts of life of competing in the snack-food business, Frito-Lay pays close attention to its constantly changing business landscape. Consider the questions that stare the company in its face every day:

- How do we sense changes in buyer demand?

- What are the geographies where we are losing market share to our competitors?

- How can we get new products to market quickly?

- How can we replenish depleted stock in a timely manner without overstocking?

- How do we monitor and rapidly respond to competitors' moves in the market—at a local level?

Not unexpectedly, Frito-Lay has organized some of the world's most sophisticated information systems, and has incorporated data-gathering processes and advanced technologies into its daily practices. Literally, the company knows the location of every package of product that leaves its manufacturing facilities and when that package is sold. Route salespersons and managers continuously gather information with handheld wireless devices on competitive product prices, aging, shelf-space allotments, and promotions and tie-ins. This information is fed continuously into real-time decision-support systems to authorize on-the-spot price and stocking changes as well as to update production schedules and supply chain activities. Local, regional, and national trends in customer buying behaviors are closely monitored and factored into these business decisions.

Frito-Lay is an outstanding example of a company providing very simple products—snack foods—in a highly sophisticated manner, driving returns that are well above average and sustaining its dominant position in the market. The role of Frito-Lay's information systems in its business success cannot be overstated. In many ways, Frito-Lay *is* its information system. Its products are secondary, for the company moves information first and products later.

The Corporation as a Living Organism

The great 2nd century physician and philosopher, Galen, introduced the concept that the human body is composed of specialized parts that need to work together, but that require an equilibrium between its four main bodily fluids, or humors, to sustain health and vitality. While his concept has been greatly refined over the last 1800 years, Galen's fundamental medical principles still underlie the teaching of anatomy in medical schools today.

The concept of the human body as an organized collection of specialized organs that must function in equilibrium to sustain the overall health of the organism provides us with a good analogy for the conditions required for sustaining the health and viability of the corporation.

Humans manifest differing body characteristics: shapes, sizes, colors, features and blood types—yet in each of us the underlying metabolism and biological functions are the same. Corporations that differ in size or operate in different markets also have different characteristics, yet the underlying economic principles and functional units are also the same. The body works like a corporation, and vice versa. In fact, the Latin root of the word "corporation" is *corpus*, which means "body."

Food intake, blood supply, the metabolism of oxygen, sensing the environment, neural activity, and cellular regeneration all have their corporate counterparts: raw materials procurement, cash flow, working capital, market sensing, decision making, and growth. And just as illness in any one biological function threatens the health of the entire body, the breakdown of any core functional process in a corporation threatens its overall economic health. Just as the human body marshals resources to combat an illness or injury, if a particular process is functioning poorly in a corporation, then the corporation must channel resources to fix the problem or eliminate it altogether.

The means by which the human body links its various functions and controls the complex interactions between them through a central nervous system is not unlike the electronic information systems found in companies. The nervous system not only provides real-time information about the state of the body and its environment to the brain for decision making; it also conveys the outcome of these decisions to the appropriate body components—muscles, organs, and glandular systems—for implementation. Bodies whose nervous systems or other body components are not functioning properly tend to suffer serious physical consequences.

Organisms that cannot sense and respond effectively to changes in their environment quickly find themselves at an evolutionary disadvantage to organisms that can sense these changes and respond appropriately. Similarly, companies whose internal functions are not properly connected and are not transmitting necessary information to the right decision maker at the right time tend to suffer serious economic consequences. A properly functioning information system is absolutely essential to the health of the company. Much as we say that a well-functioning human body is in "robust" health, we characterize a well-functioning and dependable information system attuned to the needs of the company as a robust information system. Such an information system is essential to business success because it supports and integrates the internal operations of the company. But today, even this is not enough. The emergence of electronic commerce—the transaction of commerce through electronic media—has raised to an even higher level the importance of having good information systems.

Perhaps the most important and fundamental concept in e-commerce is that it is not an alternative or "bolt-on" to traditional commerce. E-commerce is Everyday commerce—as basic as telephones and faxes. E-commerce is the movement of business information across the network of constituents critical to the success of the business: suppliers, customers, retailers, manufacturers, partners, transporters, etc. It is basic to the conduct of business, except that it uses the Internet as a conduit. It should not be managed or executed outside of the mainstream business organization and its processes, but should be embedded in and integrated with them. Companies that create self-contained e-commerce divisions do so at their own peril, and initiatives that are "e-this" and "e-that" and "e-the-other" are legless and faceless until it is fundamentally understood that e-commerce is simply another everyday way of managing commerce. Functionally, e-commerce must enable transparency of supply and demand across the entire supply chain. That means all key network constituents should be informed of changes in demand, disruptions in supply and deviations from the operating plan at all appropriate tiers.

Often, supply chains span multiple industries. For example, the oil and gas industry interacts continuously with the automotive, pharmaceutical, fertilizer, consumer packaged goods, and plastics industries as providers of raw commodities and compounds. The semiconductor industry similarly provides individual components all the way up to "computers on a chip" to industries as diverse as aerospace, automotive, consumer electronics, large appliances, medical equipment, and telecommunications.

The advent of electronic commerce increases the need for companies to operate at equilibrium and with all functional units interchanging information to keep their respective functions coordinated. Electronic commerce extends the internal information systems outside of the traditional boundaries of the company to link the suppliers, customers, and employees of the company into closely interoperating networks.

Case Analysis: Steelcase

Headquartered in Grand Rapids, Michigan, Steelcase is the world's largest manufacturer of office furniture, with 2001 revenues of $3.9 billion. The company offers more than 500 product lines—including storage, seating, lighting, and complete office furniture systems—to help its customers create a high-performance workspace. Steelcase's brands include Leap, Pathways, and Turnstone; its products are manufactured in some 50 facilities around the world and sold through some 800 dealers in more than 120 countries. Steelcase competes with Herman Miller (another world-class company also in Grand Rapids), with HON, and with a multitude of other manufacturers from all over the globe. Let's apply the Business Alignment Model to Steelcase.

Strategy

The strategic challenges for Steelcase are multiple:

- How can we enhance our global presence?

- How can we achieve growth and profit in our market segments? What products to evolve? What markets to master? Where must we focus our innovation?

- How can we increase dealer effectiveness and efficiencies?

- What must we do to maintain our reputation for speed and reliability?

- How can we systemically reduce supply chain costs—especially material and transportation costs—in order to compete globally?

Every question above must be translated into critical requirements in terms of supply chain execution, flawless business processes, and a foundation of technologies that can support all these strategic aims.

Supply Chain Execution

The fundamental supply chain objectives for Steelcase are managing daily contentions between maximizing customer response and minimizing supply chain costs while leveraging the current asset structure.

As we have mentioned before, the shadow of "cost-time-value" looms everywhere. It is present in manufacturing, which faces material constraints and capacity constraints, and must prioritize customer orders. It is present in procurement, which has to determine when to buy and how much to buy. It is present in transportation, which must decide how much to ship, when to ship, and how to synchronize backhauls so that the cost-time-distance equation can be managed in an optimal manner.

Steelcase must answer specific questions every single day:

- When we get a customer order, which plant should make it?

- Should we split the order for manufacturing efficiencies?

- What criteria must we use to split the order? Should we reduce setup time, idle capacity, the cost-structure differential between different plants, transportation cost from plant location to customer, the time available until shipment due date for the customer, etc?

- When will the plants make the products?

- Do we make sub-assemblies during idle times and store them, or do we make everything after an order has been received?

- How much do we order from our suppliers? When should we order? From whom?

- Is procurement driven by plant needs or overall production requirements?

- How much to store and for what periods? When to ship? From where?

Many of these questions can only be answered by optimization software. However, the overarching drivers are minimizing the time-flow from order-entry to delivery, minimizing the time for the product to flow throughout the factory—as they say in the furniture industry, "from coil to carton"—and being able to ship the perfect order.

The *perfect order* is the goal: correct, completed on time, free from defect or damage, arriving when requested by the customer. One of Steelcase's core strategic objectives is to *minimize material and transportation costs so the company can be competitive in multiple markets*. To achieve it, Steelcase must have a clear insight into its constraints, into its ever-changing product mix, into current production loads and their corollary—which is idle capacities. The company must know the promise dates for different customers, and the availability of trucks. Cost reduction does not happen because of a CEO mandate, a policy, and a silky slogan. Supply chain is a daily battle. Cost overruns can occur because of bad decisions anywhere along the supply chain. The subtleties and nuances of daily orderprocessing and scheduling must be understood. That is why the supply chain layer of this four-layer model is critical.

Take another strategic objective of Steelcase. The company wants to *maintain its reputation for speed and reliability*. Simply translated, this strategic objective means minimizing order-to-ship cycle-time. Let's take another objective: the company is committed to *enhancing its global presence*—and to do that, the company needs capital. What's the best means to realize this objective, if not by compressing its order-to-cash cycle! Once again, that is the result of an efficient supply chain.

As in any business, reduction of work in process, in raw material inventory, and in the time it takes to correctly quote a customer the exact ship date are all daily requirements for Steelcase as well. To manage this maze of challenges, is it any wonder that the underlying processes must be well designed, smoothly run, and monitored by management and employees on a consistent, committed basis?

Domain Processes and Decision Structures

Let's look at domain processes and decision structures that underscore the whole business. We list below some key areas and what is required for their success.

Product design

- Cut the design time to a bare minimum.

- Modularize design and reuse modules so as to compose a portfolio very quickly.

Order management

- Make transparent an entire order with all its details and its disposition at any given time.

- Aggregate orders for efficient fulfillment—using meaningful criteria.

Product configuration

- Configure the product correctly with its features and options.

- Prevent impossible combinations from occurring.

Pricing

- Make the pricing formulation clearly understood by customers as well as by appropriate internal personnel.

- Reflect any price changes immediately.

Forecasting

- Allow all key stakeholders to see for each product the relationship between supply and demand and the effect of constraints on them.

- Make appropriate adjustments and communicate them in a timely manner.

Planning

- Master plan to aggregate production—distributed across factories—and then individually plan and sequence orders by factory, taking into account all necessary constraints.

- Correctly and concurrently plan material and capacity and resource requirements in the face of supply/demand fluctuations.

Supplier cultivation and material coordination

- Create and communicate clear purchasing requirements.

- Coordinate receipts, monitor quality of supplies, and correct aberrations.

Freight planning and cost-effective transportation—inbound and outbound

- Determine freight requirements, sources, destinations, load-bearing capacities, delivery times, constraints, and delivery requirements by customers and sister plants.

- Extract efficiencies for consolidation, backhaul, timing, and load-splitting so that freight costs are kept to a minimum.

Billing and invoicing customers

- Ensure that what was ordered, what was shipped, and what is being billed are all congruent.

- Ensure correct, timely billing and create invoices that are easy to understand.

- Collect money owed from customers on time.

Payments and reconciliation

- Establish a clear audit trail for revenues, costs, profits, and margins by order, by product, and by customer.

- Highlight customer profitability and supplier costs.

- Alert management regarding any aberrations.

Handling complaints and resolution

- Establish the transparency of the complaint and its root cause.

- Initiate prompt resolution of complaints.

All the above processes are interrelated; they are like a spider's web—but not all neatly concentric and geometric. What spells success is the streamlining of all these processes so that there is no duplication and double entry, and no delayed flow of critical information. Let's take another strategic objective of Steelcase—the company's desire to *increase dealer effectiveness and efficiency*. The daily drama of invoices, orders, shipments, inventory levels, product specifications, promise dates, in-transit inventory, returns and refunds, exchanges, status notification, etc., will be a successful play only when every step in a process propels the product close to the customer. Every process must make it easy for dealers to know exactly where they stand vis-à-vis their orders.

IT Infrastructure
Every process listed above is a constant flow of transactions. These transactions lead to innumerable decisions, and decisions lead back to transactions. Both must have an audit trail. There must be visibility, viability, and validity to the ongoing pattern of decision making. Consider these questions:

- Does senior management at any given time know exactly how the company is doing? Where it is going?

- What kind of decisions are made? By whom? What specialized reports do they need?

- How should systems support quick reconfiguration of engineering changes, customer-requested changes, price changes, product changes, design changes, and manufacturing changes?

- How quickly can replanning be done, given the assault of daily disruptions?

- What should be the reliability of the systems?

- What operating standards should be set for all communication and transactions with dealers?

- How can Steelcase make itself easy to do business with?

From Grand Rapids to its dealers to its manufacturing plants to its transporters—Steelcase is making sure that all these people can connect, communicate, and collaborate. *The sole purpose of IT infrastructure is to minimize the information cycle-time for everyone.* Hardware, software, speed of data transfer, format and frequency required by stake holders, reliability of systems, interoperability of geographically far-flung systems are all considerations—but only to answer constantly the questions at the heart of the business: How can we know if we are making money? Where we are losing money? How do we know we can promise correctly? Process orders flawlessly? Produce efficiently? Parcel economically? Please customers consistently? Preserve our brand value daily? For every business is in business to make money—and every business must ask these questions all the time.

A Shift in Thinking ... Analysis Before Acronyms

Traditional approaches to the development of IT infrastructure were based on an arduous and time-consuming process of formally defining requirements. Requirements definition assumed static business needs, and further assumed the ability of the system's users to precisely articulate what information they would need for daily activities and decision making. However, these functional requirements were often discrete and discontinuous, and did not take into account a full view of the movement of a product from one end of the value chain to the other.

In short, requirements definition as the preliminary stage in building an information system architecture did not take into account a supply chain view; it was a stack of silo views sewn together in the name of an RFP. These were translated into technical requirements that were then handed off to teams of programmers to develop, modify, and implement—often weeks, months, or even years later! No wonder so many systems projects have failed to achieve their expected results!

Any business professional has likely experienced the following scene, and some have experienced it perhaps many times in their career. Put more than one IT professional in a room to discuss information systems, and the acronyms start flying. J2EE, TCP/IP, HTTP, FTTP, SMTP, HTML, XML, WAP, CDMA, LAN, WAN, SAN, MAN—the list is endless. It's also virtually incomprehensible to line management and non-IT professionals alike.

Corporations often become their own worst enemies because there is no single thread that connects corporate talk in all those cables running unseen beneath the floors. The fundamental business strategy is not aligned with other operational elements of the company. Companies are fragmented by software, by local solutions, by separatist sensibilities. A lack of alignment can cause a company to cannibalize its own efforts and compete against itself.

What on earth is this?

·These challenges are pervasive. When disciplines in a corporation compete with each other, they confuse themselves and unwittingly splinter the corporation, resulting in endless frustrations. Ultimately, these frustrations drive the organization to succumb to a state that I have decided to call *corporate technocide*—a slow, painful death caused by ineffective execution and inappropriate technology choices.

The dots in a corporation have to be connected in the same way a product moves from end to end—from the supplier's supplier to the customer's customer. In a rapidly changing

Technocide in progress

world, what is required for building a successful information system is, first, that a company's managers must thoughtfully examine the corporation before capitulating to acronyms and asinine abbreviations. It is mandatory to have a detailed understanding of the interrelationships between strategy and the elements required for its execution—and not just inside an individual company, but across all the people who touch the products or the services offered, either physically or by accessing information about it. Aligning the supply chain, the analytical processes, and appropriate technologies must form an optimal relationship.

The Business Alignment Model composes these relationships, calibrates their current states, and coordinates the multiple elements required for success. Let's look at another company where the Model can be applied—and where it makes sense.

Case Analysis: Polo Ralph Lauren

Polo Ralph Lauren is a powerful global player that has succeeded in an intensely competitive market, one characterized by fickle, fast-moving, unpredictable consumer tastes. The company offers products under the brands Polo, Lauren, Chaps, and Club Monaco, and designs and markets apparel, fragrances, home furnishings, and accessories. Yet Polo doesn't actually manufacture any products itself; instead, it coordinates the operations of scores of licensees and more than 300 contract manufacturers in the U.S., Asia, and South America. The firm retails products through over 1,400 department stores, 2,000 golf stores, and 150 company stores in the U.S. alone, and has hundreds of authorized licensees worldwide.

Polo operates in a demanding business. The sector is made more complex by the long lead-times in its design and production cycles, and by its reliance on a global supply chain. The fundamentals of demand in this market fluctuate constantly, driven by a broad range of considerations: fashion trends, seasonality, holidays, geography, gender, sizes, etc. Forecasting demand is made even more challenging by the choices available to customers, including material, color, texture, shape, functionality (right down to decisions about zippers vs. buttons vs. hooks!). To satisfy global customer demand, Polo must operate as a high-

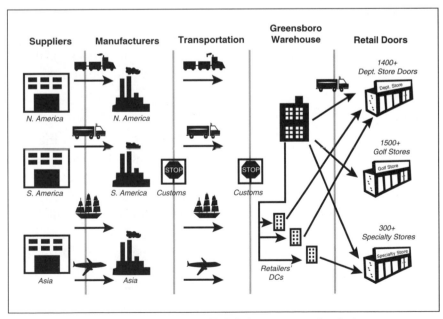

Figure 4-4   The Polo Ralph Lauren supply chain

volume, highly distributed business. It must plan sales and assortments by store, by geography, and by the ephemeral nature of fashions. Since the fashion planning cycle is more often than not closer to eighteen months than six months ahead, the long lead-times for sourcing, shipping, and merchandising can sometimes outrun the tenure of the fashion itself.

Strategy

At the level of its strategy, Polo Ralph Lauren faces the question of how the company is going to maintain and build its already successful business. Unlike Frito-Lay, which consistently achieves profitable operations, Polo's business is much more cyclical, and is therefore subject to wide swings in profitability. Recently, the company acquired Club Monaco in a bid to enhance its appeal to younger buyers, and doubtless it is constantly considering other acquisitions that would help broaden the company's portfolio of products. Managers will consider if the company has gained the maximum possible strategic leverage from its combination of apparel, fragrances, accessories, and furnishings products.

There are other questions. Should other product lines be introduced to extend the reach and value of the brand, as Martha Stewart has done? How well has the company done in predicting the combinations of styles, fabrics, and colors demanded by buyers in its various markets around the world? Where could it improve? Has the company compressed its cash-to-cash cycles to the fullest extent possible to minimize working capital requirements?

These questions are not one-time questions in setting strategy; they are a continual part of strategic evolution, flexibility, and business success.

Supply Chain Execution

In retail fashion, supply chain management and planning are particularly tricky, mostly because of the seasonality and the inherent fickleness of the industry. Most important, the company must be able to correctly assess demand months in advance. If Polo should estimate too high, the company winds up with excess unsold merchandise, a condition that kills profitability. If it estimates too low, it leaves itself vulnerable to losing market share to competitive brands. The precision of this process is also impacted by the need to maintain sufficient inventory levels to match fulfillment as well as the short selling windows inherent in seasonal merchandise.

Polo's supply chain issues are further complicated by the

company's reliance on its network of overseas manufacturing partners, with all of the currency hedging, collaboration, and information exchange issues associated with extended supply chain operations. The following are the daily challenges facing the supply chain team at Polo:

- Late deliveries to retail, lowering shelf life and risking price erosion

- Wrong deliveries to the wrong places, which increases transportation cost

- Size mismatches, leading to returns

- Cumbersome tailoring at the store level, shortening shelf life and increasing possible returns

- Lack of visibility of items in transit, customs, storage, and up-to-date status of customer orders, leading to customer service challenges

- Matching demand streams from multiple seasons, which complicates decision making

The number-one goal for Polo is to *maximize its retail sales at full price*. Translated, this means that the critical success factor is a focused, high-velocity supply chain—notwithstanding the numerous constraints of the business. This supply chain must incorporate conceiving, designing, developing, manufacturing, transporting, and delivering the right combination of size, color, and style to the retail doors. The various entities involved in this global dance, both inside and outside Polo, include design, merchandising, production management, sales, customer service, suppliers, and the company's wholesale and retail customers.

The direct effects of making sure that the products are delivered in the right mix at the right time are

- An increase in full-price sales

- Reduction in retail returns

- Reduction in excess inventory

- Lowered transportation cost throughout the supply chain

What is critical for the all of the above to happen? Simply put, it is the visibility of data at the retail doors, day in and day out. It is the matching of sizes, colors, and styles between production and merchandising. It is the reconciliation of point-of-sale data, budgets, unit plans, and assortment plans. It is the integration of vast and various streams of data and being able to analyze clear demand patterns, with production capabilities, transportation schedules within the shipping window, and unfailing delivery to numerous warehouses and retail doors.

Domain Processes & Decision Structures

The critical driver for Polo's business success is having the right product at the right time in the right place—then ensuring that the supply operation delivers that product with sufficient efficiency to earn the desired rates of return. Key considerations for achieving business success revolve around knowledge of the market, inventory management, distribution, and customer care.

Knowledge of the market involves being able to accurately predict future demand and having the right products manufactured. Maintaining optimal but not excessive inventory means being able to fulfill customer demand without unnecessarily tying up working capital and warehouse space. Getting the right product to the right locations at the right time means being able to move products to specific locations, and being able to readjust deliveries in response to shifts in consumer buying patterns.

Customer care is particularly important in a consumer-driven business. It is the retail "moment of truth." Handling exchanges and returns in a manner that ensures a high degree of customer satisfaction and loyalty while minimizing customer abuse (e.g., wearing an item to a special event and then returning it, or purchasing an item on sale and attempting to return it at list price) is a tricky balancing act. It must take into account the lifetime value of the customer. Further complicating the decision structure is the fact that it will almost always be a retail employee, not Polo's corporate managers, who will make such point-of-sale decisions.

So there are numerous processes to consider and decisions to make. They extend from opening a line to walking models along the catwalk. They reach from creating samples to managing orders and coordinating with suppliers. They involve the contractors managing retail analysts who assess buyer relationships to the merchandisers; they involve managing returns to sewing budget plans with merchandising projections and assortments. They extend all the way to calibrating replenishment based on point-of-sale data while upholding the integrity of the brand.

IT Infrastructure

Polo's IT infrastructure must efficiently support a far-flung global operation with significant real-time data acquisition, analysis, and distribution requirements. Delayed or inaccurate information can have devastating consequences for the company's overall business performance. Polo's IT platforms must be flexible enough to handle all manner of new business needs and uses of information while also operating in informational relationships with a wide range of supplier, retailer, and distribution systems around the world.

Imagine the vast ecosystem of people who either touch Polo goods or deal with information flows. Consider the global network of contractors—coordinating design, production, and delivery. The need is first and foremost informational. Consider the logistics entities, the innumerable handoffs, the suppliers of raw materials and numerous planners. The infrastructure must support a sea of information that flows globally, across various hardware platforms, and various software applications, through numerous protocols, and then eventual agglomeration and analysis by various entities.

The purpose of an effective infrastructure is to ensure transparency in supply and demand information. In this model, a pair of khaki pants, at size 36 x 32 men's with zippers and loops but without cuffs can be seen by all streams of demand, by store, by unit. In this model, the company knows what quantities are currently produced and what is in transit. It knows what is in inventory in different warehouses, what is being returned, what has been returned, and why. It knows the revenues, profits, costs, and margin implications of its current situation. And it strives to understand what trends are emerging by geography, by store, by style, by size, by color, and by brand, all on the basis of this comprehensive visibility in the company's information systems.

To meet these complex business challenges, Polo relies on an integrated information system. Senior management is able to execute highly targeted marketing campaigns and product development initiatives, while closely monitoring its extended supply chain. To optimize product placements and reduce distribution costs, Polo constantly monitors its sales at all its stores and wherever Polo products are sold. Point-of-sale information is fed through powerful analytical systems to determine what products

The Heart of Commerce

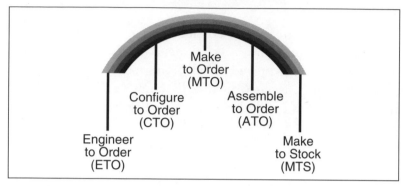

Figure 4-5a   It is volume and variety chasing each other

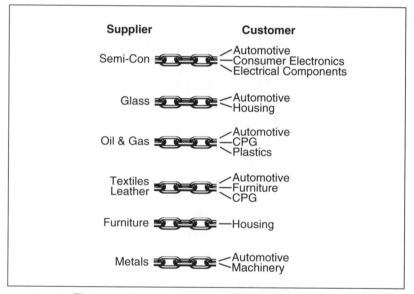

Figure 4-5b   It is cross-industry supply chains

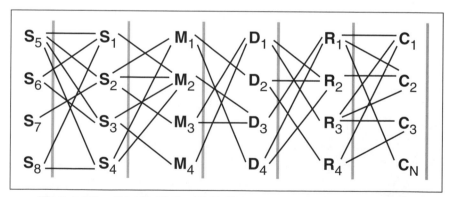

Figure 4-5c   It is Multi-tier (suppliers, manufacturers, distributors, retailers, customers)

are selling in multiple stores and geographies. Polo integrates customer information across multiple transaction systems, and provides brand managers with timely information about customer preferences and buying behavior.

As a result, Polo has its fingers on the pulse of the movement of its products, not only in all its selling locations, but in monitoring all shipments, all receipts, and all inventory in transit. In the entire flow from designing, budgeting to sales, assortment planning, and merchandising, all the way to sourcing from all over the globe, and extending to customer service and deployment, Polo strives to amalgamate every relevant piece of information in a timely manner. In the highly competitive international markets for apparel, fragrances, home furnishings, and accessories, Polo Ralph Lauren can clearly differentiate itself and command higher margins because of the quality of its information systems. At Polo, information is sewn first and clothes later!

What Is Common to All These Companies?

Frito-Lay and Steelcase are similar in that both have complex supply chains, though, while Frito-Lay has to deal with perishable goods, Steelcase does not. At both companies, product variations are virtually endless. Unit margins are higher for Steelcase; unit volumes are higher at Frito-Lay, which is fundamentally a high-speed, high-volume process manufacturer. Demand management issues for Frito-Lay are far more profound than for Steelcase. Higher volume is distributed to innumerable retail outlets, which exponentially increases transportation complexity for the food products company. But design and manufacturing complexity are far more sophisticated at Steelcase, and scheduling and sequencing issues are therefore more complex.

For Polo Ralph Lauren, the key question is global scale. For Frito-Lay, it is local presence. Frito-Lay and Polo businesses face challenges with high-volume and high-distribution business models, but have different approaches to demand management. Both companies have complex supply chain issues, and managing those issues is critical.

Despite the differences in their respective products and services, Frito-Lay, Polo Ralph Lauren, and Steelcase share key business issues. Whether you make shoes, shoe polish, nail polish, furniture, food and beverages, or chemicals, microprocessors, pharmaceutical products, automobiles, semiconductors, or satellite dishes, senior management at virtually any company must constantly work through a series of similar complex business issues.

What are these issues?

Revenue, Growth, & Profits

- Create, sustain, and kill products
- Determine which markets to enter and exit
- Holistically manage growth, sales, and costs
- Identify, execute, and integrate acquisitions
- Compress cash-to-cash and order-to-cash cycles
- Create and manage demand

Product Mix

- What kinds of variations of the product are needed for increasing the current customer base?
- What makes the product susceptible to liabilities?
- Where can the kinks occur from design of the product to the ultimate delivery to the customer?

Customers

- What kind of post-sales services can we provide, and to whom?
- How do we create secondary markets?
- What kind of promotions should we offer—where and when?
- Should we enter into co-branded and joint marketing initiatives?
- How do we acquire new customers and retain existing ones?

Suppliers

- What are their strengths and weaknesses, and whom should we cultivate?

- How can we leverage mutual competencies and build the right supplier base?

Supply Chains

- Are we assessing and forecasting demand—and properly matching fulfillment?

- Are we maximizing customer response at the least cost?

- Are we optimally organizing channels and distribution locations?

- Are we minimizing total supply chain costs?

The above issues affect all of the organizational structures of a business, requiring precise alignment and information management across core business cycles and processes. From the design of a product to its ultimate sale to a customer, several organizational units are involved. These include marketing, sales, finance, field operations, planning, purchasing, manufacturing, distribution, human resources, facilities, and all alliance partners.

Building Robust Information Systems

What are the organizing principles for building robust information systems? I believe there are seven simple yet profound areas where a conscientious effort will yield tremendous results. They are as follows:

One Full Business Cycle

As simple as this may seem, the business cycle is where many companies do not even know who influences what decisions and on what products.

- What are the top ten questions asked by anyone who touches a product, either physically or through accessing information?

- What people will be affected by these decisions? How? Where? When?

- Can you produce a simple flowchart that will take a product from its design to the completion of its business cycle by sale and service to a customer?

- Are all the information requirements organized by product or by service, therefore making it a self-contained whole?

Architecture

Information systems are critical to a company, but they are not sufficient unto themselves. Hardware, software, and a technological gallery of routers, switches, and alphanumeric protocols will not alone guarantee success. The single most important concept is that robust information systems must be designed, implemented, and managed as if they were the nervous system of the organization and not just repositories of data. It's not enough to statically support business needs; information systems must guide business decisions. They must enable decision makers to orchestrate swift responses to changes in the business environment, either internally or externally. A train is not intrinsically valuable; it is judged as valuable because of its ability to carry goods—in what condition those goods arrive, and how soon the train has arrived. So, too, the purpose of an information system is to mobilize business strategy.

Every company has its own unique combinations of hardware, software, and networks, but there are fundamental axioms for decreasing the information cycle-time.

The malediction of *data-rich, information-poor* afflicts every company. Minimize the number of data residencies, which simply means that there should be a central area where key information regarding a product or a customer is kept constantly updated and continually monitored.

For example, if the marketing department has numerous databases, then it must incorporate all the key information into one central residence that is meaningful to all.

Minimize or completely eliminate the time it takes for uploading and downloading information.

All the transactions that relate to a product should be seen in one central area, and all transactions must be transparent.

Audit Trails

Just as all transactions must leave an audit trail, so too must there be an analytical audit trail. By this, we mean being able to perceive a continual thread of cause and effect throughout the system. Ask yourself these questions:

- Are the root causes and reasons known for aberrations such as late shipments, excess inventory levels, margin erosions, high transportation costs, supplier cost increases, new pricing, etc.?

- Are there "alerts" or alarm messages for all the appropriate people, which can be automatically triggered for certain conditions, to mount a swift response?

- How easy is it to trace the specifics of a customer order or a transaction?

Decision Integration

In Chapter Two, I urged companies to reorganize their corporate strategy as product destinies. The destiny of a product depends on its health in four areas—Innovation, Rationalization, Integration, and Orchestration. To promote *decision integration*, ask yourself these questions:

- Does senior management look at the status of the company through common lenses?

- Do all employees understand how their revenue calculus is faring with respect to their products, costs, profits, channels, sales, shipments, volumes, advertising expenditure, customer loyalties, current customer base, quality problems, etc.— through a common lens?

- Is there a common navigational dashboard comprised of key indicators, with cause and effect, with reasons, with all the information that the senior management has to know, *regardless of domain affiliation?*

- During the planning cycles, how is business strategy translated into informational equivalence throughout the whole company?

- If you are a CEO reading this book, will you consciously promote cross-functional understanding among your senior executives, or will you take it for granted?

Knowledge and Learning

All systems in nature adapt themselves to changing conditions. Often, they store this knowledge in their cellular memories. The human body has what is called muscular memory, which is much different from cognitive memory. Just as the human body has conditioned responses based on its cellular or muscular memory, companies can build responses in a competitive manner based on history and extending possibilities into the future. In a corporate information system, there are innumerable transactions that are captured everyday, yet what learning can be extracted from them? In a company's business cycles for different products, what patterns emerge? What possibilities occur? What new positions are possible? Are there clear mechanisms that extract key causal relationships between products, markets, customers, and value? What is IT really doing about this? Will it analytically dissect business cycles for learning such things as consumer behavior, production patterns, periodicity of price increases, inventory levels and patterns, cost structures and aberrations, quality issues, customer satisfaction issues, and so on?

People and Culture

Cross-functional competencies must be rigorously cultivated in a company. Our educational system produces too many functional experts who are purblind to the full view of the company. They are "silo sultans," if you will, who look out only for themselves. That same system produces our marketing mavens, financial wizards, and the strategy gurus who do not see past their own domain. Fixing this blindness between functions is the first step companies must undertake in order to build conceptually connected corporations. No longer will functional expertise suffice. A new generation of managers and corporate navigators is required. Companies can no longer afford to be fragmented by functional areas, fractured by individual perspectives, and failing because of lack of cohesion. Whether one is a product designer, marketer, planner, manufacturing executive, customer services worker, transportation executive, accountant, consultant, or student, he or she must comprehend the holistic nature of decision making in a company.

The Environment

A company is nothing but a collection of its products and their supply chains. A company will be the net sum of a product trajectory. Multiple tiers on the customer side and the supply side will become as one. The coming-of-age of the Internet has collapsed the walls separating the various tiers on both ends of the value chain. As companies become more aware of the vital importance of the supply chain, traditional silos that have persisted and plagued information flows will begin to erode. Domain functions and underlying processes across companies will become integrated and almost seamless. How quickly a company can bring about a cultural transformation that has informational democracy at its core will determine the expeditiousness with which decisions are made and communicated.

The four layers of the Business Alignment Model will affect every supply chain constituent and every product or service. This concept extends deep into both customer-side and supplier-side discussions, where the strategies and operating processes of the central organization impact multiple tiers. Any industry structure can be better understood when its drivers from the customer side and supplier side are known, and when discontinuous technologies that will fill a white space are clearly identified.

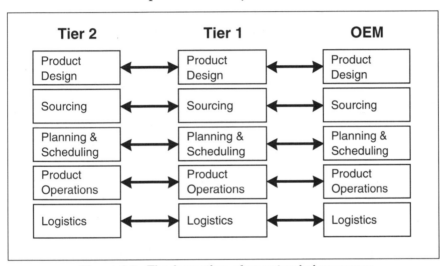

Figure 4-6 *The formation of an extended company*

The information requirements for a product or a service when structured through the Business Alignment Model will connect the destiny of a product to its daily execution. It illuminates the friction points for each product, signals where fatalities can occur, isolates failure zones, and identifies a deficient process, a delayed data transfer, a defective design. It can help pinpoint inaccurate demand assessment. It can provide insight into whether a company has the wrong strategy for the right market. Pinpointing the root cause in the success or failure of a product is critical to focusing corporate effort. The Business Alignment Model is not only a locational diagnostic tool, but the composite for the success of any product.

One Unassailable Truth

What really matters is making products that matter and making profits. Whether we are wired as a civilization or go wireless, or whether we beam our thoughts from our third eye in the course of our imminent psychic evolution, the invisible hand of Adam Smith will still be omnipresent in late 21st-century business just as it is today. Fundamental laws of supply and demand, as well as the ability to serve customers, will continue to drive business success, regardless of models and technologies that may evolve in the future.

The old Zen expression "Chop wood, carry water" invites us to appreciate that it is in the daily activities of living where we must seek our greatness. The great Persian poet and mystic, Jalal Rumi, declared that "Life is movement from moment to moment." If Rumi were alive in today's less meditative and more material culture, perhaps he would say that "Corporate life is movement of goods to one customer, then another—also moment to moment."

Daily activities bring greatness, yes. But that greatness of daily life in today's corporation translates into the lingua franca for an efficient, effective movement of products to consumers. It isn't a Zen concept; and it won't happen to companies who are meditating on their desired success. It can happen only through *supply chain excellence*, and by creating systems that allow such excellence to flourish as the company grows, day by day.

Follow the Yellow Brick Road

A Blueprint for Supply Chain Excellence

Supply chain issues vary by industry as well as by company. Regardless of industry, however, companies that seek to realize robust improvements in their business must scrutinize certain fundamental areas. The best way to do this is by asking a series of questions. Evaluating each area Socratically will help create a transformational agenda for companies striving to achieve supply chain excellence.

Focusing on what to improve is one of the major challenges to supply chain projects. In many cases, it is difficult to determine what section of the supply chain needs redress. For example, to design a supply chain network, it is essential to aggregate demand plans. And to design a demand plan, it is necessary to understand the conduits in the supply chain through which goods are sold. Many areas of the supply chain are co-dependent.

Although it is comforting to picture the supply chain as a sequential chain of events and processes, such a view is not realistic. All areas of a supply chain affect each other in a web of cause and effect, and much of what happens in the supply chain is nonlinear. However, all supply chains do tend to follow certain fundamental general principles. Examining and evaluating the degree to which these principles, these "pillars of excellence," are being followed is critical to transforming a company's supply chain.

The Ten Pillars of Supply Chain Excellence

There are ten pillars to review:

- Planning

- Demand Management

- Supply Chain Network Design

- Manufacturing

- Warehousing and Transportation

- Procurement

- Order Life Cycle Management

- Metrics

- Risk Management

- Organizational Alignment

Let's ask questions of each of these in turn.

Why the dotcoms never worked out.

Pillar 1: Planning

The first pillar of supply chain excellence is planning. And the first step in planning is to define the planning process.

Typically, a company has been asked by shareholders to produce and sell a product or service—that is, an offering—to return a profit. Shareholders want earnings that meet or exceed the rate expected of investment opportunities with similar risks. The volume, price, and cost of the offering determine the profit. Market demand determines the volume. The market determines price or heavily influences it. The cost includes all of the expenditures necessary to bring the offering to the customer.

In the context of a company's goals, the planning process is the set of activities that the company employs to balance expected demand with possible fulfillment. In this context, we assume that the design of the supply chain network or the optimal arrangement of its physical facilities is already in place. The planning process determines which resources are required, in what quantities, and during what time periods, to achieve the business plan while balancing demand and fulfillment.

The bedrock for the planning process is establishing the required volume and rate of return to undergird the financial plan according to known and forecasted elements of demand and supply. Known

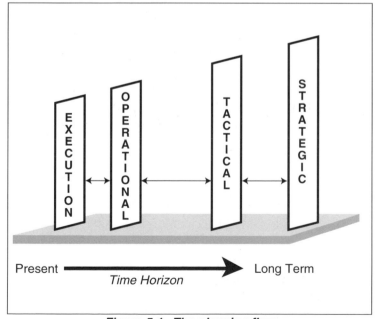

Figure 5-1   The planning flow

155

elements of demand include hard orders for the product from customers. Forecasted elements are expected levels of customer demand that have not yet been solidified through actual orders. Known elements of supply comprise on-hand inventory, committed incoming purchases, and firm receipts from production. Forecasted elements include anticipated purchases and scheduled receipts from production. The planning process compares the total demand plan over time with the total supply over time, and reconciles any differences.

Most discussions of the supply chain divide the planning tasks into four levels—strategic planning, tactical planning, operational planning, and execution—to make understanding the planning tasks easier:

- *Strategic planning* has a longer horizon—say, of one to five years, on larger time increments and an aggregation or abstraction of supply and demand elements. The strategic plan is usually broken into quarterly segments, with supply and demand condensed to accommodate product families and dollars. Usually, strategic planning takes place yearly and is reviewed quarterly.

- *Tactical planning* takes place on a semi-annual, quarterly, or monthly basis with weekly review. The supply may be buildable end items or product families.

- *Operational planning* has a horizon of days or weeks, is produced for every shift or day, and is constantly revised. The operational plan spells out exactly what resources are required on a daily basis.

- *Execution* is the completion and reporting of performance of work—a job completed, a truck loaded, or an order taken. Execution must also serve as a real-time comparison with the plan.

Depending on the company and the industry, the attributes of strategic, tactical, and operational planning can differ. Usually the lines between them blur; in reality the planning process is often a continuum.

Sales-and-Operations Planning

In the majority of companies, there is very little planning other than operational planning and execution. Polls have shown that fewer than 40 percent of companies have a functional sales-and-operations process. The sales-and-operations planning process is often highly informal, completely tactical and short-term, and not governed by principles or structure.

To analyze sales-and-operations planning, ask:

- Why does the planning not reflect the actual process?

- What are the challenges here?

- Why do most businesses fail in this process?

The biggest challenge in the planning process is the lack of common ground among functions in a company. Three company functions are utterly dependent on the planning process: sales, finance, and operations. They must stand on common ground.

The planning process should cut across functional boundaries, but it seldom does. Even in companies where the process would exist, it often fails to span some of the largest boundaries. Organizationally, the three groups are usually peers in the company, and as such they are frequently measured in ways that conflict. The vice-president of operations is judged on the basis of productivity, the vice-president of sales on top-line revenue, and the vice-president of finance on profit and cost control. With nobody directly in charge and with competing measures of performance, the planning process can easily become a low-level civil war within the company.

Take as an example a company—call it Company A—where such planning is inadequate. Let's say Company A is an industrial manufacturing firm with $1 billion in revenues, and the sales department routinely estimates what it can sell in terms of dollars and product families for the next year, by month and quarter, in support of the top-line revenue goals of the operating budget set by finance. Meanwhile, operations will present a production plan of items it can build, in support of finance's operational budget.

But no one is resolutely demanding that sales and operations talk to one another about capabilities, likely sales cycles, possible dips or temporary booms, and the longer-term prospects of the business. And by the second week of the quarter, things have changed at Company A. Sales is executing far off the plan and is blaming operations. Operations meanwhile seeks to change capacity ad hoc to keep up with the ever-changing plans, and starts pointing fingers at sales. At the end of the month, finance sweeps up the pieces and tells sales and operations that they both missed their goals for the quarter. In such a situation, sales is pitted against operations, and vice versa. Both are set against the goals established by finance. And next month, the planning cycle starts anew.

Let's imagine what it looks like at a successful company—a consumer products company with $400 million in annual sales, called Company B. At Company B, long-term strategic planning allows for a more adept management of supply, demand, sales, and production. Sales and operations work together to index forecasts and goals against supply and procurement and production capacity—building in contingency plans for anticipated scenarios, both good and bad. Procurement is not over- or under-buying; based on past experience and expert forecasting, operations can adjust to seasonal fluctuations in demand both with the required labor and production facilities; and sales, educated to the market's desires and needs, delivers on its promises of top-line revenues.

One of the main impediments to collaborative development and communication of the plan is the lack of a common denominator. Not every collaborator needs all of the information, but all need basic information in a format that they can use. Finance typically wants to define the plan in terms of the income statement, volumes of revenue, and cost. Sales wants to divide the plan by sales volume, by channel, or by geography. Often both areas are unable to specify exactly what product they expect to ship where and when. Operations would like to know exactly what the product mix would be by date so that it can plan material and capacity. Operations would prefer to have a part number assigned to the quantities on the plan, but will settle for a planning bill of material (all the items that go into making a product) at the family level. It also needs a bill of resources that can translate the plan into hours of production by machine or major work centers.

Customers want to know the volume and the timing of expected delivery. They also want to know what flexibility they will have in the event that they change their order or reschedule delivery times or locations. Suppliers want to know the requirements for components and raw material over time as well as what flexibility they will have in case of changes in timing and quantity of raw materials.

Traditionally, the lack of a shared perspective has caused a lack of collaboration and communication. Stakeholders in the planning process are all speaking different languages. The company needs a translation.

To find common ground, ask:

- How is the plan formulated?

- How is demand communicated from sales to operations, and vice versa?

- How is the plan translated into planned revenue, cost, and profits?

The company needs to establish the common data to be communicated to creators and users of the plan, both internal and external stakeholders. For instance, are the suppliers of key components or raw materials included in the planning process? How about strategic customers? How deeply into the organization does the plan penetrate? Does it stop after the vice-presidents of operations and sales have reached agreement? How is the plan conveyed to the line managers and their subordinates?

Answers to these questions and the following ones can point to opportunities for improvement in the planning process.

To evaluate the planning process, ask:

- Which internal functions are included in the planning process?

- Which partners are included in the process?

- How is the plan communicated to these players or partners?

- What are the success criteria for the planning process? Collectively? Individually?

Constrained Planning: The Reality Check

A major challenge to the planning process is the ability to constrain the plan. No enterprise has unlimited resources; for only so much capacity is available, and only so much of a critical raw material can be obtained. In the majority of cases, the plan is based on the assumption that resources are infinite. The reverse of this situation occurs when supply outpaces demand and there is a glut in the market place against a falling demand. In this case, the excess availability of resources is a constraint in itself. In both cases, the levers are the same to optimize the supply chain. The truth is that constraints, having different degrees of "hardness" or negotiability, affect any enterprise.

In times of scarcity, there may be severe constraints on a specific material. For example, in the high-technology industry, the central processing unit and dynamic random access memory chips (respectively, the CPU chips and the DRAM) periodically go on industry-wide "allocation"—rationing what is available. These circumstances limit a company's ability to meet its commitments, which is precisely what happened to Apple in the case of its iBook production, as described in Chapter One.

Another constraint is capacity—the ability to produce. Although it may not be very difficult to add a shift or schedule overtime work to increase available capacity temporarily by 30 to 40 percent, the cost of increasing capacity beyond a certain point often becomes prohibitive. At such a point, companies are challenged to reconcile demand with cost-effective fulfillment.

An important added value of the new generation of supply chain planning tools is the ability to conduct constrained planning. The company can evaluate various demand plans against existing resources to see where bottlenecks usually occur, thus revealing the effects of increasing capacity or changing the demand plan. The constraints can be considered at the lowest item or machine level, but they are typically condensed to families of items and logical aggregations of resources.

To evaluate a company's constrained planning, ask:

- What are the constraints in the business? How can they be quantified?

- What areas of the business do these constraints affect?

- Does the planning process consider constraints? At what levels?

- What are the company's rules and processes for dealing with constraints?

- Does the increase in sales justify the cost of increasing capacity?

- How are constraints in supply communicated to personnel in sales and operations?

- Does the company have a process to allocate supply in times of scarcity?

- Does it have a mechanism to capture the impact on revenue whenever major constraints are violated?

Overhauling the Planning Process

The planning process has to be inclusive, because it provides direction for many different stakeholders inside the company and out. These stakeholders must be identified; the roles of each must be defined; and how the rules of the plan are translated between and within functional groups must be defined.

Imagine a global company facing the monolithic challenge of integrating sales plans, reporting results, managing day-to-day finances, and running operations across the organization. Speed in decision making and open communication between organizational functions are imperative. So is accuracy. A bureaucratic planning process that slows the flow of information or that doesn't allow for the accurate interchange of vital information will implode under its own weight, and a decision process that runs counter to behavior for which people are rewarded will also have slim chances for success.

What bad things happen when the planning process is deficient? You can imagine the picture. Sales will be unable to meet revenue goals, because operations is unable to ship. Customer-service problems arise when operations fails to meet commitments in an unconstrained environment. Many of the products shipped will have been expedited in a rush—meaning inefficiently and expensively. Return on assets will plummet, and share value will decrease.

Pillar 2: Demand Management

Demand management is the process of creating and communicating a demand plan inside the company and out. In most companies, this process encompasses traditional forecasting. Much demand planning is striving to predict accurately what the demand for a product in a future period will be—for example, how many lollipops will be sold in Ecuador in December of next year.

Also included under the umbrella of demand management are efforts to influence demand. For example, what is the best promotion to run in Ecuador in November to stimulate sales of lollipops, to reach forecasted levels for December? Demand management strives to cull useful information about demand from past periods and market conditions. For example, what was the correlation between sales of lollipops and sales of dental floss last year?

The process of creating and communicating a demand plan is

appropriate at all levels of planning, from strategy to operations and even into execution:

- *Strategic planning* requires an aggregated long-term demand plan. For example, the question "Do we need to build a new distribution center in the Midwest?" can only be answered if the company knows what the planned demand is over the strategic horizon.

- *Tactical planning* also requires a demand plan. For example, the question "How much inventory should we build in anticipation of seasonal demand?" can only be answered if a company knows the demand and how it behaves relative to seasons.

- *Operational demand plans* confirm forecast with firmly committed orders and allow planning of crews and capacity in the short term. How fast any given organization can react to unexpected variation in demand is the purview of execution.

Demand planning, which is a component of demand management, is essential to the planning process in a corporation. A bad demand plan amplifies variability down the supply chain—and the result is the familiar ratcheting up of unmatched demand and supply in a bullwhip effect. A well-computed, reasonably accurate demand plan minimizes the effect of unexpected surges in demand and mitigates disruptions in supply.

Issues That Affect Demand

Demand planning is typically not as simple as forecasting quantities of a product by date. Some influences on the demand plan are less than obvious. Following are some issues that can affect the demand plan of a company.

Internal Data

Is your company's data on actual demand, shipments, and returns available? Does it include all sources of demand? What is the quality of this data? Is it reliable?

Seasonality

What holidays, months, and days of the week influence demand? Does it follow a predictable pattern? What industry business cycles or trends affect demand?

Product Life Cycle
How can you create a forecast for a product that you've never marketed? Is the demand expected to grow or diminish?

Promotions
What activities is your marketing function engaging in to influence demand? What is the timing of special promotions, and what is the expected impact on the rest of your supply chain? What is the "price elasticity"—sensitivity of a price change to buyer behavior—of demand? What pricing inducements can affect buying?

Competing Products
What are your competitors doing in this market, and how does their presence affect demand for your company's offerings? What product offerings of your own may compete with or complement each other?

Causal Factors
Are there predictable external events, such as weather changes, that significantly influence demand? If you can anticipate them, can you predict their impact? Can you prepare for anticipated events, such as strikes?

Financial Data
How does the predicted demand affect your costs? What about your margins? Your budget? The income statement, the balance sheet, and cash flow?

Syndicated Data
What published data (market indicators) can help predict demand?

Point-of-Sale Data
Have you access to the raw, unfiltered data on customer demand? If not, can you get it?

To discover what affects demand, ask:

- Are the foregoing issues considered in the current process of planning for demand?

- Is it necessary to include each of these issues in the demand plan?

- What is the impact of each of these issues on the overall computation and accuracy of demand predictions?

- Who are the stakeholders affected by these issues in the process of planning for demand and its fulfillment?

The Dimensional Nature of Demand

In most companies, demand is not one-dimensional. Expressing demand in terms of quantities of parts to be shipped each month is rarely good enough. Instead, demand is multi-dimensional, including the channels through which goods are sold (such as direct sales or institutional sales), along with geography, time, and products. Consider farm equipment. When John Deere plans for demand, it has to account for the fact that its channels are different dealers and distributors; that its geographic marketplace consists of countries, divisions, and territories; and its dimensions are the families of its products and models. The company's demand plan must cut across this multi-dimensional mosaic and translate between those dimensions—that is, the plan must consolidate basic requirements as well as analyze the dimensions in depth.

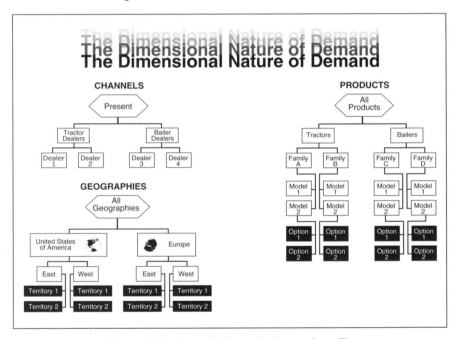

Figure 5-2   A multi-faceted demand profile

Planning for demand can benefit the whole company. Marketing may want to see yearly revenue predicted by channel. Sales may want to see potential quarterly revenue by geographical location. Production may want to see item demand by week. Each request is valid in its own right, and planning for demand must be able to accommodate the needs of different users. All parties sharing the process need to agree upon the rules for moving between dimensions. Care must be taken not to compare apples to oranges.

To find the dimensional nature of demand, ask:

- Does the company understand the dimensions in its demand plan?

- Are the rules for transition between dimensions agreed upon and understood by all the stakeholders?

- Is it worthwhile to divide the demand plan into different dimensions?

Demand-Plan Accuracy and the Dynamics of Supply Chains

The Romans sacrificed animals to Mars, the god of war; and they read the entrails for forecasts of success in an upcoming battle. Some of the machinations performed by businesses today to divine the future may be no more precise.

Why should a company care about the accuracy of the demand plan? Because the nature of a multi-tiered supply chain is such that inaccuracies will be amplified as they pass through the chain. A demand variance of one percent at the end-customer level can create a variance of 100 percent three tiers down the chain.

Lack of information about demand causes each level in the supply chain to second-guess. Each seeks to buffer against variability in the next level. And although these buffers are meant to protect from variability, they actually tend to amplify it.

How to Improve Demand Management

There are two major ways to improve management of demand: to forecast it statistically, and to communicate and collaborate within and between companies.

Statistical Forecasting

Forecasting has traditionally been a statistical game. Hundreds, if not thousands, of techniques can be deployed to create a forecast. Most systems today can apply many models to the data to pick the best "fit." Models that appear to give the best accuracy can be selected on an item-by-item basis. And different statistical models have been applied over the years to improve the accuracy of forecasts, seeking to answer the eternal question: "What tools have we to analyze past performance? Can we apply algorithms to analyze past performance to predict the future?"

Of course, no one model is best for all situations. Each suits itself to a particular demand profile. The simplest models used history as a model for the future; for example, if we shipped this many items last December, we can predict that we will ship that many again this December. Many companies still rely on such methods because of the inherent simplicity of doing so. And other mathematical techniques have been refined over the years. "Smoothing," or approximating algorithms, such as exponential smoothing and the Holt-Winters technique, are excellent for steady-state products with stable demand. But they are poor at predicting events and seasonality; they "smooth out" the variability in demand. Reactive models, such as the auto-regressive moving average method and the Box-Jenkins technique, predict events and seasonality. These are typically good for identifying recurring events but tend to "over-fit" the forecast (not approximating things that should be rounded out).

Truth is, there is no magic model for forecasting. However, a judicious application of forecasting techniques can improve accuracy, and a small improvement in accuracy can result in a large gain in efficiency for the supply chain.

Communicate and Collaborate

One of the best means for minimizing the disruption caused by variation in the demand plan is communication. Eventually, with every demand plan, a time will come when variance takes the company by surprise. Good communication can minimize the impact.

Involving all stakeholders at the outset eliminates disconnections. If marketing is planning to run a "buy-one-get-one-free" promotion to boost sales, people in purchasing, manufacturing and transportation have to know it, so all of them can plan for the surge in volume. Purchasing can then arrange for the extra materials, manufacturing for extra capacity and shipping for better consolidation.

As discussed in "Pillar 1: Planning," the rapid propagation and sharing of the demand signal to all parties—sales, finance, manufacturing, procurement, key suppliers, and key customers—will make the supply chain more agile. Not only must the demand information be provided, but it must appear in a usable format as well. Marketing may want to be alerted to the success or failure of a particular promotion. Manufacturing needs to see demand changes for each item. Key suppliers want to know what will be demanded of them. Customers want to know how much of the allocation of a scarce part they can expect. If the information is rapidly available, it will replace the need for buffering and help mitigate the bullwhip effect—the phenomenon of supply and demand in which companies either over- or underproduce. It is critical that employees within a company communicate with each other not only face-to-face, but also through their computer systems in a way that keeps the firm connected in a daily manner.

One of the topics receiving the most attention recently has been Collaborative Forecasting and Replenishment (CFAR). The initiative came primarily out of the consumer packaged goods industry. CFAR is a process in which the companies providing the goods share demand-and-supply information with their customers, and vice versa. This sharing can be as simple as a purchase order or as elaborate as a contract of expected needs for the year, so that the supply side can plan better. It can mean giving access to demand data about the ultimate customer to partners deeper in the supply chain. This sharing of information allows partners to agree and avoid second-guessing.

The extent and depth of collaborative demand planning depends on the industry. What's appropriate in consumer packaged goods may not be applicable in engineering-to-order. In many industries there are "supply chain dominators"—that is, companies so influential that they dictate the information to be shared, the process for sharing it, and the format in which it may be shared. Examples of supply chain dictators are the big automotive manufacturers and some of the dominant retailers.

To encourage communication and collaboration, ask:

- What demand planning information do we share with our customers and suppliers?

- In what format would the demand data have to appear to be useful for different stakeholders?

- What measurements can all parties agree on and enforce, to more closely align demand management with fulfillment?

Pillar 3: Supply Chain Network Design

Supply chain network design is a modeling process that allows a company to use enterprise data in making decisions about the structural supply chain. As such, supply chain network design can help with infrastructure design, facility location and sizing, resource allocation, transportation and inventory strategies, service-level analysis, and profitability scenarios. This type of modeling is useful for enterprises that have large, deep, or wide supply chains.

Network design is so called because it treats an enterprise as a network of *nodes* that consists of suppliers, manufacturing sites, warehouses, distribution centers, and customers. Products and services move between these nodes by means of *lanes*.

Each node and lane has capacity and constraints. Lanes have minimums and maximums, as well as constraints that relate to the product itself. For example, only refrigerated trucks can transport frozen food. Supply sites can provide a maximum or a minimum quantity. Manufacturing sites have production rates with low and high limits as well. Warehouses and distribution centers have minimum and maximum storage and processing standards. Customer demand must be met and desired customer-service levels achieved. All these capacities and ranges are quantifiable.

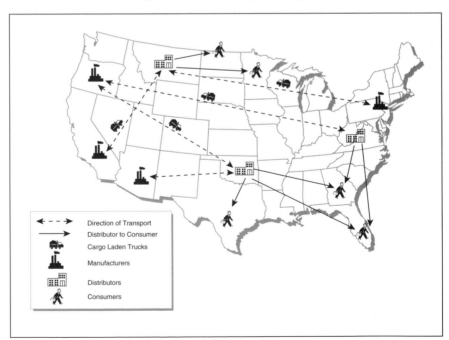

Figure 5-3   A supply chain network

Each node and lane has an associated usage cost. Each product incurs costs as it moves through the network. Typical cost components include

- Procurement

- Transportation

- Storage

- Production

- Tariffs, duties, and taxes

To configure the elements of the network, ask:

- Is the company's supply chain large enough to benefit from network design?

- Is the data available for building a model representative of the company's supply chain?

- In what form does the data appear? Are all the constraints and costs known?

- What is the total cost to serve a customer or a market segment?

The Value of a Good Network Design

The main advantage of supply chain network design is that it can allow for a view of the enterprise's supply chain that transcends specific roles, functions, and sub-organizations. In such a development, an entire multi-tiered supply chain can be visualized as a flow of product and information to the customer. This perspective will allow managers to conceive of solutions that could not be visualized at the tactical level.

Supply chain network design is also useful in a supply-driven supply chain—common in agriculture, where the question is not how to fulfill demand but what the best way is to benefit from overproduction. Agriculture is like a machine that cannot be turned off. With continuous supply, the network model can help find the best way to deploy excess supply.

Supply chain Network Design can Address the Following:

- Infrastructure design—including optimal site location and recommendations for opening, closing, or consolidation of sites

- Transportation strategies—including volume recommendations, lane choices, and mode selection

- Inventory strategies—discerning how much to hold and where to hold it, to achieve the required level of service

- Capacity strategies—establishing when and where to add capacity

- Reasoning behind mergers and acquisitions as they relate to supply chains

- Modeling the impact of the competition's network—i.e., can we model the competition's cost to deliver?

- Resource allocation—finding the best way to allocate existing resources

- Inbound sourcing—determining the best way to source from existing supply, given the constraints and the costs

- Customer distribution channels—ascertaining the best way to get the product to the customer

- Vendor selection—assessing the optimal number of suppliers

- Production allocation—computing the optimal allocation of products to each channel

- Transportation and inventory tradeoffs—ascertaining at what point it is cheaper to transport directly, and at what point it becomes preferable to store now and transport later

When the enterprise stretches across countries, there are new challenges to network design. Local governments need to be accommodated, and local tax laws need to be taken into account. Companies facing these constraints must consider

- How does globalization affect the company's network strategy?

- What are the global restrictions to supply chain network design?

- How does a company implement supply chain strategy on a global basis?

Recommendations provided by supply chain network design are

frequently brick-and-mortar decisions: to build a new plant, to close a distribution center, to consolidate warehouses. These suggestions can result in considerable savings for companies. Also, because it encompasses all of the sites in the enterprise, the network design can save millions in inventory, capacity, and time, by pointing to unnecessary buffering between sites.

Analysis can reveal the possible impacts of changes in the network model. Network design can help a company model an enterprise and compare different scenarios involving the tradeoffs among profit, cost, utilization, and service.

Pillar 4: Manufacturing

Much of the focus of supply chain theory started within the four walls of the factory. For some reason, manufacturing facilities are susceptible to crusades, and manufacturing companies in particular seem inclined to get whipped into an intense fervor, riding the crest of the latest wave of innovation—some less worthwhile than others. Such fervor is an excellent means of implementing change quickly, but in the long run such intensity cannot be sustained; it consumes what it produces.

Consider some of the crusades that the manufacturing floor has witnessed over the last twenty years:

Manufacturing Resources Planning, Generation 2
Through the 1980s, manufacturing companies implemented the second generation of manufacturing resources planning (MRP 2), to organize business data and compute requirements for manufacturing and procurement. However, these systems assumed an infinite capacity of resources and did not perform constraint-based analysis to reflect the true feasibility of plans.

Total Quality Management
Total quality management (TQM) takes as its premise that if you incorporate quality into every step of the business—from administrative paper-handling to customer service—the rest will take care of itself. The tenets of total quality management include designing quality into the manufacturing process; tracing the quality back to its source; and eliminating whatever detracts from the set standards for quality. It asks, "Why require quality control to find what is wrong just before the product is released?" and answers, "Find the root cause and prevent the flaw from occurring in the first

place." TQM brought an excellent understanding and application of process control not only to the manufacturing floor, but to business in general.

Just-in-Time

The just-in-time philosophy (JIT) requires the manufacture and delivery of products just at the time of need, eliminating wasteful storage and needless activities. This Japanese import, compliments of Toyota's manufacturing system, for a while seemed destined to be the engine that would rule the world. The just-in-time "pull" processes, as differentiated from those of the traditional "push" variety, greatly reduced the complexity of manufacturing and procurement activities. The more repetitive the manufacturing process, the better the fit for JIT.

Theory of Constraints

Dr. Eliyahu Goldratt, an Israeli physicist, proposed to simplify the entire philosophy of manufacturing by focusing on bottlenecks to resources. The premise and promise was that in a capacity-constrained environment, processing efficiency for an entire factory could be improved if the constraints were carefully addressed. Most modern scheduling systems have heuristic engines based on the theory of constraints.

Lean Manufacturing

"Lean" manufacturing, an amalgam of the good pieces of many of its predecessors, is the latest crusade in manufacturing. It uses the principles of just-in-time manufacture, producing items on a one-at-a-time, as-needed, reduced-setup-time basis. However, it also incorporates the tenets of designing quality into the manufacturing line, such as removing steps that contribute nothing. Finally, it uses Henry Ford's traditional assembly-line techniques to manage the flow of goods in the factory. Like all popular trends, lean manufacturing even has a counter-approach to rail at traditional scheduling systems.

Demystifying the Management Trends

No single approach to manufacturing is a panacea, and each must be adapted to the individual needs of a business. Is the value of JIT philosophy, for instance, which is ideally suited to repetitive manufacturing, sufficient to warrant force-fitting it into an engineer-to-order (ETO) environment? It is important not to be carried away by the magic of a new approach.

All of these "bodies of knowledge" have their own pros and cons. Just-in-time and lean approaches tend to create localized efficiency— good in some parts, but bad in patches. These philosophies encounter trouble extending beyond the four walls of the factory. Unless complementary views of supply chain planning are added to paint the big picture, one can create marvelously efficient flow lines that pull from one big pile of inventory, only to unload onto the next.

Further, some of these approaches falter under the variability inherent in many businesses. To maintain the flow of an assembly line and accommodate all the options and sequencing rules is a challenge. The assembly line begins to resemble a Copernican universe of loops and curlicues.

To accommodate routines, ask:

- How good is the fit of the chosen technique for the company?

- If you are a manufacturing executive, how can you influence change in your company without being a heretic?

Manufacturing Transformation

The American Production and Inventory Control Society (APICS) defined the standard business functions that made up the core of manufacturing resource and enterprise resource planning systems in the late 1960s and early 1970s.

When those APICS standards were designed, relatively little computer power was available. Planning systems took advantage of what little there was in two ways. First, these systems segmented the planning process so that the computer could work on one component at a time. Second, they used regenerative, disk-based processing (called "batch processing") to take advantage of then-current architecture. This approach resulted in first separating the material-requirement computation from the capacity-requirement computation, and then running each sequentially and slowly.

In the 1990s, as everyone now knows, computers became thousands of times more powerful than they had been in the 1960s. Available memory increased by orders of magnitude almost every year. This allowed planners to plan material and capacity concurrently instead of sequentially. RAM-based manufacturing planning tools decreased computation time—the time required to generate a feasible manufacturing plan—one-hundredfold. By solving the material requirements concurrently with the capacity requirements, a company can now obtain a feasible answer that is capacity constrained. Simply put, the planning system will not recommend a solution that is impossible because it is unrelated to capacity. Every work order released will be supported by both material and capacity, thus making manufacturing viable.

Concurrent planning is different from finite-capacity planning. The latter loads a work center to capacity and then moves on (either forward or backward); it makes no attempt to synchronize capacity with material requirements that have already been determined by manufacturing resource planning. Purists will argue that, by performing multiple iterations of sequential material and capacity plans, the information eventually will converge on reality. In actuality, though, the data never converge, rendering finite-capacity planning an inadequate approach.

Modern advance planning and scheduling systems consider the material and capacity requirements concurrently. Synchronizing the material and capacity plan eliminates shortages and waiting time. The systems also synchronize the dependencies among all the orders in the shop floor to increase "throughput" (the amount produced per unit of time) and to decrease cycle-time—simply, the time it takes to make the product. Other constraints—such as number of employees, employee productivity level, tools, and physical space—can also be considered while a company is planning a feasible schedule.

Traditionalists frequently assert that there is no way the computer can produce a schedule as good as theirs. That is simply not true. If 300 manufacturing orders are competing for capacity across 50 machines and 15 routing steps, it is virtually impossible for a human mind to try all the possible choices and predict the optimal results. Computers can—and now they do.

Learning to Master Tradeoffs

Manufacturing is inherently a play of tradeoffs. Everyone would like to ship 100 percent on time as requested by vendors, with 100 percent utilization of production machinery and zero inventory on hand. But there are obvious tradeoffs. Consider the tradeoff between reducing setup times and using machines. Setup time can be minimized and maximum machine use ensured for only one product, but this will disrupt the on-time delivery of other products that require the same machine—a recipe for disaster with regard to

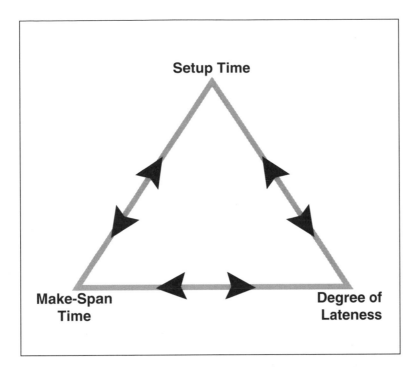

Figure 5-4 The triangular time conflict in manufacturing

on-time delivery and customer satisfaction. The result is contention between localized efficiency and on-time delivery.

Typical advance planning and scheduling (APS) systems allow managers to fine-tune such tradeoffs. Typically, the "knobs" for effecting such adjustments are on-time delivery, setup-time reduction, and reducing cycle-time from order to shipping. With advance planning and scheduling, the tradeoffs are highlighted for the users as cogent choices. For example, are you willing to sacrifice one day of on-time delivery for two hours of setup-time reduction? Or are you willing to delay five orders in order to reduce the cycle-time on just one order? If you complete this one order on time, three orders will be late, and you endanger delivery for another two. Scheduling is a complex balancing act. To add to the complexity, the tradeoffs are not linear but multi-dimensional (a change here will have an impact on five other places by varying degrees). The way an APS system accomplishes this balancing act is by weighting the choices that it makes according to how the user has set the knob.

Localized efficiency is common in complex manufacturing environments. A planner or scheduler will improve one step in a multi-step process. The result is that the *step* becomes very efficient, but the overall *process* becomes less so. It is important for companies to understand the tradeoffs—and not to build one-legged stools.

To consider tradeoffs, ask:

- How is the manufacturing schedule created? How reliable is it?

- Where are the problem areas? Where are the perceived bottlenecks?

- What are the tradeoffs among setup-time reduction, cycle-time reduction, and on-time delivery? How can the negative impact of these tradeoffs be minimized?

- What is the industry norm for cycle-time and delivery performance?

- How do customers perceive your tradeoffs?

- What are the perceived risks? What are the potential cultural fears and roadblocks?

Pillar 5: Warehousing and Transportation

Many companies use the term *logistics* to mean *supply chain*. This is a misnomer, muddying any meaningful discussion of supply chains. Logistics is only a component of supply chain management and is not to be confused with the supply chain itself. For our purposes, logistics includes warehousing and transportation. The processes involved are typically cost-intensive. Because of this, logistics has traditionally focused on cost savings through automation.

Although there is a tremendous opportunity for cost savings here, we must be careful not to lose focus on the main purpose of logistics planning: to get goods to the customer where and when they are wanted. Logistics managers easily fall into the trap of point solutions—instituting local efficiency but solving only one aspect of a bigger problem. The key question is this: Are there ways to enable the logistics function to move beyond cost and utility and toward value? Let's look at the components of logistics.

Warehousing

In an ideal world, goods would roll off the assembly line into the customer's hand, fulfilling the need just as the customer conceived it. They don't, of course, so warehouses came into being—and they continue to exist for a number of different reasons. Especially in make-to-stock environments, warehouses position inventories in anticipation of demand. These installations can take the form of central or strategically located storage and fulfillment points.

For our purposes, warehousing describes how companies store, move, and deploy goods. The basic functions of the warehouse facility and steps in processing are these:

- *Receiving* involves taking delivery of the product, making sure the product matches the bill of lading, checking for condition or quality, and logging receipt data.

- *Put-Away* is the temporary storage of goods and should be based on the function of the warehouse. Is this a fast-moving product? Is it in short supply? Is it on backorder? Does the warehouse operate on a first-in, first-out basis?

- *Picking* is also typically streamlined in conjunction with the put-away process for efficiency. Wave management, velocity slotting, and the analysis of inventory stratification are all techniques that promote efficiency in putting away and packing.

- *Packing* occurs once the inventory is picked.

- *Shipping* sends the inventory out the door.

- *Cross-Docking* is the rapid transfer of goods from supplier to customer without any intermediate storage. Wal-Mart has made high-volume cross-docking into a science. Suppliers transfer their goods directly to Wal-Mart's trucks, avoiding the need for intermediate storage.

- *Kitting and Light Assembling, Personalizing, and Customizing* exist especially in service environments, where there may be requirements for combining individual items into kits to accommodate customers' individual needs. The warehouse then plays the role of an assembler in a mass-customization or personalization market, accommodating the needs of a group or an individual client and thus allowing a company to postpone the creation of finished-goods packages.

- *Replenishing and Managing Inventory* is something else that warehouse personnel may now be responsible for, not only shipping to the customer but also figuring out when that customer needs something shipped. Replenishment and management have traditionally been planning functions, but now the responsibilities for these are often shared with the warehouse. This change is representative of a move toward greater collaboration and teamwork across company boundaries so as to streamline the supply chain.

- *Market Launches* also affect warehousers, to synchronize and speed up the supply chain process. The warehouse needs to know when new products are coming to market, again demonstrating expansion of the logistics function from a localized one to broader collaboration and full participation.

Automation and Technology

Warehousing is a function that makes tremendous use of technology to gain efficiency. Automation can greatly assist with such data-intensive tasks as serialization, lot control, and catch weight. Automation techniques already deployed include barcoding, radio frequency, fixed-position scanning, automated storage and retrieval systems, automatic sorting, conveyors, carousels, high-speed belts, and self-guided vehicles.

These are just some of the means used to move material around more efficiently—and some of this technology for moving material around is so fascinating that we forget the purpose of the warehouse—not to move inventory around but to fulfill customer needs efficiently.

To streamline automation and technology, ask:

- Do we need this entire inventory in this warehouse?

- How is the effectiveness of the warehouse measured? Is it by local efficiency? Or by the value it adds within the context of the supply chain?

Transportation

Like warehousing, transportation is full of opportunities for looking beyond point-solution efficiency and from a supply chain perspective. Many companies have begun to outsource their transportation function. Because of this trend, the third-party logistics industry is growing more than 25 percent per year. What started as renting trucks has evolved into renting all of the services involved in moving goods. The third-party logistics (3PL) providers are trying to figure out how to graduate from being trucking companies to full-service logistics providers. The goal of transportation planning is finding the most efficient way to move products to meet customer needs. Both inbound and outbound transportation can be advanced.

To plan transportation, ask:

- Does the company own its own fleet?

- What ways and means can optimize the movement of freight?

- Are there opportunities to consolidate freight?

- What mode of transportation is the most efficient?

- What carrier is the cheapest, fastest, most reliable, and most convenient?

- Does pooling freight offer opportunities for increasing efficiency? If so, what location for the pool point is most convenient and accessible, and least expensive?

- Should the company have a dedicated fleet? If so, what size?

- What is the most cost-effective shipment size that satisfies customer requirements?

- How can partial truckload shipments be organized into full ones?

All the above questions center around a core theme: determining the most efficient use of resources to fulfill the customer's need. The mechanics of transportation planning are also an exercise in tradeoffs. Myopic companies measure success in terms of fewer trucks and drivers required. This is neither practical nor workable; success instead should be gauged in terms of sensible fulfillment of customer needs. There are several practical components of a freight transportation strategy:

- *Pooling* is the process of bringing multiple small orders (less than a truckload) to a common point before combining them into larger loads for freight efficiency.

- *Dedicated multi-stop routes* are preplanned routes that the company maintains. For example, "Our truck goes to Burlington on Monday, St. Johnsbury on Tuesday, and Manchester on Wednesday, and then it returns."

- A *purchased multi-stop route* uses another company's assets. Cross-docking allows for skipping the put-away step at the distribution center. Receipts and shipments are scheduled so that the material is received and shipped without being put away.

- A *continuous-move route* has equipment coming and going from two or more destinations continuously, e.g., from the Manchester distribution center and the Burlington distribution center.

Routing

Delivering the product is the domain of routing and route planning. Until recently, only certain industries dealt with a routing problem so large as to make solving it a necessity to ensure profitability. Now industries such as small-package delivery or residential trash pick-up need routing.

The routing process begins with designing the routes, at which

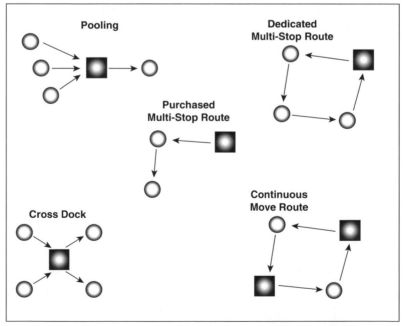

Figure 5-5   A sample of freight transportation strategies

time it is necessary to pose the following questions:

- What is the most sensible way to divide territories in terms of delivery time, schedules, and frequency?

- Should companies opt for fixed or master routes?

- What frequency of delivery would accommodate customer needs?

- What size should the fleet be?

Once routes and fleets are in place, the order load on the individual routes should be examined. This may be done weekly, daily, or on an ad hoc basis to accommodate the order load to the route schedule. Routing is essential in any large-delivery routine, and clearly private or dedicated trucking fleets have the most potential for routing. Vessel and rail routing must address unique needs that have special constraints, such as port and draft restrictions. And routing is typically coupled with a quasi-warehousing function known as yard management.

Considerations of cost for transportation are so imperative that bidding for carrier services has become essential. Supply chain modeling tools are available for reconciling the shipping requirements with the available option of carriers—to determine the optimal shipping volumes. This process has been greatly facilitated by the Internet.

Integration—Not Abdication

Sharing among business partners and visibility of information have become increasingly important. When a company outsources its logistics function, it trusts a third party to deliver its products on time in a pleasant and professional manner. Often, this is where many companies drop the ball by divorcing themselves from the responsibility of ensuring timely, high-quality service. For example, why can the driver of a furniture delivery company not talk directly to the customer? Why does the customer have to be put on hold after dialing a toll-free number just to learn the status of his or her delivery? When companies construct barriers between their processes and their customers, they lose.

Traditionally, one of the largest functional fissures in companies has been between manufacturing and distribution. Means for improving efficiency are to be had within the domains of each.

Point-solution cost reduction in the logistics realm yields diminishing returns and eventually becomes counterproductive. Local optimization can impose constraints on the companies' overall profit drivers. It is not enough to throw responsibility over the wall to distribution anymore. Downstream warehousing and delivery have to be integrated with upstream fulfillment activities. Only through such integration can the entire process of getting the goods to the customer be streamlined.

To analyze logistics integration, ask:

- How do we create valuable partnerships between our company and our logistics providers?

- How do we apply the simple value of one another's good ideas to foster co-innovation?

- What synergies and dissonances exist between our manufacturing and distribution activities?

- How do we consolidate across brands to gain delivery advantages?

- How can we reduce the time to reach a customer? What are the tradeoffs? What options are most advantageous?

- What are the areas of mutual benefit and shared services?

Pillar 6: Procurement

Approximately 50 percent of the cost of the delivered product is associated with procuring goods and services. For example, in the United States today, more than half of each dollar in manufacturing revenue is ascribed to purchased components. That is why procurement is a sensible target when the goal of a company is to increase earnings by lowering costs.

Procurement can be defined as buying the right items and services at the right time for the right reasons at the lowest overall cost to fulfill a customer's or a company's internal need. It is a critical link in any company's supply chain, and many supply chain initiatives originated in the purchasing domain. However, procurement is only one pillar of supply chain excellence, although companies often embark upon the procurement initiative as if it were a salve to all the ills of the business. Such companies realize sooner or later that a stand-alone initiative, one not part of an integrated effort to boost business, will often defeat itself. In these cases, the remedy can be worse than the disease.

What are some key elements that companies must address to streamline the procurement function? Companies must first understand the distinct classes of goods and services they procure:

- MRO items are those used for maintenance, repair, and operations. Examples include paper cups, nuts, bolts, screws, and office supplies.

- Non-MRO items are the basic raw materials, components, and sub-assemblies or services that are critical to producing a finished product.

Collaboration—The Path to Improvement

One of the most important steps a company can undertake to improve procurement is to minimize its supplier base, to whittle down the total number of suppliers that source a company's components and services. The traditional paradigm has been to use many suppliers so as to reduce the risk of supply variability and availability. Although this approach still has merit in the procurement of commodity items, most purchases of critical items should be executed with vendors with whom a company has a strategic relationship, that is, one in which the customer and its supplier share information and plans freely, define success in the same way, and have a vested interest in each other's success. As partners, the two share processes, protocols, and performance standards. Such relationships are difficult to cultivate when vendors are numerous—hence the need for decreasing the number of suppliers. The value of vendor or supplier relationships rapidly diminishes as the number of vendors for the same product increases. Even companies such as General Motors and Ford, which traditionally had thousands of suppliers, have now begun to pare down dramatically their suppliers to a valuable few.

What are the different levels of relationships? The first level is an arm's-length, "purchase order" relationship in which there is minimal sharing of information. Such relationships are characterized by a simple buyer-seller mentality. The next level is one in which the partners share information, such as forecasting data and building schedules. This kind of information sharing allows for collaboration on important decisions.

Later stages of collaboration involve process-to-process integration between a company and its critical suppliers. Plans, schedules, the status of orders, and any disruptions are constantly shared personally rather than communicated via information systems among all involved parties. The information systems of these companies connect to and communicate with one another. This ensures that products and information flow as easily between partners as within the companies themselves.

The higher the level of collaboration, the greater the shared risk. But with that shared risk comes a higher value as well. The challenge for companies is to figure out how to create such relationships with a chosen few vendors.

The distinctions among competitor, supplier, and customer are constantly changing. In a world rife with unpredictable mergers and acquisitions, there is much consolidation, both within and between industries. "Coopetition" is a term that was coined to describe how companies can be competitors, customers, and suppliers of one another at the same time. The high-technology industry is a classic example of this trend, in which many large players (such as Intel, Sun, Hewlett-Packard, IBM, Toshiba, and Fujitsu) have ambiguous and complicated supplier relationships even while they offer competitive products or services.

To consider collaboration, ask:

- Do we have too many suppliers for a single part?

- Do we have the right suppliers?

- Have we created adequate performance standards for our suppliers—in terms of time, quality, service, exchange, and return policies, etc.?

- What should be the appropriate relationship with those suppliers?

- How can our partners' relevant processes be integrated with our own?

- Who are our competitors, customers, and suppliers? What are their interrelationships?

- What are the risks associated with, and the perceived value of, our procurement relationships?

Stratification—Everything in Its Place

Another important element to consider is how to position anything that influences the quality, performance, cost, and utility of a finished product. On the one hand are raw materials and components that directly affect the item itself. On the other are the office supplies and equipment required to do business. Each of these categories has its place; each requires specific business processes and supplier relationships. And there is a hierarchy of relative importance. Items needed for maintenance, operation, and repair—the cost of doing business—can be bought online. Obtaining a critical product component or raw material, however, requires establishing a relationship with a vendor.

Consider, too, the relative risks involved. Buying pencils and paper clips online is pretty routine, but a company's very existence can be threatened by failure to procure the right microchips or other components. That prompts further important questions:

- What are some of the issues of *stratification,* or prioritizing the levels of processes, which the company must face?

- Which parts are strategically important to the company and its customers?

- What can be done to standardize the use of certain components company-wide?

- How can the product design process be streamlined through reuse of existing components where it makes sense to do so?

- Does the company have processes and definitions for raw materials and product components that are distinct from those needed for maintenance, repair, and operation?

- Does the company have secondary suppliers for primary components?

Companies in the 1990s realized that the process of buying maintenance, repair, and operating items was in itself expensive for little increase in value. Electronic procurement applications streamline the acquisition of these supplies, reducing operating costs and controlling employee spending. Online, Internet-based procurement processes pool requirements for purchasing power to select the best deal automatically.

With the current excitement over Internet-based business-to-business procurement, it is important to realize that the reason for buying a part is more critical than the process for executing the purchase. The convenience of online buying is no substitute for the critical thinking needed for buying a part in the first place.

Pillar 7: Order Life-Cycle Management

Order life-cycle management is a critical aspect of a company's supply chain because it squarely faces the customer. Taking the customer order and delivering it flawlessly are means by which companies retain customers. Even if a company can perform flawlessly in many areas of the supply chain, it can lose its competitive edge if it fails to fulfill a customer order. Figure 5-6 depicts the flow of a customer order from initial customer contact to realizing the order as cash.

The ordering process begins with customer contact. The customer may require a bid. For an engineer-to-order item, this may be an exhaustive proposal, requiring weeks of design work. For a commodity item, this may involve conducting an Internet search. The combination of customer need and product fulfillment defines the order process, including the quotation process. From the first point of contact forward, the customer evaluates the company on the basis of the perceived value of each interaction.

To assess the order-to-cash cycle, ask:

- What customer interaction activities are involved in the order cycle?

- How long do each of these steps take in the entire order-to-cash flow?

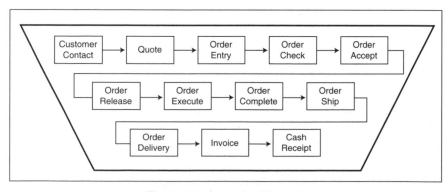

Figure 5-6 An order life cycle

- In what ways might some of these steps be failing?

- What should we do to keep these steps from failing?

- From a customer's point of view, what is the "perfect order"?

- How can we as a company enhance the overall value of a customer when he or she is interacting with us?

Typically, customers want to know whether an item is available. Sometimes they want to know when it can be made available. As straightforward as these simple questions are, they are notoriously difficult for companies to answer. They can each be addressed singly.

Available to Promise (ATP)

Available to promise is simply what the company has to offer. If a company carries a product in its catalogue, but cannot sell it immediately at any given moment, then that product is not available. Assessing what is on hand, subtracting demand, and then adding any forthcoming supply for a specific time period offers a projected available quantity for that time period. This projected availability can then be used as a basis for a promise to customers.

For example, Customer X calls to order 100 of product A in two weeks. As it turns out, the producer has no product A in stock, but is expecting to receive a shipment of 500 items from the main distribution center in the coming week. According to the order book, two other orders of 200 items each must be fulfilled in the next two weeks. So the company faces a challenge of availability. Can A's stock be promised to customer X? What is the projected availability of A's order in the second week? A supply of 500, minus the demand for 400, equals 100 projected items available. Assuming that the supply and demand numbers can be trusted, it should be possible to promise the remaining 100 to customer X. Had Customer X ordered 200 instead, there would have been a shortfall in availability.

A whole class of order-promising systems has sprung up to support answering the question "What is available to promise to customers?" Originally, the concept developed by the American Production and Inventory Control Society was designated ATP, or "available to promise." This was a quantity to which the uncommitted portion of the master production schedule could be committed. The master production schedule records the time needed to produce the standard items to be built over a given period. Such a schedule can serve as a statement of supply at the end-item stage. Theoretically, customer service representatives can safely promise up to the amount that can be produced during this time—if the customer is ordering a known standard item and is willing to wait for it to become available.

The concept of assessing what product is available for promise works well for standard items with stable production schedules. It does not work so well for custom-configured items. The world is moving toward a paradigm wherein an increasing number of products are designed to specifications that meet the differing needs of particular groups. There are fewer "standard" items and more items that are configured from options available to meet specific requirements. So what can a company do when there is really no defined "standard" item? How can the company confirm availability in a build-to-order environment? When components are mass-produced for customized assembly later, standard ATP figures no longer apply.

Another challenge to simple, standard ATP projections is that the dates and amounts are based on a master schedule that may not be realistic. The number available is based on projected demand and projected supply. The validity of these numbers determines the validity of the availability statement. Projected demand may be based on forecasts, actual orders, or some combination of the two. But how good is the forecast? How often do customers change their minds about orders? The supply information is based on on-hand inventory, incoming supply orders, and anticipated supply, which in turn is configured on the basis of the planning system. From the previous discussion of unconstrained planning tools, we may conclude that any number derived from an unconstrained master production schedule is suspect. The question of managing availability becomes still more complex when it must encompass multiple supply locations. The product may be available at one of ten sources; the company needs a method to determine which sources it gets its product from. Single-site availability may be easy to ascertain, but true multi-site availability is frequently much harder to determine because it must cross company boundaries and embrace disparate information systems.

Capable to Promise (CTP)

Then comes the question from a customer: "So when can you make them?" To answer, a company's customer-facing personnel need to know what goes into a product and how it is made. In a configure-to-order process, the material (bill of materials) and resource requirements (routing, bill of resources) are configured as the customer places the order. At the point of quotation or order-entry, the customer chooses the options to be included in the product. Once these requirements are known, the configured bill of material and routing must be evaluated against capacity constraints and material availability. At each level, the bill of material for the product must be checked to determine whether each component must be bought or built. If the component should be bought, is it already available? If the component is unavailable, how long will it take to procure it? If a component has to be built, are the resources available to build it, right now? What effect will this have on existing shop orders? If the new customer order is taken, how will other orders be affected? Are other work orders competing for resources?

In other words, before one states what one's company is capable of promising, one must consider the entire supply chain for that single order, the availability of all material, and the time and resources needed to fulfill it. These can be determined according to either a fixed date or a fixed quantity. The fixed quantity that the company is capable of promising (CTP) answers the question "How many can I have by this date?" The fixed date CTP answers the question "What is the earliest date that I can get this quantity?" Across a multi-tiered supply chain, establishing dates and quantities may be an extremely complex proposition.

The whole point of CTP is to enable a company to give the customer a realistic expectation of when goods and services can be delivered. Companies should be able to ascertain what the impact of different customer-order fulfillment scenarios will be. This ability increases the customer's confidence in a company's process of setting and meeting expectations. Customer confidence enables a company to acquire new customers as well as retain existing ones.

To consider what can be promised, ask:

- What does the customer really need to know?

- How can we provide it?

- Where does the information for calculating product availability and promise dates come from?

- How reliable are the processes that create this information?

- Is there a clear cause-and-effect link among sales promises, marketing promotions, and manufacturing capabilities?

- Is the inventory stored by the company at whatever location visible, clearly accountable, and congruently auditable?

- Are there clear rules to understand the "customer's priorities and priorities of customers"?

- What are our competitors offering their customers that we don't offer ours?

Configuring the Order

To configure an order is to capture the details of the order and communicate them to whoever will touch that order before it is satisfactorily fulfilled. In this age of customization, configuring orders is more and more important. Recording the details and communicating them to each link in the supply chain ensures not only operational efficiency, but also the health of the customer relationship. Configuring the order requires understanding and interpreting the correct product design, manufacturing specifications, delivery details, price, and service expected as well as the financial arrangements for the transaction (i.e., the credit and payment terms), in order to execute every step to a customer's satisfaction.

Understanding customers' requirements determines whether they get what they want. Care must be factored into the design of the order-to-cash cycle (refer to Figure 5-6) because the result, when it goes wrong, can be a whole series of mishaps—not the least of which is creating the wrong product. One misstep can mean the loss of a customer.

Configuration software helps this process by eliminating the options that are not feasible and guiding the customer easily through the order process. A configuration system, when set up correctly, will not let the customer order something impossible to produce.

Delivery and Follow-up

The last step in the supply chain is delivery and follow-up. This is where a company can shatter all of the goodwill built up to this point. On the other hand, a good delivery system, one that benefits the customer, can sometimes compensate for an operational glitch or two that may have occurred along the way. Consider the following scenarios:

Scenario 1

A customer buys some furniture. The furniture company asks the customer when delivery is wanted. The customer suggests a specific date and time. The company commits to that specific date and time and, on the day before the order is due, confirms that the date and time are still in effect. The product arrives exactly when the company said it would. Delivery personnel carry the furniture in and assemble it. A pillow is missing from the delivery. A delivery person calls the company and orders a pillow shipped overnight.

Scenario 2

A customer buys some furniture. The furniture company informs the customer that it can deliver the product to that area on Monday or Wednesday. The customer chooses Wednesday but has to take a day off work to wait for the delivery because the furniture company cannot commit itself to a time more specific than the day, probably in the morning. When the customer calls on Wednesday morning, no further detail on the shipment is available. At 11:30 A.M., delivery personnel unload the order on the sidewalk, make sure the shipment is complete, obtain a signature from the customer, and drive away.

To assess delivery systems, ask:

- Which scenario provided the better experience for the customer?

- What is the customer likely to tell friends when asked about either company?

- Which company has a more efficient supply chain?

- What is the value of improving the supply chain process that squarely faces the customer?

Tracking the Order

Customers also want to know the status of their orders. Tracking can be as simple as using the United Parcel Service tracking system on the Internet to locate the place where the package was last scanned, or as complicated as telling a farmer when his tractor will come down the assembly line so that he can see it being made.

The company needs to be able to track the progress of the order through the order-fulfillment cycle and to provide status information. This may be of no value to the operation of the company, but it certainly goes a long way toward building customer trust. Nothing causes the loss of a customer faster than a company's not meeting commitments and expectations. The systems and processes designed to facilitate customer interaction help instill realistic expectations and help the company follow through to meet them.

To assess breach of trust, ask:

- When was the last time something promised to a customer was not delivered on time or not delivered at all? What caused the problem?

- How can the company prevent such situations from arising in the future? What are the root causes of delivery-performance problems?

- How can the company develop a system in which the order is fulfilled to the satisfaction of all?

Pillar 8: Metrics

Many times, what is measured determines what gets done. Having the supply chain perspective of a business necessitates reexamination of the ways in which metrics, or performance measurements, are applied to gauge corporate performance. Metrics have to be aligned in two ways. First, metrics should be horizontally aligned, across organizational functions (such as sales, marketing, finance, manufacturing, and logistics), to span the company's entire supply chain. Second, metrics should be vertically aligned from the board room to the stock room (from executives to line employees), and vice versa, within a company.

Alignment of Metrics across the Supply Chain

The supply chain view of the enterprise considers the flow of information that cuts across functional lines. The supply chain considers the business from the point of view of an overall cash-to-cash *cycle* (time lapse between payment and receipt of money). Measuring the business as a *process* is essential to supply chain success. Its basis is the direction and speed with which the objectives of products and information at the enterprise level must be converted into action down and across the organization.

Traditionally metrics promoted individual-function efficiency and was in contention with the supply chain overall. Purchasing, manufacturing, and distribution each had their own systems of performance measurement. The benefits gained in one place were achieved at the expense of loss overall.

An example of this phenomenon is measuring the performance of the manufacturing function in terms of units shipped. Manufacturing can be rewarded for achieving the wrong objectives—for producing goods that the market may not demand. Manufacturing will then be creating products that cannot be sold.

Another example typical of process manufacture is rewarding on the basis of utilization levels for equipment alone. Typically, to increase utilization of equipment, orders are re-sequenced from small into large batches to minimize setup time. The problem is that the best utilization may result in scores of delivery-performance problems. Metrics must be aligned in a way that does not reatrd, disrupt, or prevent the flow of material and information across the supply chain.

Vertical Alignment of the Metrics

Many initiatives, such as the "balanced scorecard" (measurements that encompass financial, operational, customer, and organizational realms), have been tried in recent years to solve the problem of how to align metrics vertically. Two things have to happen. First, enterprise strategy must be subjected to execution-level metrics. Second, application of lower-level metrics must be relevant and conveyed back to the enterprise level.

Types of Metrics

The types of measurement systems employed by businesses vary. They include corporate, customer, and cost metrics—which often overlap. The effective combination of these metrics often depends on a company's willingness to look at itself from many perspectives.

- *Corporate Metrics* are the measures that can be used as a means for determining the direction of the company. Typically, corporate measures are revenue-based, asset-based, cost-based, equity-based, or time-based.

- *Revenue-Based Corporate Metrics.* Revenue growth by sector can be an indicator of market share and market penetration. When these metrics are coupled with the related profit-and-margin information, they enable companies to gauge the effectiveness of revenue gains. The direction of the profit margin is a key indicator of the success of both sales and operations.

- *Asset-Based Corporate Metrics.* In asset-intensive companies, the key measures are asset utilization and return on assets. Asset performance can be an indicator of how well a company is making use of its infrastructure.

- *Cost-Based Corporate Metrics.* Some industries have key cost elements that serve as bellwethers for the entire enterprise. In some, the market price of a key commodity, such as crude oil, drives all other considerations.

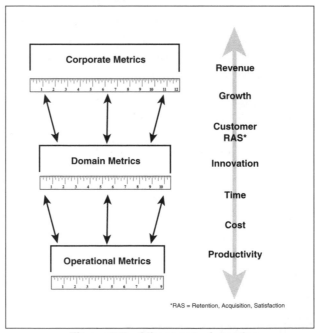

Figure 5-7   Alignment of metrics

- *Equity-Based Corporate Metrics.* In the 1990s, many companies began to emphasize the measurement of their expenditures in light of the return each expenditure gave investors. This forced companies to compare each outlay with all other investment opportunities in the free market world. Measures such as "economic value add" (EVA) and "market value add" (MVA) forced many comfortable public companies to rethink their approaches to valuation.

- *Time-Based Corporate Metrics. The* supply chain is dependent on the flow of products and information. Flow rates must be measured and good practice reinforced. As the cycle-times are reduced, the company becomes more agile and responsive to the customer. This agility leads to increases in revenue and market share.

Each segment of the supply chain has its own cycle-times: the physical cycle-time (the time required to move goods from one location to another), the information cycle-time (the time between the occurrence of an event and the purposeful communication of that information to other links in the chain), the component cycle-time (the time required to complete production of an individual component), and the overall cycle-time (the time required for a product to pass through all stages of production). For example, a company would need to estimate the physical cycle-time needed to move canned goods from its warehouse and place them on a retail store's shelves. One would refer to information cycle-time in computing the time between knowing that the shelves are empty and starting the wheels in motion to rectify the situation. Obviously, reducing component cycle-time reduces overall cycle-time.

To extend the image: within the component and overall cycles, like wheels within wheels, are other cycles. Efficiency demands that a company consider what each entails:

- *Manufacturing cycle-time.* How long does it take physically to manufacture the product? Assuming no constraints, what is the minimum "touch time"—the time required to perform each activity?

- *Procurement cycle-time.* How long does it take—from point of need to receipt of ready-to-use product—to purchase material?

- *Planning cycle-time.* How long does it take to develop the plan? The area of plan development itself can become problematic if the time required to plan exceeds the "plan horizon," the duration of the problem.

- *Order-to-cash cycle-time.* How long does it take to progress from the customer's expression of need to the supplier's receipt of payment? Cash keeps a company moving. How can a company decrease the time needed to receive timely payment?

- *Order-to-ship cycle-time.* How long does it take to perform all the internal functions required to process an order and get it to the shipping point?

- *Cash-to-cash cycle-time.* How long does it take to reach the point of receiving cash before spending it? Reducing cycle-times enough can enable a company to run a customer-funded business.

- *Information cycle-time.* How long does it take to get any kind of information about company performance through its systems and processes? How long does it take for key supply/demand disruptions to be reported to all the key personnel? For example, if the company's retailers are out of stock, how long does it take for the company to know about it?

Examining the cycle-times honestly across the supply chain will reveal buffering of product and information flows. Eliminating such buffering can be extremely lucrative to the company.

Customer Metrics

Customer metrics should measure what is important to the customer. How can a company find out whether or not it is meeting customer expectations? Obviously, delivery performance is a critical metric. Is the company measuring delivery performance from the customer's point of view?

Too many companies measure themselves with delivery-performance metrics that are irrelevant to the customer. For example, a 100 percent fill rate (the percentage of the order filled in the first pass) is not the same as 100 percent shipping (the percentage of orders shipped on the dates to which a company commits itself). The customers see fill rate as 100 percent of what they asked for *and* when they wanted it.

Cycle-times are also important to the customer. Too often, companies measure cycle-time as a particular step in the fulfillment process. The customer sees cycle-time as the time from placement of an order to the time of receiving it. Do not confuse internal-operation metrics with customer metrics.

To assess interaction with the customer, ask:

- How do we evaluate our interaction with the customer? How effective is that interaction?

- How do we measure our ability to acquire customers?

- How successful are we at retaining customers?

- Have we extended the company-customer relationship?

- What is the rate of customer attrition?

Cost Metrics

Cost is accrued as a product makes its way along the chain. Obviously, it is to be hoped that value is accumulated at a faster rate. Traditional costs consist of direct labor, material, and overhead. Cost seems straightforward, but it can be hard to isolate. To make matters worse, many organizations are seldom quick to update their standards for costing. Once developed, standards are often implemented for far longer than they remain accurate or useful.

Newer manufacturing methodologies, such as the theory of constraints and flow manufacturing, advocate that cost be considered a result of process and flow rather than of a per-piece measurement—the argument being that if processes are efficient, the cost will ultimately take care of itself. There is truth to this. Cost metrics have long been the bane of supply chain practitioners. Traditional piece-based cost accounting tends to promote local efficiency over supply chain efficiency.

An example is a capital-intensive industry in which there is a large, expensive piece of machinery. The metrics will invariably be tied to the use of that machine, which is being amortized in the form of overhead in relation to each piece being made. The problem with this approach is that the local utilization rate of this machine may have very little to do with the overall efficiency of the supply chain.

Workers, however, know the basis on which they are being evaluated, and they will keep that machine running—even though they are making a product that the company does not need.

In the early 1990s, activity-based costing became popular as a way of overcoming the distortions created by traditional costing. Activity-based costing is intended to compute accurately the direct cost of the product and points out the effect of indiscriminate overhead application. This effort is more direct, but does not change the overall structure of traditional costing.

Supply chains should be measured in terms of least overall cost and optimal profit. When constructing local financial measures, make sure they support the overall supply chain flow. Some examples are

Demand management

- What is the profit on all orders?

- What is the profitability by market segment?

- What is the profit by product mix?

- Do we understand the costs incurred because of demand inaccuracies?

- Is the bullwhip effect clearly understood in terms of extra cost to the company?

Procurement

- Does the company know the cost of ordering?

- Does the company know the cost content of the product?

- Does the company know the cost of quality?

- Does the company know the cost of carrying inventory?

Manufacturing

- Does the company know the correct labor costs?

- Does the company know the scrap costs?

- Does the company know the setup and expediting expenses?

- Does the company know the machining costs?

- Does the company know the handling costs?

Transportation

- Does the company know the relationships among time, distance, and load and delivery stipulations for each product, by product groups and by packaging configurations?

- Are all the costs from end to end visible? Can the company trace, track, audit, and agree to them?

"Owning" the Metrics

Metrics aren't enough. Anyone who serves a function in a company must understand and "own" the metrics. Key executives must be compensated based on the common good, as opposed to local heroics. Supply chain excellence in a company can result only when there are collective metrics to which every department must contribute. Establishing a culture that rewards cross-functional performance is the first step to creating an aligned organization.

Pillar 9: Risk Management

A company needs to identify and isolate areas prone to risks in its end-to-end supply chain. By definition, business risk is a prevailing or potential situation that can jeopardize any part or all of a company. A few years ago, the Coca-Cola Company had some well-publicized problems in Europe that financially hurt the company. Up to this point, the company's operational efficiency and share value had made it the pride of Dow Jones. Did Coca-Cola properly assess the risk of adding new suppliers of ingredients? Did it monitor the quality of new suppliers? If you are selling soft drinks, high-quality ingredients cannot be compromised. Certain critical elements of a business need to be safeguarded. No matter how good the coordination between demand and fulfillment, poor risk management can leave the company vulnerable.

What are some of the risks that companies face?

Process Risk

Certain critical processes have to work right in a company. There is no such thing as "close enough" or "partial credit" for these processes. For example, in a chemical business, the waste-removal system must work reliably. Failure of this process can derail a business. Contamination is a critical risk in the consumable and food markets. The process of testing and certifying a product with suppliers is a key to success or even survival.

People Risk

People are a key link in a supply chain. The wrong person in an important position creates a major risk. A British financial institution with a history of hundreds of years was put out of business by one rogue trader buying on margin. Why was he permitted to take this risk? A better question: why had systems not been installed that could flag his behavior, corroborate its falsehood, and impose necessary sanctions on his trading capacity?

One bad sales representative can lose a million-dollar sale on a key account. One impaired sea captain can pollute a coastline. Companies must find ways to identify people who potentially precipitate a business-threatening risk. The only way to do this systemically is to insist on quality throughout the company's operations—and to meaningfully examine risks according to their relative significance.

How do companies identify weak links? How can they find and prevent these links from breaking the supply chain? Perhaps it means learning to be mindful of the Peter Principle. Perhaps it means testing for people who have been promoted into positions in which they impede the process rather than advance it. A common example of this is promoting schedulers and planners without training them adequately, before they are put in charge of a supply chain planning project.

There are other risks. How can companies mitigate the risk of having critical people leave, taking trade secrets with them? That means identifying the critical information and formally copyrighting it.

Infrastructure Risk

Infrastructure is a tangible risk. How are company assets deployed to support the supply chain? Just as one person in the supply chain may be a weak link, an asset may be a weak link tactically. Even as ancient Rome's rulers realized the importance of the grain supply from Egypt as a link to be protected from risk in its supply chain, so companies need to find and protect their own. Does weather play a role, for example? The risks must be identified before they can be addressed.

Unique machinery in a supply chain may warrant risk assessment and protection. Consider, if a production line goes down or does not start up on time, the Big Three automakers lose millions of dollars per day. If a company is to deploy assets in remote foreign environs, it must know the quality of the power supply and water as well as what the risk in available transportation routes may be. If a train of cars bearing sulfuric acid should derail, any company that relies on that railroad for transport must know immediately. Any time a company depends on a sole source of supply, there is a risk. What will an orange producer do if frost or a hurricane wipes out its only orange grove? What is a viable program to mitigate such risk?

Information-Technology Risk

Information-technology deployment is fraught with hazard. Introducing new software or hardware into a company's core business processes can interrupt the cash-to-cash cycle. How can the liabilities in information-technology implementation be minimized?

Bad data can present dangers. What is the effect of one too many zeros on the check? What is the impact of sending a key player the wrong salary information? What is the consequence of reporting financial results incorrectly? What could be the result of quoting the wrong information to a customer? What danger accrues from not having the right information to make timely decisions?

Risk is inherent in sharing information as well. Who should be allowed to see what? Just having data in the system opens up the possibility that the information could be used against the corporation. What risks are involved in information sharing? Which ones are appropriate to take?

Supplier Risk

In well-intentioned efforts to minimize the supplier base, many companies have worked themselves into single-source strategic relationships. These relationships may be of tremendous value to both companies, but single sourcing introduces a degree of vulnerability that must be anticipated.

Some well-known computer makers have been hurt recently by single sourcing memory chips. Strategic partnerships cease to be worthwhile if they hold up shipments to customers. What happens if the single source fails?

Just-in-time production can compound the risk by removing

any buffer from the supply chain. When employees of an essential automotive parts plant go on strike, the whole chain shuts down within a week. How can a company recognize and plan for the precariousness of supply availability?

Legal Risk

Business always involves some legal risk. The key is to recognize this and be prepared. How do you protect your intellectual property and patents? What are the legal ramifications of manufacturing your product and marketing it? If you are producing car seats for children, for example, what is the risk of malfunction? How do you identify and remove, or at least prepare for, legal risks associated with your products, markets, and customers?

International Risk

Supply chains are becoming more international. How can a company prepare for the risk associated with doing business worldwide? When a new government nationalizes a company's assets, the company loses. How can companies prepare for the possibility of social and political upheavals?

What is the cultural impact of your business on the global environment? What risk does your company run of operating plants where protests and boycotts may occur in primary markets? How can you, as an executive, identify and reduce these risks in your organization's supply chain?

Environmental Risk

We still cannot control the weather. Building a distribution center in Buffalo, New York, requires dealing with exposure to snow. Massive earthquakes in Taiwan last year shook the memory-chip market. Hurricanes routinely ravage the southeastern United States in the fall season. Monsoons pelt Asia with periodic regularity. Supply chain planning needs to address these environmental risks and their potential impact on your business.

Pillar 10: Organizational Alignment

When supply chain theory was first implemented, the traditional organization structure was the biggest barrier. Most companies are still organized along military models. They are hierarchical, having split domains of control down the organization ladder. Decisions start at the top and work their way down. This system becomes a major impediment to supply chains that need process, product, and information to flow across the functional domains.

Aligning with the Supply Chain

From design of the product through delivery to the customer, everyone should be doing something that improves the efficiency of the chain of decisions. Roles and responsibilities to the supply chain's efficiency must be clear through each step of the process. Is everyone clearly responsible for something? Are the releases after completion of the stages firm? Often, there are no clear process definitions in a company. If departments oppose one another instead of cooperating, the supply chain is disrupted. Even in companies where they do exist, the steps tend to be intradepartmental and do not support the flow of the supply chain.

Decisions—Beyond Process Definitions

How can processes be aligned to complete a business flow? In addition to focusing on the transactions, it is necessary to pay close attention to the decisions being made. Is there a decision chain? Where does it start and with what role? Is the decision being communicated? Who is informed next?

A process that has not been defined cannot be improved. Once the processes are defined, a company can concentrate on speeding up the process. How quickly can responsibility be passed to the next link without breaking the supply chain?

To assess decision making, ask:

- Where are the imprecise processes in the company? How can they be streamlined?

- What are the clearly defined steps?

Roles

Most of the time, people's organizational roles have little to do with the process. Individual roles have to be adapted to the supply chain process. Creating a project charter involves determining what the roles are and who makes the decisions across the project. Project team members see the same business through different eyes. If roles are not defined in a team of peers, nothing will get done. If you are an executive, how do you establish roles that engage everyone in working toward common goals? What is the penalty for doing nothing? For supply chain purposes, areas of responsibility across the decision chain must be clearly defined. The roles must be changed from disconnected functions to effective links in the process. This will streamline roles according to a process flow, not a structure. The supply chain is like a train that moves from station to station through a company; at each stop a stationmaster must confirm that the process is proceeding as intended.

To assess roles, ask:

- What are the roles in the organization and how do they support the supply chain flow?

- Which roles do not support the flow and how can these be modified?

- How can we modify the current structure to speed up decision making through the supply chain?

- What new competencies should we cultivate collectively and individually to understand cause-and-effect relationships?

- How soon will we rotate people through jobs?

Executive Sponsorship

One of the best means for resolving territorial battles is through executive sponsorship. A project stands a much greater chance of success if there is executive understanding and commitment. The supply chain project leader will need wisdom and restraint to allow opposing groups to figure out how to make it work.

Executive edicts are inefficient management tools when applied broadly. After hearing several such pronouncements, some employees will find ways to work around the rulings. Those who are devious can weather the storm, finding opportunities to evade repercussions. Top-level edicts may be ignored unless the executive observes his or her own decrees. Executives who make pronouncements that others must implement are absentee landlords.

The executive needs to display an understanding of the goals and means of the supply chain and to demonstrate involvement. This will encourage other employees to regard themselves as valuable implementers of a project. If the leader is an active

The Devil meets the details

participant, the workers will regard themselves as essential participants, too.

Cross Pollination

Supply chain processes need the partners in each link to understand and value the needs and contributions of adjacent links. People can be groomed to attain a broader, more functional view of the supply chain. They can learn to appreciate that what they do affects the rest of the chain.

To support this view, there may be a need to cross-train or "cross-pollinate." One way to do this is to rotate people through each step in the process. Conceptually connecting the people in an enterprise takes more than an office party once a year. Successful companies will share the skills of employees with customers and suppliers to extend supply chain appreciation further. This leads to valuable co-innovation and synergies in which one plus one often equals ten.

Where does a company start? The supply chain appears as a long road disappearing into the distance. With no map in hand, it is difficult to start the trip. Attending a wounded patient requires starting with some triage. Where does it hurt the most? Assessment is essential.

In most companies, sufficient opportunity exists for improvement in any one of the ten pillars of supply chain excellence. How do we choose which pillar to concentrate on and what to do first? What are the mile markers that will put us on the road to success?

Creating a Circle of Excellence

A supply chain "circle of excellence" symbolically demonstrates the dynamic nature of the key elements that support supply chain transformation. The circle represents both connectedness and completion. In applying the circle-of-excellence philosophy, it is important to analyze every area of the circle to ascertain its value, the time taken to effect improvement, and the associated cost.

Value

An effective way to separate the wheat from the chaff in supply chain assessment is to use the yardstick of value. How can the value of a firm be increased by making improvements in each area? Analyze

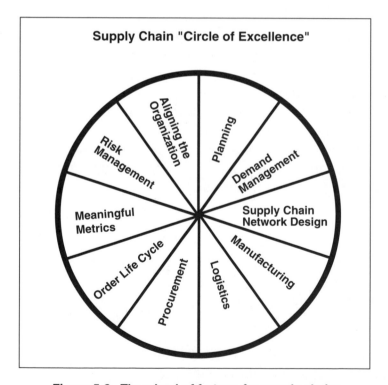

Figure 5-8   The wheel of fortune for supply chains

each area's value and quantify that value as much as possible. How much inventory will modifying routines save? How much will the increase in customer-service levels be? How much more revenue can be engendered? Remember that most of this value is conditional on the commitment to and execution of modifications to follow. Identify the conditions for opportunity.

Time

Any supply chain improvements, major or minor, should be implemented in a timely fashion. Time is of the essence, for at some point in the implementation process the potential value of the solution begins to decrease exponentially. Non-implemented solutions are no solutions at all. Measure the time to benefit. Break up any long-cycle processes into smaller ones. Devise the implementation to deliver value consistently and incrementally over time, not in balloon payments at the end. Otherwise, people will stop waiting and stop believing in the payoff long before getting there. Short-cycle implementation may produce less return on investment but can nonetheless result in value increases faster, with less cost and risk.

Cost

Most solution providers prefer to talk only in terms of value, but there is also an associated cost. What is the cost of this improvement? What is the cost in terms of people and in terms of tools? What are the one-time costs and the ongoing ones? What is the timing of those costs: Are they "front-loaded" or spread across the duration of the improvement project? Costs, like value, also come in ranges. Value is a one-legged stool unless couched in terms of expected cost.

Risk

There have been recent horror stories of companies embarking on improvement projects that have ended with shutting down the business. Take steps to understand the risk. How much will it cost to mitigate the risk? How can the project be divided into less risky segments to gain proficiency that counters the risk?

Quantifying the Tradeoffs

Placing the variables into a matrix such as Figure 5-9 and using a collective criterion removes the emotion from the decision and encourages quick consensus.

Types of Improvement Activities

In any company, some activities are exercises in belt tightening that

Supply Chain Pillars	Value	Time	Cost	Risk	Total
Planning	4	3	-7	-4	-4
Demand Management	9	4	-3	-9	1
SC Network Design	8	7	-1	-6	8
Manufacturing	7	7	-3	-3	8
Logistics	6	1	-8	-5	-6
Procurement	3	1	-2	-3	-1
Order Life Cycle	3	1	-3	-4	-3
Metrics	7	3	0	-5	5
Risk Management	0	2	-9	-9	-16
Organizational Alignment	0	6	-9	-4	-7
Best = 10					**Least = 0**

Figure 5-9 A holistic evaluation tableau

result in cost savings. These operational routines allow the existing supply chain to function more efficiently. Cost-saving operational improvements are easy to sell to the organization and have solid, low-risk, reasonable returns. Operations improvements tend to be limited, however, inasmuch as they are bound by the current paradigm.

Other activities explore new territory and fundamentally change a process. Improvement activities that fundamentally change the way business is done tend to be a harder sell at a tactical level. These are risky in the sense that they veer from the current structure. However, such innovative activities are frequently the ones that produce the greatest returns.

The batter that swings for the fence every time hits many home runs but also strikes out a lot. The key is to balance both types of activity and to understand the risks and rewards. Creating the supply chain circle of excellence is a prerequisite to crafting a winning business model.

What IS on the Outside?

Understanding the Interplay of Industries

On July 2, 2002, as in every year, most Americans will prepare for the Fourth of July vacation—and a celebration of 226 years of sovereignty for the United States. Millions of them will do exactly what they did the previous year. They will plan to cook out, at home or with friends; they'll buy hot dogs and soda, beer and burgers, potato salad, and all the attendant comestibles for the traditional backyard barbecue. Others will pack the family car and set off to a park in another state—perhaps to a river or to a resort on the ocean, where they'll swim or fish or go scuba diving. Many will just lie on the beach and relax.

On July 2, 2002, on the other hand, most Europeans will be in a frenzy of anticipation. On that day, the central banks in eleven sovereign nations will effect the full transition to a unified currency—*the euro*—and the face of Europe will change forever. The new currency will fully replace the currencies of Austria, Belgium, Finland, France, Germany, Holland, Ireland, Italy, Luxembourg, Portugal, and Spain. And, since the prices of all goods and services in those countries will also change that day, the whole world will be watching.

What will Austrian retailers do when the country's consumers discover that the new VCR they planned to buy this week—the one that was 3,495 shillings in Austria and 399,900 lira in Italy only a week before—is instantly repriced at €254 in Austria, but at €207 in Italy? Which will they buy, and how will they buy it? The Euro has become much more than the pipe dream of bureaucrats in Brussels or a funny new symbol on everyone's keyboard. Companies around the world will spend millions of dollars adapting their accounting and treasury systems to the new currency. But this is not the real impact of the switch to a centralized currency. The real impact will be the challenge for companies to create a global supply chain that irreversibly affects their European customers, distributors, transporters, retailers, and suppliers. The ongoing challenge across Europe will be to eliminate exchange-rate hassles and to make the real comparative cost of goods and services from country to country transparent across borders.

As a result, companies will experience relentless pressure to create new supply chain flows. Manufacturers, distributors, and retailers will find that the old price points do not translate, and they will have to set new ones. Will they round up or round down to set marketable price points? Without cumbersome exchanges, price comparisons across borders will inaugurate a new era of competition that some companies will not survive. Once again, a fresh round of corporate cremations and consolidations will occur. Moreover, the complexity of the revisions of cross-border taxation, including tariffs and other international levies, will be staggering. Will we see an exodus of American manufacturers to Europe? Will the Continent of the newly unified economy become a low-cost hub for industrial production?

The impending transition to the euro is only an example of what today's global companies face all the time: radical, discontinuous change. It's too easy to dismiss the advent of the unified, centralized currency in Europe as being an extraordinary and unique situation. It's not. In today's rapidly evolving competitive climate, companies face serious challenges from shrinking product life cycles, increased competition, the adoption of new technologies, shifting customer loyalty, and a porous global economy. How a company reviews, reconceives, and reconstructs its business model to adapt to such fitful change will determine that company's survival and success.

Change is a constant, but the type, manner, speed, and character of change are difficult to predict. Look at the converging landscape of media, cable, Internet, and wireless technologies. As communications technology developed in the 1980s and 1990s, traditional media companies and content providers saw new avenues for providing services and value to customers—from cable television to the Internet. Now those same companies see a new avenue in wireless systems—another discontinuous technology. These same companies are also grappling with what this potential convergence of previous technologies will entail—one that will grant access to information from anywhere, at any time, at the customer's choosing.

Consider these questions: What will happen to traditional land-line telephone service, for instance, when all communications can be received on wireless systems? What will be the fate of pay-per-view cable services when their markets are threatened by completely customized content that is delivered by wireless narrow-casting right to our TVs and computer screens? Will the public enjoy the freedom to combine any set of programs from various TV stations and radio stations in addition to news—all delivered to their computers, TV screens, or even personal digital assistants—at the exact time and sequence of their choice? Will customization acquire a whole new meaning? Will mass advertising become oh-so-unfashionable? In order to sell individually to each of us, will companies be watching "every move you make, every breath you take"? How will all this affect our public policy regarding privacy? Tsunamis of change are rising to crash on us because of the imminent convergence of these technologies.

Yet the convergence of unpredictable technologies is not the only avenue through which change will occur. Factors affecting one industry or even one company affect all other relationships inside and outside that industry or company, including its suppliers and customers. For example, when Intel began warning Wall Street of a dip in earnings in late 2000, the entire industry suffered. Personal computer manufacturers as well as the makers of peripherals plummeted in their market value. Apple lost nearly 50 percent of its stock value overnight at about the same time as Intel's announcement.

That a judgment by Intel's own forecasters could impact the entire high-technology marketplace demonstrates the disproportionate influence one company can wield. When Procter & Gamble saw its profits dip, its earnings reports suffer, and its stock price tumble by 36 percent in 1999, the company immediately blamed "unexpected" price increases from suppliers as the cause of its woes. P&G learned what every industry must understand: complex relationships exist between customers and suppliers, and those relationships extend not only all the way down the chain of its own business operations, but also all the way down to stock prices on Wall Street.

It seems obvious, but time and again companies ignored or incorrectly anticipated how changes in one industry would affect other industries in their supply chain. A dip in chemical manufacture immediately affects production of pharmaceuticals. Stalled glass production or higher glass prices impact home builders. Tighter oil and gas production ramps up prices of these key commodities, endangering both the production and transportation of consumer package goods. Vehicle repair costs impact the tool industry, which affects the metals industry.

The global economic or political situation can also change, as in the mandated advent of the euro or the unanticipated tightness in crude oil supplies that threatened France and virtually halted the economy in the United Kingdom during the summer of 2000. Companies cannot prepare for every change, but they must appreciate what change can mean for their business model, their processes, and their very structure and identity.

Individuals in organizations must cultivate a peripheral vision to see beyond their own industry. They must train themselves to see globally and across other industries in their business supply chains. Consider the following questions:

- What are the fundamental drivers of change in your industry?

- What are the changes occurring in the industries of your suppliers and customers?

- Do you know them beyond purchase orders and invoices?

- Where will the dangers and opportunities emerge from outside your industry?

- Is what is happening in these industries known only to a select few in your company? If so, how can you make sure that all who are affected have a way of knowing?

- How do the risks and difficulties beyond your own industry affect you?

- How can your company better anticipate, manage, and even initiate change to your benefit?

By asking fundamental questions about how a business

operates—the nature and characteristics of its customers and suppliers—and by understanding how trends in other industries affect their own business, managers have a better opportunity to identify strengths and weaknesses within their company and to isolate risks. And the first step in mastering change is to understand your suppliers and customers.

Understanding Business Practices

The spectrum of internal business practices delineates how a company fulfills demand for both products and services. There are five categories—an alphabet soup—into which all companies fall. They are not strict pigeonholes; they are ideals for achieving a certain type of performance in design and fulfillment.

Each of these five approaches to business has implications for supply chain management. Where a company resides along the rainbow of business practices determines how that company operates. But while certain synergies can be achieved by adopting one fixed model, many companies do not operate at a single point along the continuous spectrum of practices, but rather move from point to point along it. The position of a company along the

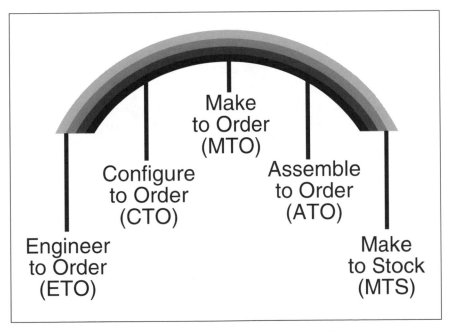

Figure 6-1 Spectrum of business practices

spectrum has different impacts on each of the following activities:

- *Demand Management:* how the business practice influences marketing, forecasting, and identifying customer demands

- *Fulfillment Management:* how the business practice influences order-taking processes and satisfying customer demands

- *Supply Management:* how the business practice influences supplier relations and procurement activities

- *Manufacturing Management:* how the business practice influences manufacturing planning and activities

- *Inventory Management:* how the business practice influences the types and amounts of inventory

- *Transportation Management:* how the business practice influences the modes and roles of transportation

Make-to-Stock

Chances are that if a product is on retailers' shelves, it is a Make-to-Stock product. Make-to-Stock (MTS) is traditional mass production at its finest. Thousands of identical parts whiz along conveyor belts, are packed into boxes, and are piled high in warehouses. Make-to-Stock describes the mass production of predesigned products, such as cereal, soup, off-the-shelf clothing, and mass-produced software.

MTS is driven by forecasts to make inventory that is then stocked in a distributor's warehouse. MTS companies buy raw materials, invest labor and equipment time, and pay for shipping— all in hopes of a sale. Thus, MTS rides on faith that "if you build it, they will come." When customers want products, they are quickly served from the inventory.

But MTS companies are forced to limit the number of product variations they make. There are two reasons for this. First, the more product variants a company has, the lower the demand per variant. The statistical nature of demand makes it impossible to profitably stock very many variants and still satisfy customers. If you sell an average of only one unit of a niche product per year, it is too easy to run out. If you stock only one unit and two customers come in to purchase it, then you have a problem. It is also too easy to be left with excess stock if you stock two units and no customers come in.

Second, MTS companies invest tremendous amounts of money to build very specialized manufacturing systems to make exactly the products that they sell. In return for their investment, these companies have very low unit costs—specialization brings efficiency. The flip side is that the machinery is only useful for making one product or a few variants. Readjusting the manufacturing line for another product is costly, both in terms of setup time and in terms of the required "warm-up" or "centering" period of adjustment.

Most consumer packaged goods companies—such as P&G, Nabisco, Phillip Morris, and Black & Decker—are MTS companies. Whether it is canning green beans or brewing beer, these companies operate on the principle that bigger is better. Retailers are the backbone of MTS production and are themselves essentially MTS companies, because they buy and carry a standard range of products in hopes that customers might later buy them. MTS is used when customers demand delivery cycle-times that are shorter than what manufacturing can deliver. MTS is also used for many commodity goods because demand is stable and cost efficiency is essential. Most Make-to-Stock products have relatively long product life cycles. Changes in the product tend to be marketing changes to boost demand rather than functional changes that necessitate a redesign of the basic fit, form, or function.

Because MTS companies risk their resources on the speculation that customers will buy the product, demand management plays two essential roles. First, demand managers must accurately forecast demand so that the right amount of stock can be made. Second, demand managers, marketers, and salespeople must persuade customers that they will be satisfied by one of the limited array of products made by the company and sitting on the shelves.

Fulfillment management in MTS companies is driven by the goal of efficient mass production, creating a stream of suppliers' raw materials that are then converted into finished goods. A reliable supply stream is important because of the high cost of downtime on MTS companies' expensive manufacturing equipment. Sophisticated inventory management is important to MTS companies because overstocks and stock-outs are anathema. The large and steady volumes for MTS production also dictate the need for efficient transportation to move goods from manufacturing to a multitude of distribution points and on to final consumers.

How to minimize inventory in the distribution network and still maintain a low cost delivered item with a high level of service— this is the biggest challenge in MTS companies.

Make-to-Order

Whereas Make-to-Stock companies make products in hopes of selling them, Make-to-Order companies wait for a firm order before actually performing the bulk of the manufacturing, making a product only when a customer requests it. But Make-to-Order companies are similar to MTS companies in that they make only a finite, predesigned set of products. Make-to-Order means the order-driven production of predesigned products and services that can be sold as commodities such as furniture, specialty software, boats, die-cut or molded fittings, house-cleaning services, and income-tax preparation.

Typically, then, Make-to-Order (MTO) companies thrive in situations where demand is unpredictable, such as common industrial products like motors or pumps, special orders at retailers, or in situations where the product is expensive, such as aircraft, machine tools, or power-generation equipment. The MTO model also applies in restaurants, where the product is valued for freshness.

Companies that make industrial products often practice MTO because they have many different models, and demand for any one of them could range from none at all to several each year. MTO is also practiced when the cost of making and carrying inventory is too high. Item by item, big-ticket products such as machine tools, aircraft, boats, and power equipment all vary enough to make inventories of each variant prohibitively expensive. Certainly this would be true of a company such as John Deere.

The special order process at many retailers is an example of Make-to-Order because the retailer does not work to buy and deliver the product without instructions and commitment from a customer. Whereas Make-to-Stock companies are worried about where their product is located, MTO companies worry about when the product will ship. They will not carry a finished goods inventory, although they may create and manage inventories of work-in-progress (WIP) or of materials from suppliers.

Managing demand at MTO companies involves creating forecasts based on past and expected needs. It also depends on persuading customers that the standard array of product variants is adequate to their needs. Because any given product variant can have uncertain demand, these companies will aggregate demand forecasts across product categories, across underlying work activities, or across supplied raw materials. These forecasts drive capacity planning and allow the company to confidently purchase some supplies or to create commonly used sub-assemblies. Manufacturing is a significant aspect of Make-to-Order companies only because customer orders often contend for the same set of resources. Therefore, scheduling, sequencing, and capacity management in the shop floor are all crucial issues in MTO companies.

In MTO companies, the fact that customers must wait for their orders also puts pressure on fulfillment. Timely planning injects each customer order into the stream of activities in the company, and careful tracking ensures that the company can meet lead-time promises. The MTO manufacturer typically does not have the volume to justify any investment in transportation infrastructure. The MTO business has very little ownership of the outbound freight, as the order goes directly to the customer, and there is no distribution network.

Assemble-to-Order

Assemble-to-Order (ATO) companies create finished goods as defined by a customer's order by quickly assembling the finished product from a set of component modules. Whereas Make-to-Order companies start with raw materials, Assemble-to-Order starts with a series of pre-manufactured modules. Whereas both MTS and MTO have a limited set of product variants, Assemble-to-Order offers an exponential range of options, depending on an order-driven assembly of different components. Examples include products like computers and specialty engines.

Assemble-to-Order is a centaur—the mythical animal composed of different parts, front and back. The back half of the ATO company operates in MTS mode, facing its suppliers, ordering parts, creating requisite modules, and stocking these modules. The last stages of manufacturing—the front half facing customers—operates in MTO mode, completing a product only when a customer order defines the required combination of modules. Customers can witness the lead-time of the assembly and shipping process, but will not see all the work that went into creating the modules.

Assemble-to-Order makes sense only when two essential conditions are met. First, the highly modular design of products must permit last-minute assembly of orders; and, second, the available combinations for product assembly are too numerous to allow stocking all variants at any one time.

The exemplary ATO company is a computer company like Dell, one that lives off mail order, telephone, or web-based sales. Computers are highly modular and can have thousands of combinations of processor speeds, memory, disk drives, CD-ROM options, monitors, keyboards, mice, software bundles, and other accessories like networking cards, sound cards, graphic accelerators, and so on. Customers can pick and choose their favorite combination of features, ordering from a menu of components. The ATO manufacturer receives the order and then pulls modules from inventory, snaps them together, tests the product, and ships it. Other companies that adopt the ATO model are cash-machine makers like Diebold and telephone equipment makers such as Lucent or Nortel. While automobile buyers do not yet get to pick their own combinations, automakers also embody Assemble-to-Order principles in offering an extremely wide range of options for cars (colors, engine model, power gadgets, interior configurations, sound systems, and on and on).

ATO has a clear implication for supply chain management. Companies must have available all the modules or optional components that might go into the assembled product. Thus, demand management at ATO companies must create useful forecasts for future demand at the module or options level. The back half of an Assemble-to-Order company must manage all the supplier reliability, manufacturing efficiency, and inventory management issues of a Make-to-Stock company. The front half of the company has all the lead-time and work-stream issues of an MTO company.

Configure-to-Order

Configure-to-Order (CTO) takes customization a step further than Assemble-to-Order. In Configure-to-Order companies, customers can themselves "design" certain elements of the product, and CTO manufacturers use application, design, or engineering information from the customer to compute the design parameters of the desired product. CTO therefore goes beyond the fixed set of products available in Make-to-Order or the fixed set of options available with Assemble-to-Order; instead, it offers unbounded product options within certain design-concept or product-family limits. Configure-to-Order describes order-driven design and manufacturing customized to particular users.

Configure-to-Order is economically feasible today because, with little human intervention, contemporary engineering and manufacturing software can compute the dimensions of component parts and command machine tools to make the part. For example, a pump company might let a customer select the flow rate, outlet pressure, shaft RPM, and so on, for a particular assembly. Once the customer has specified the desired properties, the pump company creates the custom design—that is, it computes the exact diameter of the pump bore necessary to meeting the other specifications of the customer's design. Then it makes the customer's specific pump.

Configure-to-Order is used for many custom applications for common industrial products: motors, transformers, and electrical enclosures are all ideal CTO products. Other examples of companies include print shops, where the customer defines the design (text and graphics), colors, paper stock, and page size; while the company translates those specifications into the settings of its printing, collating, trimming, and binding machinery. The prerequisites for using CTO are that the design or engineering rules for the product are well understood and that the basic design concept remains the same over some range of size, performance, or particulars.

Demand management at CTO companies is similar to that for ATO companies: it is impossible to predict demand for any unique product, but it can be useful to forecast demand for product families and likely raw materials. For example, the aforementioned pump company might forecast demand for each size class of pump. And fulfillment for CTO tackles many of the same issues that ATO does—the back half acquires raw materials and creates the WIP inventory that the concluding steps in manufacturing rely on to customize the product. For example, the pump maker might make partially completed pump casings in each size class to minimize the amount of machining needed once an order comes in.

Configure-to-Order often has more custom labor and activity than ATO. However, some manufacturing coordination issues for CTO are similar to those of Make-to-Order: that is, CTO companies strive to minimize lead-time by efficiently coordinating each order as it wends its way across the manufacturing floor. Inventory and transportation issues are similar to those of MTO or ATO: there is no finished goods inventory, and each order is shipped when completed.

Engineer-to-Order

At the far end of the spectrum are completely customized products run more as projects than as products, such as the design and construction of hospitals, airports, bridges, and dams. This is the realm of Engineer-to-Order (ETO) companies, where the process is largely driven by the up-front design effort to define exactly what is built and delivered. ETO is used when the customer's needs are unique and no standard product or slightly customized product suffices. ETO companies are geared toward producing extremely low volumes of fully customized, uniquely designed products. Most of the construction industry—from high-rise architects to local homebuilders—follows ETO practices. Other ETO companies include outsourcers for certain services such as contract manufacturing, consulting, service contracts, and website developers.

In ETO, to varying degrees in different situations, three sets of people—customer, company, and supplier—work together to develop a feasible, cost-effective design that is then built and delivered. In each case, the needs of the customer intersect with the capabilities of the company to create a customized solution. Engineer-to-Order is driven by complex sales efforts involving requests for proposals. In proposals, engineers work out the implications of the customer's specifications and try to reliably estimate the time and costs of the project. They also try to persuade the customer that the company can create an innovative and desirable result.

If the company wins the project, then it faces implementing the proposed work within the time and budgetary constraints detailed in the proposal. Engineering work includes refining the design, collaborating further with the client, translating the proposed effort into a detailed schedule, and executing against the adjusted schedule to create the refined design. In this environment, milestone deliverables and interim payments are common, and truly major ETO projects may even see the creation of entire MTO or MTS factories to ensure project completion, such as the cement factories created for building the Hoover Dam. The Hoover Dam epitomizes the result of the ETO practice—a distinctive product filled with highly specialized machinery.

Manufacturing and inventory management are idiosyncratic at ETO companies because such companies usually have no regular manufacturing or inventory activities at the core of their business. But each project may require manufacturing management as well as acquiring and storing raw materials or an inventory of work-in-progress. Therefore, these companies often create a cadre of trusted suppliers and have developed competence in finding new suppliers or subcontractors.

Forecasting for ETO is generally limited to projecting backlogs of business and penciling in possible project leads to gauge the future volume of business. Correspondingly, managing demand in an ETO environment entails being aware of project leads and being ready to respond to requests for proposals.

Managing supply becomes important in ETO because engineering companies use a wide range of raw materials and supplier companies. When a proposal opportunity arises, an ETO company may immediately coordinate with several suppliers to fully work through the expected costs and schedules. Because each project is unique, an ETO company might need to line up a supplier to serve some novel purpose. During implementation of the project, the ETO company would then delegate appropriate segments of the effort to its preferred suppliers.

If supply becomes a matter of working with subcontractors and partners, transportation management is even more straightforward at ETO companies. It generally consists of simple outsourcing because the irregular levels of materials handling in ETO companies cannot justify creating a dedicated fleet.

The Customer Decoupling Point

Where a company resides in the spectrum has a large effect on its attributes. For example, who inside any given company knows which activities are for which customers? While every company is affected by orders, the depth to which each customer's order penetrates into a company varies across the rainbow depicted in Figure 6-1.

At the MTS end, orders do not penetrate far at all. Only people in the warehouse have any awareness of which inventory is being shipped to which customer. Manufacturing staff may have no idea where the product is going, either because when they make the product there is no firm order, or because a given batch may be divided among many customers at multiple destinations. By contrast, nearly everyone in an ETO company is aware of which project they are working on and who the customer is. Individual customer orders penetrate to nearly every point in the organization.

There are other differences. The following attributes have low values in MTS companies and progressively higher ones toward the ETO end of the spectrum:

- The total number of products and product variants
- The day-to-day variation in people's jobs
- Customers' tolerance for lead-times
- Commitment by customers before work starts

Conversely, the following attributes have high values in MTS companies and progressively lower values toward the ETO end of the spectrum:

- The size of production batches
- Importance of demand forecasts in setting work activities
- Ratio of production workers to engineering or design professionals
- Amount of finished-goods inventory

Moving along the Rainbow

The five business practices described above, then, are "ideals" for a pure form of a particular practice. In real life, most companies blend these practices to manufacture different products for different markets at different locations. A company like Lockheed-Martin might use MTS principles for consumer-oriented products, MTO for business applications, and ETO for military applications. Another—like IBM—might use MTS to create work-in-process for an ATO final assembly or CTO operations. A large automobile manufacturer may well use ETO to build an assembly line for MTS, MTO, ATO, or CTO practices, while using MTS to handle the bulk of demand and MTO for emergency orders or fleets.

But mixing and matching the different business practices also has limits. Design principles, business processes, worker training, and equipment all tend to be narrowly attuned to a particular business. A company that can produce a million copies of a product would have a hard time creating a single customized copy, and vice versa. Changing from MTS or MTO to ATO requires changing the product design to a more modular product so final assembly really is fast and efficient.

Of course, that would mean reexamining the business—and perhaps reinventing it. The real point is not the mix or the challenge of the mix; it is that, paradoxically, companies are moving toward a combination of more customization and more replication of such customized execution. This movement is mass customization, and in a changing world, regardless of the industry you are in, you will want to understand mass customization and its effect on your company.

Several major factors drive movement along the mass customization rainbow:

- A perceived opportunity to create a new market

- A perceived opportunity to service a market that is underserved

- A perceived opportunity to take market share from a competitor

- An effort to maintain growth by expanding into new markets

- A desire to counter a real or anticipated loss of market share

- A desire to gain cost efficiencies

- A desire to improve customer service

- A desire to change perception of one's company in the marketplace

Mass customization requires more flexibility than MTS but more reliability than ETO. To increase product variation while still manufacturing goods at a reasonable cost requires a serious change in business practices. But there are many good reasons why companies are moving to the center of the rainbow. Partly it's because they are routinely pushed toward mass customization from all sides of their supply chain: from the customer side, from the supply side, and by the internal dictates of running an efficient business.

All of these conditions suggest that your company must answer the following critical questions:

- Do all markets crave variety? Don't some reward standardization? Is variety always the antithesis of efficient production?

- Is not an automated ATO process just as efficient as, if not more efficient than, a traditional MTS process? Why, then, do companies move around?

- What makes a company with a history of success in ETO decide that it needs to standardize its product offering?

- What makes a successful consumer packaged goods (CPG) manufacturer decide that it has to configure products to be successful?

Mass customization is widely applicable, but it is most applicable to companies that offer a wide range of options or accessories. These include vehicle makers like Mercedes, Mack Trucks, and Deere & Co., which offer combinations of engines, exterior styles, interior styles, and numerous optional accessories. As discussed in the first chapter, Natuzzi—the Italian furniture maker that offers an enormous range of combinations of styles, sizes, colors, and surface materials—would also be thought to have mastered mass customization, along with rival Miller SQA. The list also includes companies like apparel maker Levi Strauss, Ross Controls—makers of industrial components such as pumps, valves, motors, and enclosures—and Dell Computer.

Mass customization means moving away from both the MTS and ETO ends of the spectrum of business practices. In the new arena of competitive global markets, companies must reliably and repeatedly deliver products and services that are tuned to local needs. MTS is too unvariegated and too unresponsive to individual customer demands. ETO is too unreliable and too costly to respond to volume. Mass customization is neither some bandwagon to be jumped on, nor a narrowly defined approach to business. Instead, it identifies a trend toward economically and reliably producing a greater range of goods and services for customers who are ever more demanding. It entails asking, "What is the best mode of operation?" Given the range of options, there is no correct answer or optimal practice. The approach deployed depends on the type of products being sold, the market, the customers within that market, and the value those customers derive from the products and services.

The concept of mass customization applies across the board to any industry for both product and service companies. The appeal of mass customization is that it provides a framework for analyzing how any business practice could be altered or expanded to better suit the dictates of an industry. Mass customization is the first step to identifying opportunities within one's own industry.

Understanding Opportunities across Industries

Think for a moment about the number of supply chain constituents whose actions can impact Ford, GM, or Daimler-Chrysler. Major manufacturers of automobiles rely on power companies for their assembly lines, on tire companies, on petroleum by-product and chemicals companies for carpeting, on tanners and plastics manufacturers for upholstery and trim, and on glassmakers for glass and mirrors. They depend heavily on steel production; on tool-and-die parts manufacturers; on builders of pumps, radiators, flywheels, and gears; on specialty engine manufacturers and suppliers; on makers of wire, hoses, and belts; and on electrical experts for resistors, capacitors, solenoids, plugs, connections, and distributors. Increasingly, they even rely on makers of silicon chips—not only because today's cars require computer controls, but because the heavy equipment these companies design and build to help automate

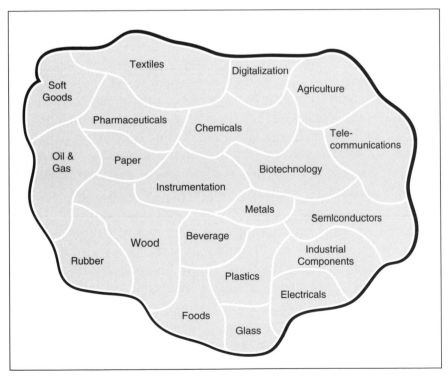

Figure 6-2   A sample cross-industry kaleidoscope

their assembly lines is also reliant on computer-controlled programming and functionality.

The example of an automaker is useful for a further reason. From one perspective, automobile manufacturers represent the ways supplier and customer relationships are intertwined across industries in multiple sectors. But it's even more useful to consider that the automobile industry is a *convergence of industries* and that all the relationships between different manufacturers and suppliers are continually in flux. This means not only that opportunities can arise at intersections in the web of relationships, but also that other opportunities can arise even where intersections don't yet exist.

In Figure 6-2, a cross section of industries is represented as existing in a kaleidoscopic relationship: they all intersect with one another; they all interact with one another, they all illuminate one another. White spaces are the possible intersections between industries—and those white spaces mean opportunities.

The best way to understand these opportunities is to look at the ways different industry sectors can converge and a new product emerge—hopefully creating its own market. In the 1970s, the Wrigley Company spent millions to promote sugar-free gum to sell its product to people who were fearful of tooth decay. But, in 1999, when SmithKline Beecham introduced its new dental gum under the Aquafresh name, it promoted a new chewing gum— which is traditionally a type of flavored candy—as an aid to both dental care and oral hygiene. The company suggested that consumers use their Aquafresh dental gum as an adjunct to brushing their teeth. In this way, SmithKline Beecham crossed the perceived boundaries among a candy manufacturer, a provider of dental hygiene, and a supplier of oral hygiene products, blending desirable attributes of all three in a new product and thereby creating a new market.

Nor is this the only example of cross-industry opportunities. Consider the technology of liquid plasma displays—one of the fastest growing technologies in the world. It is a combination of two very different fields—electrical engineering and synthetic fibers or textile technology. In the healthcare sector, Bausch & Lomb is attempting to create a canopy of total healthcare by converging three distinct industries: vision care (contact lenses and glasses), surgicals (medical instruments, disposables, and so on), and pharmaceuticals.

The questions for companies to ask are

- What competencies, processes, and technologies do we have that are transferable across the intersections between industries?

- Where can we create new solutions and solve new problems?

- Where are the new growth areas?

- How can we provide full solutions that combine the attributes of different industries?

Creating a Full Solution

Cars combine microchips and metals, software and soft leather, manufacturing and marketing, repair and consumer finance. In constructing the full supply chain, car companies must bring together a very wide range of competencies, seeking mutually

Convergent, cross-industry, collisional

complementary abilities in supply chain partners from a range of industries.

At the same time that supply chain partners should share similar business principles, they should also have some dissimilar aspects, bringing complementary, interlocking pieces of a solution together. For example, you might choose to emphasize innovative product design and marketing, while your various supply chain partners emphasize customer credit, efficient manufacturing, and order fulfillment.

Optimal dissimilarity in a supply chain is especially apparent in convergent industries such as the automotive industry. Although the business models for car manufacturing, car sales, car financing, and car repair are all very different, they must mesh at certain crucial interfaces. Cars must flow from manufacturers (with a production-based business model) to dealers (with a consumer-retail business model). Likewise, car sales are linked to financing (whose business model emphasizes managing its risks and collecting monthly payments) because a particular customer wants both the car and financing or lease qualification. These flows and links represent connection points in a supply chain.

Explicitly choosing these connection points is where your supply chain strategy meets your business model. Important elements of your business model will need to match corresponding elements in your supply chain partner's business model. If there is a gap between where your company's processes leave off and where your partner's processes start, there will be problems in the supply chain and opportunities for you, a partner, or a competitor to add value by filling in the gap.

It is important to recognize that in a vastly changed economy, driven by information technology and the Internet, traditional relationships between certain types of companies also change. Today, we see a new role played by companies that act as aggregators and disseminators of information: *infomediaries*. These companies exist in cyberspace as well as on *terra firma*.

The Constituents

To understand how supply chain relationships work in the web of economic conditions surrounding every company, you should understand the concept of archetypes. An archetype is a dominant process that defines a company's value in the supply chain.

Following are some principal archetypes.

First, there are two types of *doers* in the supply chain:

- The *Transformer* is a company on the solid line between raw materials and consumers.

- The *Incrementor* executes a small step in the flow of a supply chain.

Second, there are three types of aggregators in the supply chain:

- The *Supplier-Side Aggregator* helps many chains converge into one.

- The *Customer-Side Aggregator* helps one chain diverge into many.

- The *Dual-Side Aggregator* helps many chains converge and then diverge.

Third, there are companies that play roles as creators in the supply chain:

- The *Product Creator* creates new stock-keeping units (SKUs) in a supply chain.

- The *Customer Creator* creates new downstream flows.

- The *Industry Creator* creates new market spaces with new supply chains.

An archetype is an ideal characteristic in its pure form. No company is purely one archetype or another. The markets in which companies operate dictate that businesses develop a portfolio of competencies. In many cases, then, archetypes also describe pieces of the company. For example, the purchasing department might act as an aggregator archetype for all your company's suppliers. Or different business units might appear as different archetypes because of the various products, services, or channels they focus on. Different archetypes represent different functions and different units in a company.

Archetype: Transformers

The Transformer archetype is perhaps the one most associated with traditional industrial production. Transformers are companies or parts of companies geared to converting some primary, elementary raw material into a valued-added product. The best examples are petroleum refiners, chemicals producers, metal smelters, electricity generators, and generic pharmaceutical manufacturers. Transformers are valued for their ability to efficiently convert one type of material (often a commodity) into another more valuable product (that might also be a commodity).

The transformers' business models are primarily defined by their cost of production; these companies leverage an often large capital asset base of equipment to efficiently convert raw material into product. Such companies worry about sourcing the raw material, controlling inventories at various stages of production, and avoiding downtime. Transformers also face the greatest risks from fluctuations in both commodity prices and demand. Commodity price fluctuations roil transformer-type industries, hurting some companies and benefiting others. Differences in pricing of contracts for raw material and contracts for supplying product can make or break these companies. Companies can easily get locked into paying high prices for raw material and getting a low price for products, or vice versa.

Demand fluctuations also present risk. If demand drops below the industry's normal operating capacity, then cutthroat price competition can ensue. Small differences in efficiency can make the difference between winning and losing customers. Losers sink deeper into trouble because of the high fixed costs of their asset base. Even high demand can be troublesome, as it forces transformer companies to make major investment decisions about expanding their capacity in the face of uncertainty that the high demand will continue.

To a lesser extent, all consumer packaged goods companies and many discrete products companies conform to the Transformer archetype. Most of these companies are concerned with efficiently manufacturing products from an incoming flow of component parts.

Archetype: Incrementors

Incrementors do the small things that fill the gaps in every supply chain; they are the spackle of the economy. For example, in the pharmaceuticals industry, certain companies specialize in packaging bulk pharmaceuticals into pills, syrups, and ointments, and stuffing them into appropriately labeled bottles, blister packs, tubes, boxes, and so on. While not as intensive in using capital equipment or technology as synthesizing the drugs, the job of the packager is still important. These companies have local knowledge regarding governmental packaging and labeling regulations; they can meet preferences regarding flavor and form of medications; and they understand the marketing preferences of their customers (in box design, quantities per package, and so on).

One might think that incrementors have much in common with transformers. However, the magnitude of their contributions in the supply chain differs greatly. Where transformers must be extremely efficient, incrementors can compete on the unique value added by their services or processes. The incrementor title is no insult. Even though one might argue that they do not add much, what they add is essential in the context of the supply chains that they serve.

Archetype: Aggregators

The Aggregator archetype is widespread in the transportation, logistics, and complex manufacturing systems. Aggregators manage a multitude of assets (such as trucks, trailers, aircraft, and freight cars) to support a vast multitude of jobs (shipping a load, moving a passenger, or delivering a package). Rather than materially affect what they handle, aggregators mostly move and track. Indeed, most never even own the goods they handle, in contrast to many other businesses.

Many companies play a middleman role, representing either multiple suppliers to a customer or multiple customers to a single supplier, or both. These are aggregators, providing one-stop shopping or a single point of contact to a large and fragmented market. Although the aggregator often owns the good for a time, the goods handled by a pure aggregator pass through its hands almost unchanged. An aggregator's value is not defined by product features but by its logistical, marketing, and transaction-handling services.

The business model of an aggregator is defined by the need to support large numbers of relationships, either on the supplier side or on the customer side. Processes that create, maintain, and service each relationship are important to an aggregator. An aggregator must also handle transactions in a way that splits the transaction among the multiple parties that it is servicing. While one side of the aggregator's supply chain sees a single monolithic transaction, the aggregator must track the components of the transaction. Accounting systems, account management systems, and order management systems handle deaggregation and reaggregation processes. The archetype of the aggregator can be organized into three subcategories: supply-side, customer-side, and dual-side.

Archetype: Supply-Side Aggregators

A Supply-Side Aggregator handles many suppliers on behalf of a single customer. Examples of supply-side aggregators include the procurement departments of most major corporations, dedicated inbound logistics service providers, and Assemble-to-Order manufacturing. A supplier-facing aggregator model works where multiple supply chains converge into a single stream.

The key processes for this type of aggregator are defined by its ability to manage multiple suppliers and properly deaggregate both purchase orders and payments, while reaggregating inbound shipments and invoices. Thus, this business accepts purchase orders or work orders on the customer side, which are then broken down into orders to the multiple respective suppliers. The suppliers send the requested goods, and the aggregator tracks the completion of the purchase order, sending the assembled order to the customer. The customer pays one invoice, and the supply-side aggregator divides the payments among the suppliers.

A supply-side aggregator usually works on behalf of the customer who does not want to be bothered by the details of procurement. As such, the aggregator will also help qualify suppliers, seek competitive prices, find second sources, notify the customer of delivery, and generally take responsibility for ensuring timely delivery of requested items.

Archetype: Customer-Side Aggregators

A Customer-Side Aggregator supports multiple customers on behalf of a single supplier. Examples include franchise retailers and the distribution departments of most major corporations. A customer-side aggregator model works where multiple supply chains diverge from a single stream.

The converse of a supply-side aggregator, a customer-side aggregator has processes that manage a multitude of customers, maintaining local inventories so that each customer's order is fulfilled without needing to call on the supplier. This is one of the reasons that a supplier might use a customer-side aggregator, who aggregates demand into bulk orders. As such, a customer-side aggregator is much more likely to maintain inventory than a supply-side aggregator. The customer-side aggregator handles many accounts and transactions on the customer side and relatively few transactions on the supplier side.

Customer-side aggregators provide a number of value-added services to their supplier. They handle order fulfillment and transaction support for small orders; they gather knowledge of local markets; they support marketing and field service; and they handle customer credit and accounts receivable. But most of all, they let the supplier concentrate on making things in economically viable bulk quantities.

Customer-side aggregators do face a diminution of their value if mass customization becomes prevalent. Although they will still offer many local services, they will not be able to fully insulate the manufacturer from multitudes of individual customer orders because it will presumably be the manufacturer who executes some mass customization Make-to-Order process. One work-around for this challenge is in-channel configuration, such as is used by Compaq's distributors, who can customize orders by adding memory, disk drives, and accessories.

Archetype: Dual-Side Aggregators

Dual-Side Aggregators create a nexus or marketplace on behalf of both multiple suppliers and multiple customers. They are actually quite common, with examples including many retailers, distributors, and wholesalers as well as the financial exchanges (such as NASDAQ or NYSE) and online marketplaces (such as eBay.com or Amazon.com's ZShop service).

Dual-side aggregators combine the processes of customer-side and supply-side aggregators. For example, the traditional department store lets each customer buy any combination of goods from any combination of suppliers all in one transaction. At the same time, suppliers can sell to multiple customers, all in one bulk sales transaction.

Dual-Side Aggregators can put themselves into a position of turning their suppliers into customers of a sort. The best example of this is Charles Schwab, which provides a number of services to both mutual fund companies and to financial advisors. Schwab provides the back-office systems for the advisors, making them customers of Schwab at the same time that the advisor's clients are also Schwab customers. In the retail arena, the practice of slotting fees, which suppliers pay to receive space on store shelves, illustrates the fact that suppliers are actually customers of retailers, too.

Archetype: Product Creators

Product Creators create new products and services to fill the market spaces that they occupy. They are found in many industries, including consumer packaged goods companies, high technology, aerospace, and even financial services, where companies create new financial instruments or customer account services. Engineer-to-Order companies (such as construction) are consummate product creators, because every project requires skills in leveraging technology to meet unique customer requirements. Examples include idea laboratories or idea "hatcheries," along with contract manufacturers.

Product creators present a mix of competencies related to the technologies that go into products or services, or to meet the needs of customers that might buy those products or services. Their key processes include gathering knowledge from the marketplace on unmet needs, research and development (R&D) processes to create or leverage technology, engineering processes to design new products, and marketing processes to spur acceptance of the new products. Product creators may include features or processes from the Transformer or Incrementor archetype models to manufacture the products or outsource to companies of these archetypes.

Product creators are a source of new value in supply chains because so many industries now compete on the basis of innovative product and service features. Product creators can benefit from tight supply chains by collaborating on new product designs with either component suppliers or with customers.

Archetype: Consumer Creators

The normal transaction-oriented sales model assumes that all transactions of a given product through a given channel have the same profit margin. But some industries and products feature extraordinarily high up-front costs before they execute the first transaction with a customer. In such industries, it is not sufficient to create a new product. Companies must focus on creating new customers. These are Consumer Creators.

The classic example of such a company, dating back more than a hundred years, is Gillette—and its innovation with the disposable razor. The handle for holding the disposable blades is a relatively costly product to develop and produce. To gain broader market acceptance of this new shaving concept, Gillette sold (and still sells) the handles at a substantial loss. By contrast, the blades are sold at high margin, offsetting the initial loss as long as the customer stays loyal and buys enough blades and as long as a generic maker of the blades does not arise. This tactic lets Gillette create new customers.

Other industries that use a consumer creator business model include manufacturers of

- Printers and cartridges (or photocopiers and toner)

- Videogame players and game cartridges

- Cellular phones, often offered free with service

- Reduced-cost personal computers that provide subscription Internet service

The consumer creator archetype contains a major source of risk: the rise of generic makers of the consumables. A consumer creator company must charge a price that is higher than cost for its consumables to recoup the money lost on the initial investment: the razor handle, for instance, or the printer or game player. If another company can provide the same consumable, it will be able to offer the product at a much lower price because it is not defraying the cost of the initial unit. Obviously, consumer creator companies protect themselves from this in a number of ways, including aggressive patent and trademark enforcement (coupled with licensing) or with marketing that suggests that third-party consumables are inferior. Companies like cell phone and free-PC companies also have the option of demanding return of the equipment if the consumer cancels the service. Online trading exchanges are also consumer creators because they create a new nexus in the supply chain, bringing suppliers and customers together.

Archetype: Industry Creators

The most innovative and powerful archetype is that of the Industry Creator—a company whose products and services create entirely new market spaces that did not exist before. Although every major company attracts a small cadre of attendant service and support companies, industry creators distinguish themselves by actively helping these non-customer, non-supplier companies.

Thus, a major element of the industry creator's processes is the support services that help other companies join the nascent industry. Open standards, engineering support, development kits, developer communities, and careful product-change processes all enable outsiders to join the new industry. Industry creators cannot be greedy. They must leave a lot of the money on the table for others. But by creating a new market space and helping others join it, they reap tremendous profits for themselves.

An excellent example is 3Com's Palm Computing division, makers of the Palm Pilot. Among competing handheld computing devices, Palm organizers are neither the smallest nor the fastest on the market; they are not the most feature-packed; they do not have the best handwriting recognition. But Palm has done a good job of fostering third-party add-ons, including hardware (keyboards, wireless modems, printers) and software (productivity applications, vertical market applications, games). Palm could easily have staked out a wider footprint in its market by developing more of these accessories itself, but it didn't.

The result is that Palm significantly increased its market during

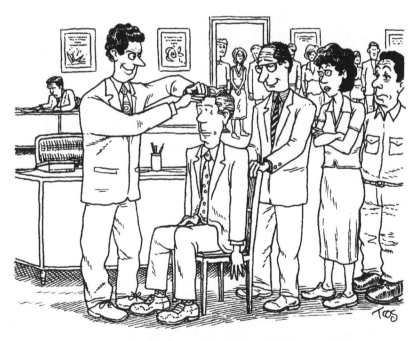

WITH THE VULCAN MIND MELD, BERNIE WAS
ABLE TO UNDERSTAND HIS SUPPLIERS AND CUSTOMERS.

What is to come?

this period, despite the presence of computer-industry behemoth Microsoft (who actually lost market share in handhelds). And the Palm division contributes much more than its fair share to 3Com's profits. As an aside, the Palm phenomenon is also partly due to Motorola, which makes and supports the DragonBall processor chip inside these devices. Supporting both hardware and software developers is both a critical success factor for and a core competence of technology companies like Motorola.

Industry creators walk a fine line between under-profiting from and monopolizing the market spaces that they create. While IBM has certainly under-profited from the PC industry it helped to create, both Microsoft and Intel have been accused of monopolizing the market. Microsoft has angered other software developers by aggressively usurping parts of the functionality created by those third-party developers. Intel has made PC manufacturers nervous by getting into the business of making PC motherboards, which make Intel both a competitor and a supplier to these PC makers.

What Will Your Company Do Next?

How can you masterfully drive your company into the future? Change across industries can be more predictable than many people believe. New technologies evolve, but business follows cycles or patterns that continue to recur. Rather than fall victim to change, any company can map its future and evolve its business model to meet or beat these predictable patterns.

To do so, get a clear grasp of the structural attributes of the business practices of your suppliers and customers. Most change occurs when companies want to avoid pain, and most pain comes from day-to-day irritations. Understand the business archetypes that dominate different industries. Look at all the crevices and chasms across your own industry. That is where dramatic but episodic opportunities lie. Ask yourself:

- What new products and services will we offer?

- What markets will we go after? What customers will we serve?

- What value should we offer to differentiate ourselves?

- What are the new revenue streams for the company?

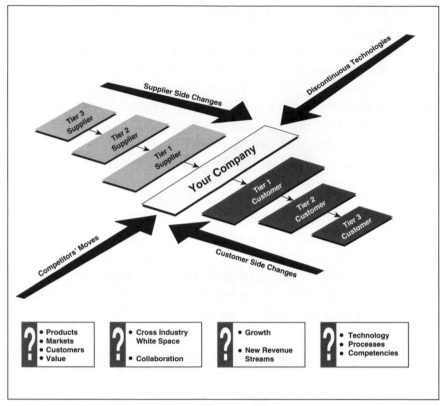

Figure 6-3   Learning to see peripherally

- Who will be our new collaborators and partners?

- What will be the new growth areas?

- What technologies and processes will we adopt and utilize?

- What are the cross-industry white spaces?

- Whom must we acquire and why?

- What will be the new employee competencies?

- What will be the next phase of innovation? What is a full solution in our industry?

- Who will be our new competitors?

The answers to these questions will not be found solely by management or articulated in a meaningless corporate mission and vision. Rather, the answers must be drawn from and understood by everyone in the company—from front-line factory workers to customer service representatives and all the way up to the boardroom. Only then can companies respond to market needs and the imperatives of change in a unified effort.

In addressing all these questions, corporations must find the means and will to unleash their collective creativity. And that brings me to the final chapter: a review of the opportunities and the techniques for unleashing human creativity and the imagination within the confines of your company's operations.

What IS on the Inside?

Unleashing Corporate Creativity

Creativity is the ability to look at the world through a kaleidoscope of possibilities where none existed before. A creative act fuses originality, courage, passion, and artistry, thereby transcending the ordinary. The real winners of the future will be those who continuously create, recognize, and implement new concepts, applying them to ever-changing business situations. Ask yourself: How close is your company to creating the next e-commerce/supply chain strategy breakthrough? The following one? The one after that?

Why a Mandate for Creativity

Creativity and innovation are essential in a world driven by change. New competitors and new business models require new strategies and new tactics. The proliferation of products and services, markets, and customers (not to mention the sheer rate of change in the global business climate) demands a new paradigm, one that establishes creativity as a core corporate function, like accounting, marketing, and shipping.

Humanity is moving from the Internet to the "innernet," tapping into our innate abilities and dormant creative energy. In this century, self-expression and creative contribution will underscore corporate success more than ever.

In the past, companies paid lip service to creativity; they did not regard it as a mainstream function and prime activity of a corporation. In fact, most current corporate processes still stifle the generation and promotion of valuable new ideas. Many companies fail to realize that having creative thinkers and creative products in the marketplace is critical to survival.

The Impact of Creativity

Low corporate creativity is a degenerative disease; it does not kill outright but cripples its victims until they lack the strength to succeed. The symptoms include diminishing numbers of new customers (sales only to existing customers), lackluster product launches, an anemic company atmosphere in which people just bide their time, and loss of valuable employees to higher-risk startups. Victims of this disease slip from positions of market leadership into a gradual decline of market share, sagging margins, and plummeting stock price.

One challenge to recognizing the warning signs is that business momentum masks the onset of low creativity—the healthy glow of market dominance hides the company's basic weakness. There is often a lag before customers and industry analysts recognize that a former top-rated organization has slipped from the ranks of the innovative. Competitors are emboldened by the former leader's decline. Stockholders express their dismay by studying other investments. Loyal customers and dependent suppliers wring their hands and wonder about the company's future. Eventually, however, they too abandon the dying firm. Moreover, reversing the downward spiral is hard when an entire company has degenerated into risk-averse costcutters who lack creativity. The prognosis is not hopeful.

Creativity is more than just devising some clever ideas; it is also the basis for retaining the best and brightest employees. Why do top-flight executives consistently leave leading companies to join high-risk endeavors? Employee loyalty is often directly related to how people's creative energies are tapped, challenged, and rewarded. People stagnate without change. Productivity, loyalty, and industriousness are the direct outcome of the way people are treated, whether they are given opportunities to move forward, and how their creativity is rewarded.

The penalties for low creativity are intensifying. Today's accelerating competitive environment offers less time for resting on one's laurels. Remember how quickly Netscape rose and fell as a market darling in the browser market. One fundamental reason that companies will fail in the 21st century is lack of innovation. Approaches that were effective even ten years ago are anachronistic today.

Human potential is the ultimate form of energy, and harnessing it offers the ultimate competitive advantage. How a firm uses the potential of its contacts (employees, suppliers, and customers) will determine its long-term success. People have the potential for great innovation, if only they can work creatively to release it.

How does creativity change a company? A creative company is a competitive company. Corporate *rigor mortis*—fear, uncertainty, and doubt—arises from the lack of free, creative ideas being produced, managed, and manipulated to solve pressing business problems. Creativity improves a company's ability both to accept and to drive change in industry.

The Scope of Creative Endeavor

One thing that's crucial to the success of creative companies is that creativity is not defined as belonging strictly to one area. Creativity is not useful just for research and development or marketing. Creativity certainly drives traditionally idea-intensive areas such as marketing and product development, but it also propels manufacturing, finance, and shipping. Creativity is a corporate asset, so companies must learn to recognize and nurture it. They must consciously foster innovation and imagination.

Consider accounting. Although "creative accounting" is usually frowned upon, a legitimate accounting system benefits from creativity. Companies can innovate in how they create a transparent and auditable accounting trail, how they collect and manage account transactions, and how they use this data to provide leverage for driving intelligent business decisions. For example, Dell Computer reduced its capital requirements for inventory to less than zero by creatively timing different accounting routines. Dell is now paid for the computers it sells five days before it has to pay for the parts in those computers. The accounting categories and calculations may be regulated, but the use of data to drive cost and revenue improvements is open territory for creativity.

Even the invention of activity-based management was creative.

Once all the possible avenues for cost were identified, the process of controlling costs followed in natural sequence. Although general audit and accounting procedures (GAAP) and accounting fundamentals (such as debits, balances, and credits) will not change, innovation will spring from how accountants and managers capture and control costs.

The Basics of Creativity

The first step in attracting and fostering people who generate ideas is to understand how creativity and the human brain work. Then a business can implement initiatives, incentives, and infrastructures to encourage innovation. The second step is to optimize how creativity is used in the organization. Systematically directing human creativity and devising a creative culture enable a firm to go into uncharted territories, areas with unexplored regions and the opportunity to reap profits as yet unrealized. Creativity redefines boundaries for exploration.

The Internal Mental Layout of the Human Brain

Most researchers agree that the brain has four quadrants, which are roughly established by a left-right split and a cerebral-limbic

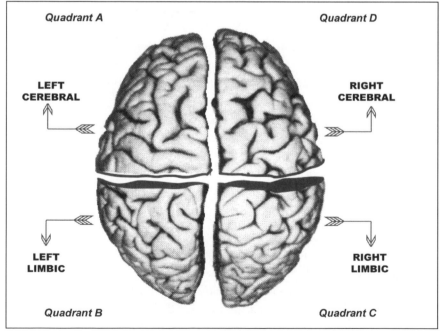

Quadrant A   **Quadrant D**

LEFT CEREBRAL   **RIGHT CEREBRAL**

LEFT LIMBIC   **RIGHT LIMBIC**

Quadrant B   **Quadrant C**

Figure 7-1 The quadrants of the human brain

split. It is suggested that each quadrant corresponds to a dominant style for mentally processing and working with ideas on the part of every human being.

The four quadrants and their defining characteristic styles can be summarized as follows:

- *Left-cerebral*—a preference for hard facts and analytical clarity

- *Left-limbic*—a preference for clear procedures and well-defined organization

- *Right-limbic*—a preference for emotional connections and human potential

- *Right-cerebral*—a preference for future-oriented visions and imaginative exploration

Right-Brain and Left-Brain Styles

The easiest way to understand the difference between the right and left sectors of the brain is to remember that dominance of the left-brain is marked by a preference for sharp, yet narrow, facts. In contrast, right-brain dominance results in a preference for broad, less-defined concepts. The stereotypical "left-brain person" is analytical and detail-oriented. He or she prefers concrete facts, logical deduction, and meticulous procedures over imaginative thinking. As employees, people with left-brain dominance get things done, but they may not question whether what they are doing is the correct thing to do or the best way to do it.

By contrast, the stereotypical "right-brain person" is more conceptual and is oriented toward the big picture. He or she prefers expressive metaphors and affective experiences. As employees, people with right-brain dominance may not stay exactly on task, but they are likely to devise interesting new ideas.

Including right- and left-brained people in the same team can offer checks and balances that stimulate the flow of ideas but provide necessary confines. It can also give rise to problems, however, if people are not aware of each other's thinking styles. To left-brain people, right-brain thinking may appear too emotional and impractical to be useful. To right-brain people, left-brain thinking may seem rigid and boring. Both styles are creative and productive in different spheres of activity. Whereas left-brain thinkers can logically combine and refine creative concepts, right-brainers can intuitively envision new vistas and possibilities.

Cerebral-Limbic Styles

The brain is more than just the two hemispheres that define the left-brain/right-brain divisions. The second major division that predicts brain preferences appears to be the central limbic axis, dividing the upper and lower regions of the brain.

The cerebral-limbic brain sector essentially divides regions of the brain into thinking and doing areas. The disparity between cerebral and limbic thinking styles can sometimes be as great as that between left- and right-brain thinking styles. The cerebral style is analytical, favoring the application of thought processes. The limbic style is more visceral, favoring action. People whose style is predominantly cerebral may regard limbic-style thinkers as too quick to spring into action without considering the whole situation first. By contrast, limbic-style people may see cerebral-style thinkers as too abstract in their thinking and not pragmatic enough. The creative contributions of cerebral and limbic brain styles are markedly different but equally beneficial to business.

Mr. Spock, of Star Trek fame, personifies Quadrant A, the left-cerebral style of employing logical processes to reason through problems. Being grounded in objective facts helps left-cerebral-style thinkers dispassionately dispose of sacred cows if they see the cows as having outlived their utility. The creative output from left-cerebral employees is defined by relentless linear deduction and precise logic, not visionary insight. This thinking style is not well suited to interpersonal problem solving, however, because the cold logic used to drive the solution focuses on the practical, not the emotional or human, impact of the decision.

The left-limbic style typifying Quadrant B is embodied by the stereotypical bureaucrat—who values clear procedures and well-defined organization and who relentlessly follows strict rules and procedures. Left-limbic employees emphasize efficient control and do not solicit other opinions, encourage change, and take human emotion into consideration to any great extent. Established order is most important to left-limbic-dominated people. Although this style is not essentially associated with creativity, the drive to organize and control efficiently can work wonders at distilling order out of chaos. The positive side of rigidity is a dependable stability that gets things done.

The right-limbic style, Quadrant C, is embodied by the people who connect emotionally and intuitively with those around them. These people are grounded in reality, although it is a reality of emotion and human energy that sometimes fails to be guided by logic and fact. Right-limbic-dominated people can be very innovative because they are the first to catch the subtle shifts in emotional energy that precede more objective changes in a group of people (such as customers). Their lack of interest in objective requirements and confidence in emotional realities, however, can frustrate left-brain-dominated people.

Quadrant D, the Right-Cerebral Style, is exemplified by future-oriented people—those who have vision and who value imaginative exploration. A love of excitement and experience prompts these people to seek out interesting ideas, although right-cerebral thinkers may not attend to all of the details. Employees characterized by the right-cerebral style can be extremely creative but may seem ungrounded. Although good at creating a vision, they may not pursue any single vision to its end or be able to implement their ideas without the help of people with left-limbic styles. The founders of many high-technology companies embody this style.

Each of the foregoing quadrants has a set of associated skills. Understanding the strengths that people from each quadrant possess helps companies direct them to apply their creativity effectively. Forming patterns, making productive analogies, visualizing abstract ideas, producing physical models, kinesthetic thinking, aesthetics, play-acting, role-playing, manipulative skill (hand-eye coordination), playing, and experimenting—all these have roles in generating imaginative ideas.

Combinations of Styles

Most people display a combination of styles, with one or two styles perhaps predominating and elements of the others less evident. Often, a person's thinking style is defined not so much by a conscious preference for one but by a subtle discomfort or disconnection with the extreme opposite.

To understand how styles combine, consider two examples from different professions. An engineering manager may possess both the left-cerebral skills for analytically developing engineering designs and the left-limbic style for efficiently executing big projects according to plan. But the engineering manager may—and should—also exhibit a little of the right-limbic style that helps him or her relate with consideration to employees and clients. A sales manager, on the other hand, may reside mainly in the right-brain stylistic camp, envisioning exciting new pitches that inspire salespeople and customers alike. At the same time, a little left-limbic skill ensures that the manager can effectively supply the monthly numbers that are sent to corporate headquarters.

Stylistic issues drive creativity in two ways. First, different brain styles can tap into different types of innovation; and, second, enhancing the brain styles of everyone in the corporation will make the company more broadly creative. The point is that people possess a mixture of styles that can help them function effectively in modern organizations.

The External Interface to the Brain

Of course, the brain does not operate in isolation. It has a connection to the world, and that connection affects creativity. Just as people have different internal modes of thinking, so do they have different modes of interacting with others and the outside world. The three principal stylistic modes of interacting are visual, auditory, and kinesthetic. These modes affect how a person filters information and communicates it. The style of interaction even affects internal processing and thinking styles. Everyone uses all of these modes, but we are usually more comfortable with some than with others.

The Visual-Interaction Mode

For those who interact best through visual means, ideas are images, and images are ideas. Other people may find a visual thinker's images intricate, confusing, or abstract. The good news is that often the visual thinker's pictures really are worth a thousand words. A visually oriented person will choose a picture over words every time.

The combination of the four internal thinking styles with the visual style of interacting reveals itself in the content of graphics. Left-brain thinkers will select images such as engineering drawings, organization charts, or spreadsheet graphs—factual images tied to a controlled, concrete reality. Right-brain thinkers will opt for more abstract, stylistic images, and right-limbic thinkers will make people or emotional tone the focus of their images.

The Auditory-Interaction Mode

Did you hear these words as you read them? The world of the auditory person is one of sounds and language, especially spoken language. Auditory people hear the words even if they are reading them. Of the three styles of interacting, auditory people are the most comfortable with language, but they prefer speaking to writing and prefer listening to reading. Others may find the auditory person's use of language too complex or too verbose. On the positive side, however, auditory people can often inspire with their writing or entertain in their speeches.

The four internal thinking styles drive what an auditory person prefers to listen to or to create. For example, the left-brain thinker looks for logic, precision, and order in sounds, be they the words of a speaker or the melody of the music. By contrast, a right-brain person might enjoy a flowery turn of phrase or connect to the emotions aroused by music.

The Kinesthetic-Interaction Mode

How can someone learn anything when nailed to a chair? Kinesthetic people use motion and physical activity to learn by doing. They are keenly aware of physical locations, physical orientation, and physical movements. For example, aerobatic pilots rehearse their stunts by moving their hands and contorting their bodies through the sequence of orientations through which they intend to put their airplane. People of other styles may think that kinesthetic people are merely restless, fidgety people who cannot pay attention. On the positive side, such thinkers demonstrate energy and vitality.

Again, the four styles of internal thinking can combine with the kinesthetic style of interaction, although the kinesthetic style usually correlates with the physically oriented limbic styles of thinking. A left-brain kinesthetic person (especially a left-limbic thinker) uses controlled and repetitive motion to instill logical order (such as typing commands to control a computer or practicing to perfect a good golf swing). A right-brain kinesthetic person (especially a right-limbic thinker) uses body posture to connote emotional energy (such as in dance).

Assembling a Balanced Mix of Styles

What do these styles mean for you as an executive and for your organization? Mental styles, both of thinking and interacting, are of more than academic importance. Differences in style cause miscommunication almost as great as that caused by people's speaking different languages. Worse, these styles are so embedded that most people do not recognize their own styles or the styles of others. The result is confusion as people grope for meaning.

The keys to successful teamwork are matching the styles to the tasks and ensuring members' stylistic compatibility (or at least stylistic awareness). Individuals and corporations also must enhance their brain styles to strive for greater balance, using a richer array of styles to solve tough business problems.

For individuals, the issue of brain styles drives career choices, defining which jobs and companies may be best for them. If brain styles are like languages, finding out about the styles associated with potential career choices is like finding out about the languages spoken at potential vacation spots. For companies, the style issues are crucial for hiring, assigning team members, and making job assignments.

Whether you are looking at the style issue as an individual or for a corporation, there are three steps to success:

- Identification of the styles of people, activities, and teams helps people understand each other.

- Alignment of styles among people, activities, and teams helps people work more efficiently together.

- Enhancement of styles of people, activities, and teams helps people perform better.

People process learning, express themselves, and absorb knowledge differently. Companies must uncover that knowledge and apply it in the way they train people and benefit from their talent.

Identification: Who has What Style?

Before an enterprise can avail itself of employees' creativity, it must understand the personal styles of particular people, activities, and teams in the workplace. Individuals and companies can identify employees' underlying thinking styles for short-term company efficiency and long-term performance.

We can identify brain-dominance styles formally, through carefully scored and professionally validated tests that may determine mental styles, or informally, through casual comparison of people or activities to the list of characteristics of each style. A formal program for identification of employees' personal styles might include creating a database of their stylistic-preference scores. Remember, these tests are not judgmental; there are no good or bad scores.

And basic styles aren't obvious. We are often misled by people's superficial characteristics. The vagaries of career choices result in people's thinking styles not always meshing with their credentials, educational background, job histories, or outward appearances. For example, each of two people might have an MBA in marketing and have similarly impressive progressions of job positions on their résumés, but might differ widely in their respective thinking styles. The first person might have an amazing knack for analyzing marketing data and spotting the trends before the competition does. The second person might be uninterested in numbers but remarkable at translating dry technical specifications into inspiring campaigns that sell products. Both people could be achieving impressive marketing results but in utterly different ways. Identifying these different characteristics should stress looking beneath the surface without being intrusive.

Moreover, an identification process can be used for more than just categorizing people, activities, or teams because it also fosters awareness. When people learn about their own thinking styles and those of others, they become more attuned to stylistic differences. As a result, identification starts the crucial second step of complementing mental styles—blending styles cooperatively by avoiding mismatches.

Alignment: Which Style is Needed Where?

Once everyone knows his or her thinking style, roles and team assignments can be adjusted to accommodate the styles. Activities can be arranged to take advantage of the stylistic variations. Not every style is equally productive in every situation. Just as a specific manufacturing method can efficiently produce certain types of products, so can each specific thinking style efficiently produce different types of creativity. Nonetheless, it is critical to bear in mind that stylistic inclinations are not a single reflection of an individual's potential. Research has shown that most human beings use only three percent of their innate brain potential. Human beings are incredibly versatile, and an inclination toward one particular style should not be construed as an inability to adapt or excel in others.

For example, a person might be very articulate, know five languages, have years of industry experience, and be an energetic, persuasive speaker. He or she might combine the best of left-cerebral thinking (coherent chains of reasoning) and right-cerebral thinking (good conceptual vision) with the ability to listen well. Yet this same intelligent business professional might be ineffectual in supervising a small work group. The failure would not be attributable to inexperience or incompetence but to thinking-style misalignment—for example, little emotional connection with colleagues (limbic-right-brain thinking) or little interest in establishing routine procedures (limbic-left-brain thinking) or difficulty communicating with the visual thinkers in the work group. The point is that people's thinking styles should be well matched to their workplace roles. Two types of alignment are needed for successful matches.

Intrinsic alignment relates directly to the work, aligning each person with the nature of the role and duties to be assumed. If a task requires analytical problem solving or conceptual diagramming or perceptive "people" skills, look for a job candidate who has a natural predisposition for those tasks. Intrinsic alignment is usually associated with a stylistic match of thinking skills, but interaction styles are also important (for example, an engineer with good visualization skills for new product designs or a call-center representative with an auditory style of interacting). Intrinsic alignment is most important for aligning employees to job functions inside an organization.

Relative alignment is the type of alignment that each person should have to the people with whom he or she interacts. Often, instead of communicating with one another, people end up communicating past one another, so one team member does not understand what the others are talking about. In many instances, the exact style is less important than ensuring that everyone is comfortable with the style—hence the name *relative* alignment.

Alignment plays two roles in increasing creativity and innovation in a corporation. Intrinsic alignment helps correlate the creative style of people with the problems they face in daily activities. The result is catalytic creativity. Relative alignment increases the transfer of creative ideas throughout the organization. It also helps reduce the miscommunication that can halt a good idea in its tracks and stifle future good ideas.

As with the identification activities, alignment can be implemented on a formal or an informal basis. An informal program might mean nothing more than an occasional get-together to talk over the issue of proper alignment. A formal program might result in creating a database that records the thinking styles of relevant constituents, be they people, activities, or departments. The same database techniques that permit delving into sales figures can facilitate studies of thinking-style patterns in an organization.

Identification and alignment, although helpful, do not solve every problem associated with differences in thinking styles. What companies need are ways to engage stylistically dissimilar people in working cooperatively. To achieve the next level of performance, leadership must begin enhancing employees' thinking styles by creating a better balance of styles to cope with a complex world that demands interaction.

Identification and alignment lay the groundwork for a third step: initiating actions that break down the nearly invisible mental walls between people.

Enhancement: The Drive for Balance

The Industrial Revolution, the rise of high-tech industries, and the recent emphasis on operational efficiency have created a great brain imbalance in today's corporations. Left-brain "number-crunchers" and process followers have inundated organizations with efficiency and productivity, but they have wrung out much of the creative vision needed for future competitiveness. The future era of mass customization, supply chain collaboration, and the "innernet" dictates greater emphasis on exploration and intuitiveness. Although

Headlong into trouble

left-brain thinkers have succeeded at creating organizations that can work efficiently, these organizations will need an increase in right-brain thinking to perform better.

Business schools have not been successful in integrating left-brain and right-brain thinking. In fact, according to some, MBA could stand for "My brain's asymmetric." Business schools reinforce the dominance of the left brain by emphasizing verbal and deductive subjects. Right-brain areas—such as music, art, and fantasy—are ignored. The result is a lack of originality and a stifling of the creative spirit.

Consider an invention such as Sun Microsystems' Java programming language. On one hand, as a programming language, it epitomizes the logical-procedural left-brain thinking style. On the other hand, as a purposefully created new paradigm in information technology, it embodies the result of generalized, right-brain thinking. The notion of advancing the ubiquitous Web browser and adding platform-independent access to software was a stroke of genius, endangering Sun's biggest rival, Microsoft. Concepts and products such as Java, which represent a combination of left-brain and right-brain originality, are the future of business. Without right-brain conceptualization, efficiency will not matter because a business cannot survive.

"So," says the corporate executive, "how can my company stylistically enhance itself?" I submit that the process of expanding one's personal stylistic horizons passes through four levels:

- *Awareness:* learning about the different styles of thinking and interacting

- *Appreciation:* learning to accept different styles

- *Apprenticeship:* practicing new styles of thinking and interacting

- *Mastery:* adopting new styles of thinking and interacting

Organizations can enhance themselves stylistically by expanding the range and repertoire of every employee. Broadening the stylistic horizons of each person increases both individual ingenuity and the flow of ideas among people. All employees become more creative because each style they encounter adds new tools to their own intrinsic creativity. Expanding perspective enables people who previously did not communicate well to share more and understand each other better.

Some people inevitably remain inflexibly attached to a single style. Sometimes it is hard to motivate people to adapt, and they may be unappreciative of the styles of others. At the same time, these people (such as a company's chief design engineer and best field sales representative) may be extraordinarily good at their particular specialties. Using "translators" for such employees—that is, multistylistic intermediaries who help connect these experts to the rest of the organization and to other companies in the supply chain—will be useful. Although not ideal, this tactic balances the need to boost creativity with the need to retain functional specialists.

But a company must make the best use of its most balanced, multistylistic people. If there are only a few such people in your organization, they can be assigned particular roles, as they are especially good at bridging gaps among people whose thinking styles differ. These employees make excellent liaisons, managers of multifunctional teams, mediators, and CEOs.

Stimulating Creativity

How can people and companies systematically increase their creativity and innovation? Creativity is more than a "Eureka!" experience, a serendipitous solution, or a mere accident. Creativity is "manufacturing" valuable originality. The innovation may be artistic, as in introducing music to calm or inspire, or viewing a painting on aesthetic grounds, but it can also be a new business model that is valued for its return-on-investment. From the perspective of fostering valuable originality, some companies and individuals have superior skills in manufacturing productivity and efficiency—they consistently and quickly produce valuable solutions to vexing problems.

Although there is no reproducible recipe for perfect creativity every time, there are many methods that can tip the odds in your favor. The following methods in essence draw on actions that stimulate creative thinking.

Encouraging Imaginative Combinations

Most creative ideas are not completely new. Rather, they arise from clever, unusual combinations or reconfigurations of existing ideas. E-commerce business models are an excellent example of combining existing business practices (auctions, markets, shopping baskets, catalogs) with newly introduced Internet-information architecture. Creating novel combinations, for e-commerce as an example, is more than just appending one idea to another (such as the tiresome practice of inserting an *e-* before the name of every business activity). Truly clever combinations interweave existing ideas to transform them into something new.

Revealing Perspectives on Problems

Many creative solutions arise from a reformalization of the problem, constraints, or possibilities. The goal of such a method is to look at the problem from a different direction. Seen in a different light, some facet of a problem may fall by the wayside or reveal the kernel of an innovative solution.

Increasing Knowledge and Experience

Systematically creative people are not suddenly, magically inspired with amazing ideas. Such people immerse themselves in their fields of expertise as well as other areas that offer them new perspectives. Alexander Fleming, who discovered penicillin, represents someone who immersed himself in his field. The story commonly recounted is that Fleming "accidentally" discovered penicillin when bacteria landed in one of his Petri dishes. What is interesting is that this chance event had occurred to three other biologists before Fleming—one of them none other than Louis Pasteur. Although each of these scientists recorded the event in his lab journal, none of them followed up on it to discover penicillin's antibacterial properties. Why not? They did not have the knowledge to realize what had happened. Fleming had that knowledge, and one reason was his deep experience with all kinds of bacteria and germs. In fact, one of Fleming's hobbies was to make "germ paintings." In a Petri dish, he created with different-colored molds as his "paints" and painted scenes such as his house, a ballerina, and a mother feeding a baby.

Amazingly, in order to create these works, Fleming had to grow the bacteria. That is, he did not simply arrange colored bacteria artistically. Rather, he began with swipes of colorless bacteria and literally grew the paintings. To do this, he had to learn which bacteria produce each color and under what conditions. He conducted experiments to learn how fast the bacteria grew, whether two or more bacteria would grow in the same medium, and whether they would interfere with one another. Imagine the tremendous amount of knowledge about bacteria that Fleming had to accumulate in order to create these germ paintings! In short, people who actively seek knowledge and experience see more options, understand more implications, and become more creative. This facet of creativity is not just an intelligence issue; even a genius like Pasteur can fail to see alternatives, without sufficient experience or data.

Soliciting Alternatives

Creativity is also more than just the springing into existence of perfect, fully formed ideas. The Wright brothers performed meticulously documented experiments to solve crucial design problems (wing shape, propulsion, controllability) to "invent" the airplane. These days, businesses can use modeling and simulation technologies to validate and fine-tune inventive business strategies.

The old saw about necessity's being the mother of invention contains an element of truth. Encouraging the creation and application of new ideas is a prerequisite for real creativity in organization. Too often employees are not rewarded for creative ideas; worse, they are punished for the impertinence of questioning tradition.

The Repertoire of Creative Techniques

Following are fifteen techniques for encouraging creativity that can be applied individually and company-wide.

Technique 1: ABCD—Establishing an All-Out Business Creativity Day

The cornerstone of boosting creativity in any corporation is providing an immersion in creative experience—it can be dubbed ABCD, an All-Out Business Creativity Day. ABCD takes people away from their offices, energizes them through ideas, and encourages them to speak freely about the company, their colleagues, processes, policies, procedures, activities, customers, and suppliers.

For ABCD to succeed, it is crucial for companies to create an atmosphere of safety, to reassure employees unequivocally that their participation and frank airing of issues will not be exploited or directed against them at any future time. Such a gesture will not only pave the way for mature participation but also, by default, foster an open, constructively communicative culture within the organization. This endeavor will

- Drag nagging organizational problems to the surface
- Allow teams to co-create and share solutions and best practices
- Transfer knowledge to and from all corners of the organization
- Allow people from all levels of the organization to meet

Where should the company take people for an ABCD? Rule one for the venue is that people meet away from the workplace—at a neutral location with few distractions. Disconnection from everyday life helps employees to step outside the minutiae of the work world. Only then can people step back to look at some of the bigger issues in the organization. Chastise anybody whose cellular phone interrupts the event!

Whom should the company invite? Cross-fertilization of ideas cannot occur if the invited (or mandated) group is too parochial. People from a wide range of professions, departments, geographic locations, and management levels must participate. Regardless of who is invited, all must be encouraged—even required—to participate and submit ideas.

The ABCD concept can be used with suppliers and customers to encourage the same sort of creative knowledg sharing and problem solving. The challenges, though, are greater than with an internal ABCD. First, the company must establish sufficient trust with these external participants. If customers or suppliers suspect that the event is the means for establishing a negotiating advantage, it will not work. The goal should be a candid exchange regarding problems and solutions.

But ABCD will not work without a high degree of commitment. Nothing is worse than lip service; it breeds cynicism and resentment. If you, as the organizer of the event, invite people to talk about problems and come up with solutions but then do not implement the ideas, you doom future efforts at innovation. Instead, the best way to make ABCD efforts productive is to request that each participant contribute at least five ideas. Use multisensory language and multisensory engagement. Bring a gross of crayons and let people draw to express their ideas.

How valuable can these crayons be? Hal Rosenbluth, founder of

Rosenbluth Travel, randomly selects 100 employees every six months to receive paper and crayons. He asks them to draw a picture of what Rosenbluth Travel means to them and how they would like to represent the company. People are not asked to sign their names, but most do. "I learn so much from these drawings," Rosenbluth said. For example, one employee pictured his career as a man climbing steps leading to heaven, but he had a computer shackled to his leg. "I called this person and asked, "What's going on?'" Rosenbluth said. The employee explained that response time on the company's computers was terrible and that the company could not move forward unless the response time improved. Investigating the problem, Rosenbluth found a telephone communication-line problem and quickly remedied it.

What if everyone cannot get together at one time? A very large global (7-day, 24-hour) organization, may not permit getting everyone together at the same time in the same place. Instead, you may use "rolling" ABCDs to bring together overlapping groups of people. If groups span the organization, the event can achieve an acceptable transfer of knowledge, and employees can discuss problems and solutions. If each person attends two or three

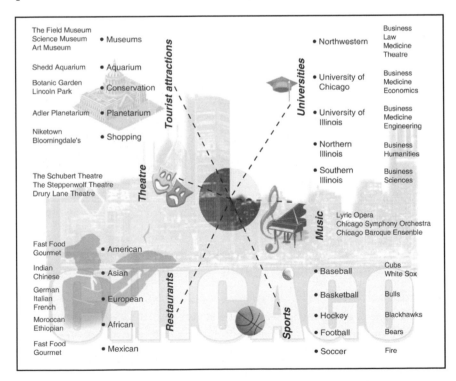

Figure 7-2   Mind map: arts, learning, & entertainment in Chicago

ABCDs with people from other spheres of the company, the transfer of knowledge is multiplied, and additional creative ideas saturate the organization. It is important to make the group as representative of the organization as possible, however. If one department or location sends too many members, they will dominate the ABCD, creating imbalance and discouraging the participation of others.

The ABCD technique is so powerful, yet so easy to implement, that it should be standard operating procedure for all companies.

Technique 2: Mind-Mapping

Mind-mapping is creating a type of drawing that expresses all the concepts and language surrounding a topic. The topic can be personal goals, a company's future, a specific problem, or another issue. Lines, small iconic pictures, and words or phrases convey information on the topic of interest.

Like drawing, mind-mapping enables one to express and remember complex concepts. Mind maps can be more effective than freer-form drawings because the "rules" for mind-mapping eliminate some of the ambiguity of the lines in free-form art. Mind-mapping permits more exploration than simple drawing does because a mind map can be progressively built and indefinitely enhanced. One team at Boeing created a 25-foot-wide mind map to explore the cause of the company's manufacturing problems.

Mind-mapping can be done by individuals, although it is an excellent team technique for engendering creativity. The radiating structure of the mind map allows each member of the team to add his or her own thoughts. Team members can easily add original ideas, start new branches of the map, or express alternative viewpoints through it.

A few tips, though, will help the mind-mapping process. Mind-mapping is not intended to be some grueling exercise or bureaucratic process, but a technique that helps get what people know onto paper to reveal the connections that may have been missed earlier. Consider the following tips for successful mind-mapping:

- Work in short bursts—five- to seven-minute explosions of creativity.

- Avoid the obstacle of judgment. Get it all down first; filter ideas later.

- Give yourself room. Use a big sheet of paper so that ideas will not be cramped.

- Start in the center and work out, not from right to left and not from the top down.

- Keep moving. Keep ideas flowing by free-associating, changing colors, or skipping to different parts of the map.

- Allow the organization to emerge. If things connect, great; if they do not, just keep going.

- Mind-map frequently. The more you exercise this technique, the more helpful the mind maps will become.

Color is vital for mind-mapping, and you can use it in two ways. First, color can simply enliven a mind map. Branches may be assigned different colors just to make them stand out. A color map can be easier to interpret than a black and white one. Second, the mind map can also incorporate meaningful color coding. Each color may represent an option under consideration, a good or bad connotation, a different time frame, a different responsible party, or any other factor. Just add a legend in a corner of the map to indicate what the colors signify. A color-coding scheme permits creating and perceiving new patterns in a mind map.

Mind maps help companies navigate tough problems, reach consensus, and communicate ideas. As a routine work tool, a mind map aids in identifying and organizing the issues surrounding business problems. The process encourages all members of a group to contribute and to consider the perspectives of others. Mind maps can serve as a reference point for preparing policies, procedures, memos, reports, and presentations. As a communications tool, a mind map shows participants the rationale behind conclusions.

Learning the system can move progressive companies ahead of the competition. The human brain stores ideas in the form of mind maps, so acquisition of the technique can become a valuable life skill.

Technique 3: Increasing People-to-People Connections
To improve the creation and spread of innovative ideas, companies can mix people together in new combinations. Studies of corporations have shown that employees rarely stray far from their offices. Co-workers have little contact with others who are more

than 50 feet away, to say nothing of co-workers on other floors of their building. These seemingly natural patterns of connection are really barriers to creativity. Randomizing your company's patterns of connection will create more interaction and more cross-fertilization.

For example, when Mobil Corporation had a major restructuring, all of its outdated collegial networks were broken by the move. Before the restructuring, little new knowledge permeated the shell of the corporation because people always called the same person to help deal with the same business problems (thereby acquiring no fresh perspectives). Worse, other people who should have been involved were left out of the loop. After the restructuring, however, everyone was assigned new duties and so could not rely only on the established patterns. Mobil created a corporate yellow-pages database in its groupware system to help employees find and communicate with one another. Online discussion databases and e-mail lists connected more people both to the experts that they needed to talk with and to the knowledge that enabled them to work effectively.

Mixing people, via ABCDs, job rotations, multiple team assignments, or physical rearrangement of offices will improve the knowledge flow in your organization. People will be exposed to new facets of the business, conceive of new solutions, and perceive new problems that they can help to solve. Encouraging cross-boundary communication and using online infrastructures help connect members of a far-flung global organization. Addressing many of the toughest business problems is like solving a jigsaw puzzle of which each person has only a few pieces. Bringing more people together will assemble all the pieces to complete the view of these business problems. Make random mixing of people a common function in your organization.

Obviously, the past must not be sacrificed on the altar of the present—or even of the future! In the rush to foster new approaches, everyone must take care not to alienate the people who can prove to be one's most valuable allies—those with experience. Channels of communication that took years to build must not be discounted as means for accelerating progress. In fact, such channels can serve as a foundation for creativity. Enthusiasm for the new is intended neither to negate the tried and true nor to disrupt what works. The goal here is, simply, not to be trammeled by tradition or bound entirely by the past. It is to expand established connections, not to replace them.

The brain, we now know, can at every age produce new synapses by continuing to challenge itself. So can the corporation regenerate itself by constantly applying its resources to new situations. Drawing from several areas and levels of expertise for specific project assignments can be a productive means of forging new connections and encouraging creativity without threatening those who have settled comfortably into a routine. In fact, enlisting the cooperation of those with invaluable experience is essential to innovation. Once new alliances have been formed on a project-by-project basis, the dreaded R word, "reorganization," will have lost its power to diminish morale. Restructuring will already have taken place—painlessly—and with a concomitant spirit of excitement about a joint endeavor.

Technique 4: Eliminating Assumptions

In fast-moving global business, the "self-evident" premises that seem true (but may not be) can prevent recognition of unique solutions to business problems. Many assumptions have long been accepted without question. Although assumptions can save time, and no one could function without them, they can also be limiting. Employees may follow "rules" that no longer apply or "recognize" something as a familiar pattern when in fact it breaks the mold.

When employees perceive a problem, they are not just seeing facts but are also interpreting them, and an interpretation is always subjective, reflecting the viewer's assumptions. Facts never actually speak for themselves, regardless of how "obvious" they appear. For example, the statement "The temperature is 50 degrees" to an Alaskan means it's hot; to a Hawaiian, it means it's cold. Inside a building, 50 degrees is usually considered cold, except in a warehouse for frozen foods. And these judgments say nothing about the assumption that the temperature referred to may be 50 degrees Fahrenheit or 50 degrees Celsius. "It's 50 degrees" may be a fact, but the statement does not tell us much by itself. Here are some examples of other common assumptions:

- "Examine both sides" assumes that there are only two sides and no other options.

- "You can't have your cake and eat it too" assumes that what you create and sell to others you cannot retain for yourself.

- "Get back to basics" assumes that old ways are always best and that problems invariably stem from change. This view ignores the fact that conditions may have changed and that what worked in the past may work no longer.

There is another class of assumptions to which we fall prey: those that we make about ourselves and our capabilities. Consider, for example, statements such as "I'm not creative," "I can't sell," or "My company can't change quickly." If such assumptions are never challenged, they might as well be true! As Henry Ford said, "Whether you believe you can do it or whether you believe you can't do it, you're right." That's the self-fulfilling prophecy of assumptions.

Sometimes our assumptions block our ability to see new ideas. Then a problem may seem impossible to solve because certain views are accepted as inviolable truths, believed so fundamental that they are never questioned. Once you become aware that they are assumptions and that you can question them, however, you will have new leverage points.

The first step to eliminating such assumptions is to become aware of our own; only this awareness can enable us to change assumptions that cannot be supported by the evidence. Here are some steps to identifying assumptions:

1. Think of a specific situation or problem about which you would like to obtain creative ideas.

2. Write down the problem you want to solve or the goal you want to achieve. "My problem or goal is that

   _____."

3. Now, disregard rules and reality for a while and fill in: "If I could break all the laws of reality (physical as well as social), I could solve the problem by _____, or "What I would really like to do is _____." (The purpose here is to articulate your wish, because the wish is a possible solution or approach to a solution.)

4. Once you express your wish, you can search for ways to make it possible since it gives you some elements with which to work. So work with it. Examine your answer to the last question and write the following: "I can't have my wish because _____." Your answer is your

constraint. It is probably an assumption—or at least a point of entry to the problem.

5. The next step is to question the constraint: Is it true? Do you have proof that it is true? "My proof is
_____." Then ask yourself: Are you satisfied with this proof? Is it enough to convince you?

At this point, you may be feeling either uneasy or liberated—uneasy because you've questioned something that you thought true, or liberated if you see a solution. To question assumptions can be disorienting; it is as if gravity suddenly disappeared. A new way of thinking takes some time to adjust to. So, if you feel some resistance, that's fine: it is a natural reaction to ideas that disrupt your models of the world. Models provide stability and understanding, so people should not throw them away too casually. Once you regain your ground, you will be able to enjoy your new freedom and suggest ideas that previous assumptions filtered out of view. As Tony Robbins, the author of *Awaken the Giant Within* says, "If you're committed enough, your brain will find a way."

Technique 5: Reframing

Changing the manner in which we look at a business problem often leads to new solutions. Reframing has to do with how people look at a problem or situation. Like a picture frame or a window frame, the frame of the situation defines what we see in the picture, what we notice.

The first step in discerning new solutions to a problem is to take conscious control of framing—to be aware of how you are looking at the situation and then to change that perspective so that you can envision different solutions. A frame directs the focus of attention, setting boundaries for what is included within it. Common frames in business include definitions of industries, product categories, market segments, or departmental responsibilities.

Not all things that are inside the frame are treated equally. The angle of view can focus attention on certain factors, leaving others obscured. Personal experience or recent events may subconsciously lead us to place some ideas in the forefront and others in the background. And all frames have blind spots that prevent us from seeing issues or realizing that some patterns are linked. In psychology, this phenomenon is called psychotoma, or selective filtering. For example, U.S. Steel (now USX) made the assumption that other large steel companies were its only competitors. The company completely missed the rise of small mills that entered the market with much lower price points and eventually winnowed away U.S. Steel's market dominance.

The knack of reframing is to learn how to view a problem from more perspectives for more comprehensive analysis of which frame provides the best vantage point on solutions. Changing these frames increases creative options. Trying out different perspectives offers a choice of responses. It opens up possibilities. The ability to reframe expands our repertoire; it enables us to see more ways to respond. Best of all, what makes reframing so effective is that the principles, once learned, can be applied to any situation.

It's true that looking at a situation from a different point of view is not easy. We are certainly not born knowing how to do it. The education expert Jean Piaget has shown that a child looking at a scene, such as a model of some geographic terrain, believes that other people viewing it from a different angle see the scene the same way as he or she does. Only at seven to eight years of age can most children consider the point of view of another in even such a simple situation.

The dangerous trap inherent in a one-frame approach is that it locks out other perspectives and other options. How often have you heard people claim that they solved a problem "the only way" that it could be solved? Such an expression often points to the failure to consider options. When people are unaware of their options, they view a problem from a single frame of reference and look for solutions only from that viewpoint. Looking at a situation from different viewpoints, on the other hand, reveals options and provides deeper understanding.

Technique 6: Drawing the Problem

However one might feel about one's artistic ability, drawing can clarify complex business problems and uncover creative solutions. The first step is to put some visual representation of a situation on paper—i.e., drawing the problem. Stick figures, misshapen circles, or wobbly lines will suffice. The purpose of the exercise is to express the problem graphically.

The reason for drawing is twofold. First, it's hard to keep many facts organized at once while you are trying to work with them. Psychologists call this "cognitive load," and there is a limit to how much information the brain's working memory (short-term memory) can retain. Nobel laureate Herbert Simon's extensive research on cognitive loads has shown that people can hold between three and seven items in working memory. If the data is committed to paper, however, the working memory is freed to address other ideas. The result is the ability to deal with more factors and to increase the cognitive load without being limited to what fits in short-term memory.

The second reason for drawing is that doing so produces more holistic and systematic thinking. Instead of jumping from thought to thought, determine at each stage what to think about next. Moving step by step is important because skipping from idea to idea disconnectedly can give the impression that a topic has been considered thoroughly when in fact you may just have gone around in a few circles. Drawing the problem will make repetitions and omissions obvious.

A drawing can simultaneously express the following:

- Inside and outside: which things are contained by other things

- Dominance: top-down order from best to worst

- Flows: arrows showing movement of materials, money, or information

- Obstacles or problems: as indicated by X's or walls to show barriers

- Mutual connections: as indicated by double-ended arrows

- Order or disorder

- Cycles and responses

In a drawing, many features are visible at a glance, whereas writing is more linear. For example, who has ever tried to explain supply chains to someone without resorting to a simple flow chart demonstrating the flows of goods, monies, and information? Behind this verity, too, is surely the cause of the overwhelming popularity and success of Microsoft's PowerPoint software—which literally puts thoughts into pictures.

Technique 7: Rotating Jobs
How can a team solve a problem if members do not thoroughly

understand it? In the stereotypically dysfunctional corporation, marketing, engineering, and manufacturing groups are all at odds (while jointly regarding upper management as the common foe). Why? Because each group does not fully understand the forces driving the decisions of the other groups. Members of one group see only the negative impact of other groups' decisions on their own group.

The solution is mandatory job rotation across a wide range of functional areas. Every person in the company should spend at least one week a year working in another area. For example, some companies make their management prospects do a stint on the "front line" (shipping for a food-processing company or managing a pizza-delivery service). Harvard Business School professor John Kotter says that examining the early career of an executive who came to be known as a visionary will usually reveal a series of assignments that enabled him or her to see a business from many perspectives.

So create a management-training program that incorporates the idea that job rotation is integral to grooming people for top management; otherwise, vital decision making will be left to those who understand only one facet of the company. Finally, besides moving people around within the company, encourage them to volunteer in community activities or to spend time outside the office at customer and supplier sites. This exercise will get the creative juices flowing!

Technique 8: Expanding Education

The view that employees should enroll only in courses related to their jobs is myopic; it perpetuates limited views. Progressive, creative companies will encourage their employees to take courses in any subject they want to pursue. Let employees take courses that broaden their horizons! Free, intellectual cross-pollination should be aggressively encouraged. Would you send a programmer to a music class? Consider Raymond Kurzweil, who developed the first omnifont-recognition machine. "I have a lifelong interest in music from my father as well as a nearly lifelong interest in computers," Kurzweil said. "My father always felt that I would combine those interests someday, but he wasn't sure quite how." Music promotes spatial intelligence and sharpens intuitive perception. The creative result can't always be predicted, but people who learn about many areas use more parts of the brain.

Remember the four quadrants? Taking courses and learning

about new areas allows people to tap into other styles. Consider the following scientists who were formally trained in art before they began studying science: Louis Pasteur, inventor of the germ theory of disease; Joseph Lister, inventor of antisepsis; and Santiago Ramón Cajal, the famous anatomist of the brain. These scientists claimed that they owed their amazing observational and experimental skills to the arts.

Why pursue an avocation such as music or painting? Because what is known in one discipline can be used in another. What usually happens is that people hold many distinct ideas in their heads without the ideas ever meeting, but creative people aim deliberately for that encounter. Johannes Kepler gave astronomy a new view of the universe by using Pythagoras' concept of the "music of the spheres." He identified a number of unsuspected relations among familiar disciplines (geometry, arithmetic, music, astronomy). He also developed the laws of motion by approaching astronomy through metaphor, to "uncover the magic of mere numbers and to demonstrate the music of the spheres."

To gain the benefits of expansive education, corporations should encourage their employees to take one course a year that is unrelated to their jobs.

Technique 9: Overlapping Disciplines

One easy way to gain a different perspective is to think like someone from a different profession. People from different disciplines often view the same situations differently. They have acquired their own sets of "tools" from their own fields.

Consider the challenge of world hunger. Nutritionists will see it largely as a problem of selecting optimal diet. Agronomists see it as a problem of food production. But epidemiologists will see world hunger as a problem of disease that increases the demand for nutrients and prevents their absorption, while demographers see it as a problem of population growth that has outstripped agricultural activity. And that's not all. Engineers view world hunger as a problem of inadequate food storage and distribution. Economists consider it as a problem of insufficient purchasing power or inequitable distribution of land and wealth.

The point is this: if we consider how someone from a different profession would solve a problem, we can uncover new tools and insights. Although no single profession has all the answers, clever combinations of answers from different disciplines can create a well-rounded solution. Multidisciplinary thinking brings together ideas previously thought disparate. It combines various techniques and objects by perceiving in them similarities where everyone else perceives differences. It imagines a problem that has assumed one form (such as a verbal question) and transforms it into a mental image or pattern, solving it by analogy. It is to be able to perceive issues in a framework or context different from everyone else's. It helps employees be creative, and gives them the chance to learn and understand more of the world than simply what is required to solve problems within a single discipline by using a single mode of thought.

Technique 10: Translating Words into Pictures, and Pictures into Words

As was discussed earlier, people possess different filtering styles, different internal styles of assimilating and filtering impulses. Some people thrive on words; when they see a car, for example, they cannot help describing it with words such as *sleek or smooth*.

We can "transform" one set of sense impressions into another by moving from the language of science to that of art. Einstein's ability to communicate his insights depended on his ability to transform a mental picture of a physical sensation into a physical picture or a mathematical equation and then to translate the meaning of this

Figure 7-3 How the mind translates Porsche

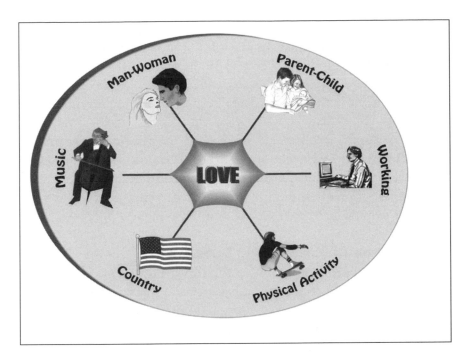

Figure 7-4 The many faces of amoré

picture or equation into words.

Playing with words themselves can produce creative, thought-provoking ideas. Roman Szpur, inventor of the first non-lens focusing system for lasers, thought of the laser as an "energy knife." Akio Morita spurred the invention of the Walkman at Sony by describing it as "portable music." Have you had your wordplay today?

Technique 11: Including the Naive Outsider

Sometimes the most creative idea comes from outside, from a fresh perspective, from someone not afraid to question the old order. What outsiders can your firm invite to help insiders see common things in a new way? Schoolchildren are a great resource for fresh perspectives. They are not locked into habitual ways of thinking; they are not convinced that they already know the answers. Their uninhibited questions and imaginative responses can yield surprising insights. Why not invite some students to your next meeting and see the magical ideas they propose for new uses of your company's product? Let them ask "dumb" questions, and if they cannot be answered frankly, maybe the questions were not so dumb! Listen carefully and look at common situations through their wondering eyes.

Customers are another source of outside perspectives. In fact, customers are a leading source of new product ideas. MIT professor Eric Von Hippel conducted a study of scientific-instrument and component-equipment manufacturing businesses. In a review of 160 inventions, he found that more than 70 percent of the product ideas came from customers. Customers inspired more than 60 percent of the minor modifications and 75 percent of the major modifications. Surprisingly, 100 percent of the so-called first-of-type ideas (complex instruments such as the transmission electron microscope) were from users. How is your company tapping into the creativity of its customers?

Technique 12: Encouraging Questions

A good question can point in the direction of a good solution. Good questions penetrate to the heart of the matter. They provide necessary information, new insights, and unusual ideas. Ask solution-oriented, win-win questions. To start, consider asking the following questions to spark new ideas:

- *Goals:* How does the situation or problem affect the goals of the organization? Does it promote or inhibit the attainment of corporate goals? Does it suggest the need for new goals?

- *Causes and history:* How or why did we get here? What constraints or opportunities are inherent in what led to current conditions? Why should we do things in the same way or in a different way in the future?

- *Pathways:* What might we do, and when might we do it? What might happen along the way? What contingencies or realities exist that could expedite or impede our progress?

- *Upside-downside:* What might go right? What might go wrong? How could we make it go right? What could we do about the downside?

- *Motivations:* Why are we doing this? Who realizes the rewards from it? How do we motivate people or create support for our chosen path? How do we create a win-win situation or fairly adjudicate among adversarial stakeholders? How do we align people's motivations with goals?

Just as good questions are powerful, good answers are essential, and answers such as "We have always done it that way" or

"Everybody else does it that way" are not acceptable. Delving deeper to understand the reasons is essential. One need not throw away every tradition, but an occasional review might reveal the need for change.

The answer "Everybody else does it that way" takes on special significance in the context of supply chains. They work only when all employees adhere to a set of standard and accepted business practices. The need to emulate best practices of other companies does not absolve innovators from questioning standard practices. Truly leading companies find ways to extend or replace these entrenched "industry-best" practices—generating new paradigms and new profits.

Another means of obtaining answers is the twenty-idea method. With this method, you ask a question and devise twenty answers to it. Pushing oneself or a team to reach that number will undoubtedly provide some gems. Alex Osborn, author of *Applied Imagination*, developed a set of questions that can help any team initiate a flow of creative ideas. A mnemonic device for remembering the questions is SCAMPER, an acronym for "Substitute, Combine, Adapt, Magnify, Put to other uses, Eliminate, Reverse-Rearrange."

Alex Osborn's Idea-Spurring Questions

- *Substitute:* Who else instead? What else instead? Another ingredient? material? process?

- *Combine:* How about a blend, an alloy, an assortment, an ensemble? Should we combine units? Combine purposes? Combine appeals? Combine ideas?

- *Adapt:* What else is like this? (What other idea does this suggest?) Does the past offer a parallel? What could we copy? Whom could we emulate?

- *Magnify:* What could we add? More time? Greater frequency? Strength? Height? Emphasis?

- *Put to other uses:* Could we modify the shape? Add a new twist? Modify motion? Uncover new ways to use as is?

- *Eliminate:* Minimize some element? Subtract something? Reduce? Shorten? Lighten?

- *Reverse-rearrange:* Should we transpose positive and negative? Rearrange components? Devise another layout? Another sequence? Turn the tables? Turn the other cheek?

The quality of creativity is determined by the quality of the questions. So ask yourself a question: Have you asked a good question today?

Technique 13: Listing Attributes

The technique of listing attributes engenders in-depth focus on one element of an issue at a time. For example, suppose the goal is to improve car safety. One might consider listing the individual attributes of the different aspects of the car: instrumentation, ventilation, fatigue-free seats, braking system, or energy-absorbing body structure.

If the aim is to improve the taste of coffee, one might look at all the factors that contribute to improving coffee taste: type of bean, fineness of grinding, hardness of water, or water temperature. What about designing a new tooth cleaner? The attributes include its form (gel, powder, cream, or solid), its main function (to polish, protect, clean, whiten, or purify), its context (where and when it will be used—in the bathroom, during travel, at morning, at night), and its users (children, pets, lovers, seniors).

Listing attributes may reveal a detail that others have missed. The goal is to list facts that could be leverage points. Another reason for listing attributes is to provide an opportunity for dividing the pieces in a new way. Sometimes all the parts of a product have been associated with it for a long time, and no one questions why the parts are included or configured as they are. Maybe all of the parts are not essential, or some can be modified. For example, reducing the number of functions performed by the product can lower its cost, as can unbundling (removing standard, nonessential components).

Attribute listing can also provide a better understanding of a company's customers, and for this reason has become the *modus operandi* for a host of marketing services firms. Customers can be judged according to the following:

- Industry

- Technological sophistication

- Strategy

- Financial strength

- Frequency of placing product orders

- Ethnic, age, or sex classification

- Psychographics

Some attributes that often go unnoticed but that can accomplish a great deal include company policies, access to information, customer perceptions, and routines or procedures. Can you attribute creativity to attributes?

Technique 14: Facing the Music

Music activates the right hemisphere of the brain. By listening to music while we work, we engage the right brain as well as the left. Research has shown that playing Mozart, for example, coordinates breathing, cardiovascular rhythm, and brain-wave rhythm, and leads to positive effects on health. It acts on the unconscious, stimulating receptivity and perception. Baroque and neoclassical composers tended to employ a constant theme, and they aimed for symmetry or integrated patterns throughout their work. As a result, their music has an orderly structure and produces a sense of well-being and relaxed receptivity.

One of the easiest, most powerful steps a company can take to creating an environment for innovation is to play classical music. Such music—especially that of Baroque composers, such as Vivaldi, Corelli, Telemann, and Bach—is the main aural route to the subconscious. Work in most organizations focuses on left-brain thinking: it is verbal, procedural, deductive. The emotional power of music also makes it an effective tool for establishing an upbeat, pleasant atmosphere. Specific recommendations for musical selections could include Haydn's Trumpet Concerto or Liszt's Hungarian Rhapsodies, to awaken enthusiasm, vision, and vitality; and Bach's Brandenburg Concertos or Handel's Water Music, to promote clear thinking. Companies should further consider arranging a "creativity room," containing paintings and having soft music playing, to create a relaxing atmosphere to foster creativity.

Background music also deserves companies' attention. Businesses can extend the same kindness to their customers as to their employees by substituting classical music for the hard-sell messages callers often hear when they are on hold. In particular, Bach's two Concertos for Two Pianos are known to calm anger; and the quiet, pleasing melodies of Vivaldi's flute concertos help relieve tension.

Technique 15: Reward Creative Behavior

There is truth in the adage "What gets measured gets done." To advance creativity, make it one of the performance measures on which employee rewards are based. Every employee could submit one new idea a quarter that he or she will execute and on the basis of which his or her bonus will be determined. When implementing this idea, businesses should make clear to managers that dismissing new ideas with "That won't work" is counterproductive. Senior management needs to encourage middle managers to solicit ideas, and bonuses should be tied to the number of ideas that come from their areas.

Consider the success that American Airlines has had with its suggestion program, called IdeAAs in Action. The program was launched in 1989, with the CEO of American Airlines personally inaugurating it, telling employees that the company needed their creativity, knowledge, and ideas in order to control expenses and generate revenues: "We want you to tell us what those better ways are. We will listen, we will respond, and we will provide rewards." In 1996, American Airlines received more than 17,000 ideas from employees, saving the company $43 million. One reason the company received so many good suggestions is that it rewards those who submit them. Rewarding creative behavior produces benefits for companies and employees alike.

Quantifying and Managing Creativity

How can we estimate creative potential? Is creativity too "soft" to justify to the accountants in management? Unfortunately, originality has the reputation for being unquantifiable for the measurement-oriented, left-brain management styles that prevail in many companies.

It is possible, however, to quantify both the creative potential of a company and the creative return on investment. Once the basis of ingenious productivity is understood, it is possible to measure creativity-related performance and increase creativity in any company. Skandia Corporation's notion of "intellectual capital" is an excellent basis for estimating such potential within an organization. Skandia's model is based on developing an analog to the financial balance sheet that reflects the intellectual assets of a company. The point is that a company's creativity depends on having appropriate intellectual assets, and intellectual capital techniques help measure those assets.

How can we estimate the return-on-investment for creativity? Thinking of creativity as the manufacturing of valuable novelty clarifies the measurement of creative return-on-investment. An analogy drawn from the world of manufacturing can be used to model creativity in any organization. Consider the following analogs for creative activities:

- New creative ideas correlate to raw materials.

- Ideas in development are equal to work-in-process.

- Bad ideas that are abandoned are tantamount to scrap rates.

- Ideas that are good but are not yet being used equate to inventory.

- The return-on-investment of ideas that have been implemented equals profits taken against the cost of goods sold.

The result is that any company can develop a measurement-backed model of its own creative productivity that includes the following:

- How many creative ideas the company is generating, developing, and using

- What the creative productivity of employees, teams, and departments is

- How much the company is investing in ideas in different areas and stages of development

- What percentage of ideas are making it into mainstream corporate activities

- How much return the company is making on the ideas

The goal is not to slot every creative idea into a little categorical-parts bin or to attach barcodes to ideas or to create stacks of paperwork for each one. Rather, the aim is to track the aggregate effects of large numbers of small ideas and to build the ability to track intensively the effects of especially big individual ideas. Some companies (such as Ford and Texas Instruments) use their knowledge-management efforts explicitly to track the conversion of creative ideas into measurable gains in performance. The results at these companies are a thousand tiny success stories and a few big initiatives that add up to major bottom-line benefits. For example, TI's efforts yielded billions of dollars in productivity gains; the ideas produced savings equivalent to the capital required to build two new fabrication plants.

As with any investment, there are certain costs associated with ingenuity and its development. Creativity incurs three categories of costs: the direct cost of spending resources on generating creative ideas, the cost of developing and implementing those creative ideas, and some indirect costs associated with the change that each idea brings. But it is not difficult to estimate and track these costs on an aggregate basis (for handling many small daily acts of creativity) or to create formal processes for determining the costs of major commitments to large-scale implementations of creative ideas. Methods such as activity-based costing are useful for allocating the costs to activities and for tracking them. The point in understanding these costs is not to discourage investing in creative ideas but to make sound decisions regarding creativity.

Managing a Portfolio of Creative Risks

How can you minimize the risk inherent in implementing each creative idea? Companies should subject individual creative ventures, especially high-investment strategic ideas, to risk-management techniques that consider the chance of success and contingencies in the case of failure. Risk management is not just another term for risk aversion but the controlled acceptance of and response to actions or events whose outcomes are not known. Techniques such as staged investment, setting of intermediate milestones, prototyping, and contingency planning are all part of risk management. Silicon Valley's process of venture capital funding exemplifies risk management in maximizing return on investment while investing in extremely risky creative endeavors. The goal of risk management is to minimize lost investment and mitigate the cost of failure on individual creative ideas.

How can you maximize total return across all creative pursuits? Portfolio management techniques often improve aggregate return-on-investment by revealing how patterns of investment in many creative activities and across a range of possible contingencies combine to create overall performance. Spreading investment across many activities reduces the risk of total failure—a diversification approach akin to that of successfully managing mutual funds. You can even seek out complementary creative ideas (for example, one that presumes a certain trend in customer needs and another that presumes the opposite trend) to hedge all bets. Whether the trend is confirmed or not, at least one of the two investments will prove profitable.

Portfolio management is a collaborative process enterprise-wide. Only when the full range of ideas across all departments is understood can one judge how the suggestions might combine to yield high aggregate return on investment for the entire company.

Building a Creative Culture
Relegating creativity to just another initiative promoted by

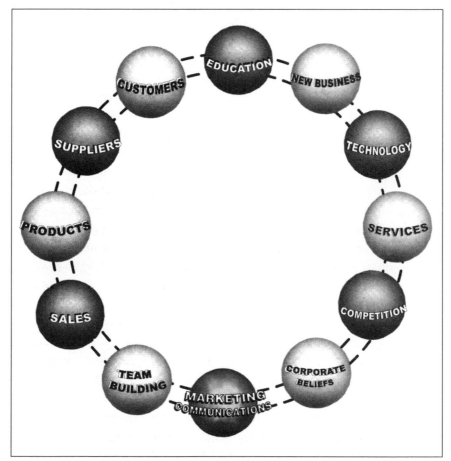

Figure 7-5   Can you apply the techniques to these areas?

Human Resources is doomed to failure. Creativity should underpin all of a company's operations. Original thinking is not just an afterthought or a one-time special event. And creativity is more than just adding curvy shapes and trendy colors to the latest product or the latest new office space. Creativity must be manifest throughout a corporate culture, explicitly advancing the power of a corporation's existing structure and combining the brain power of the entire staff. Building on enlightened perspectives is about making a product transformation, market transformation, business breakthrough, or radical industry transformation. These are Promethean changes that can fundamentally—radically—alter a company's destiny. An organization that can bring this new fire to the marketplace can bask in the warmth of success.

Where does creativity end? Creativity does not stop at the doors to your company's building. In a world that comprehends the relationships between cause and effect in today's corporations—in building supply chains, information systems, connectivity and collaboration—the value of contributions from suppliers and customers cannot be overestimated. Just as the world of information technology is moving away from closed proprietary solutions, so too must the world of creativity expand to include open lines of communication with the outside. Customers often know more about products than the manufacturer does. Suppliers know more about how to get the most from their components than you do—and you know things about your customers and about your suppliers that they do not. Extending a creative, collaborative culture out to crucial business partners increases everyone's knowledge, creativity, innovation, and ultimate success. The fire of creativity can ignite a whole supply chain, creating a blaze that burns brightly into the future.

Call to Action

In the 21st century, the rapidity with which companies bring new products to market will impel organizations to create innovative ideas and procedures. This dynamic environment will engender a call to corporate action. To produce a vital product and service-leadership strategy, companies will need to cultivate even closer relationships with suppliers. Thus, the call to action will reverberate beyond each organization. Not only must a company and its employees be in tune, but customers, suppliers, and the community must be part of the orchestra.

Executive sponsorship is essential to this call to action. For creativity to thrive, companies must structure competitively. As the quest for dominance becomes intense, how will you increase and improve your business? How will you construct a value proposition for each business segment? The creativity techniques discussed here can help to improve a firm's competitive—as well as its creative—position. If you institute a creative atmosphere, using the various techniques discussed, you are ready to consider Value-Enhancing INnovation.

Where will you mine your next VEIN of gold?

Author Biography

Dan Balan is one of the world's foremost leaders on the subject of business transformation. Applying his groundbreaking framework—which addresses the urgent need to view rationalization, innovation, integration, and orchestration of any product in relationship, he has helped propel several companies from diverse industries into leadership positions.

A veteran of the application software industry and an alumnus of SAP and i2 Technologies, he has held key positions in both Product Management and Strategic Marketing. In the course of his career, Dan has analyzed several hundred companies, large and small. He has observed that companies fail because of irrelevant products, ineffective supply chains, inappropriate technology choices, incongruent innovation – or some combination thereof.

Transforming Corporations is a result of that observation.

A passionate advocate of deliberate creativity, Dan believes that unleashing human potential at the workplace is the next frontier. Based on his business transformation framework, he personally conducts results-producing workshops for corporations and has been a popular lecturer at universities.

A continual learner with myriad interests, when not championing business turnaround efforts, Dan might be happily occupied writing, performing stand-up comedy, or dabbling in art. The founder and CEO of PMCV Technologies, an advisory and training firm focusing on business transformation, Dan resides in Chicago.

He can be reached at dbalan@pmcv.com